TEXT BOOK OF CELLULAR AND MOLECULAR PHARMACOLOGY

[According to latest syllabus of M. Pharm of Pharmacy Council of India]

Dr. Smita Jain

Assistant Professor

Central University of Rajasthan,

Ajmer, Rajasthan, India

Ms. Reetuparna Acharya

Ph.D. Scholar

Birla Institute of Technology,

Mesra, Ranchi

.

Dr. Tarak Nath Khatua

Assistant Professor

NSHM Knowledge Campus,

Kolkata, India

Mr. Ashish Maletha

Research Scholar

Siddhartha institute of Pharmacy,

Dehradun

Ms. Pragya Sharma

Assistant Professor

Amity Institute of Pharmacy,

Amity University Rajasthan,

Rajasthan, India

Notion Press

.

TEXT BOOK OF

CELLULAR AND MOLECULAR PHARMACOLOGY

First Edition 2024

Published by:

NOTION PRESS

Publisher and distributor

Head office: Notion press Media Pvt. Ltd.

7, Red cross Road,

Egmore, Chennai,Tamil Nadu 60008

Website: www.notionpress.com

TEXT BOOK OF CELLULAR AND MOLECULAR PHARMACOLOGY
NOTION PRESS
PREFACE

The authors feel great pleasure in presenting the first edition of the book **"Text Book of Cellular and Molecular Pharmacology"** for graduate and post graduate students. The present book on **Text Book of Cellular and Molecular Pharmacology** has been written according to the syllabus of B. Pharm-VII semester of Pharmacy Council of India and covers full course of the subject.

THE SALIENT FEATURES OF THE BOOK ARE:-

- *Easy to understand style of writing* which makes the book a self-study material.
- *Each new concept has been introduced through day-today problem of interest* to the students which makes the subject matter interesting.
- *The language of the book, on the whole, is lucid and easy to understand.*
- Wherever needed *neatly labeled figures have been drawn.*

The authors hope that the students, teachers and other readers will find the book interesting and to the point covering the course. We hope that the students will receive the book warmly.

I express a sincere thank you to the Management of Central University of Rajasthan, Birla Institute of Technology NSHM Knowledge Campus, Siddhartha institute of Pharmacy and Amity Institute of Pharmacy, Amity University Rajasthan for their support during the writing of this book.

Every effort is made to keep the book error free. The author will gratefully acknowledge the suggestions to improve the book to make it more useful.

Wishing our readers success in examination and life ahead. The authors feel that their efforts will be fully rewarded if the book serves the purpose for which it is written.

TEXT BOOK OF CELLULAR AND MOLECULAR PHARMACOLOGY

CONTENTS

- Cell biology
- Structure of cell and its organelles
- functions of cell and its organelles
- Genome organization
- Gene expression and its regulation
- importance of siRNA and micro RNA
- gene mapping and gene sequencing
- Cell cycles and its regulation.
- Cell death– events, regulators
- Intrinsic and extrinsic pathways of apoptosis.
- Necrosis and autophagy.

- Cell signaling
- Intercellular and intracellular signalling pathways.
- Classification of receptor family and molecular structure ligand gated ion channels;
- G-protein coupled receptors
- Tyrosine kinase receptors and nuclear receptors.
- Secondary messengers: cyclic AMP, cyclic GMP, calcium ion, inositol 1,4,5-trisphosphate, (IP3), NO, and diacylglycerol.
- Detailed study of following intracellular signalling pathways: cyclic AMP signaling pathway,
- mitogen-activated protein kinase (MAPK) signalling,

- Janus kinase (JAK)/signal transducer and activator of transcription (STAT) signaling pathway.

- Principles and applications of genomic and proteomic tools
- DNA electrophoresis,
- PCR (reverse transcription and real time),
- Gene sequencing
- micro array technique
- SDS page
- ELISA and western blotting,
- Recombinant DNA technology and gene therapy
- Basic principles of recombinant DNA technology-Restriction enzymes
- Various types of vectors.
- Applications of recombinant DNA technology.
- Gene therapy
  - Various types of gene transfer techniques
  - clinical applications of gene therapy
  - Recent advances in gene therapy.

- Gene mapping and cloning of disease gene.
- Genetic variation and its role in health/ pharmacology
- Polymorphisms
- affecting drug metabolism Genetic variation in drug transporters
- Genetic variation in G protein coupled receptors
- Applications of proteomics science: Genomics, proteomics, metabolomics, functionomics, nutrigenomics
- Immunotherapeutic

- Types of immunotherapeutic,
- humanisation antibody therapy
- Immunotherapeutic in clinical practice

5. Cell culture

- Cell culture
- Cell culture Techniques
- Basic equipment's used in cell culture lab.
- Cell culture media
- various types of cell culture
- general procedure for cell cultures;
- isolation of cells
- subculture
- cryopreservation,
- Characterization of cells and their application.
- Principles and applications of cell viability assays
- Principles and applications of glucose uptake assay
- Principles and applications of Calcium influx assays
- Principles of flow cytometry
- Applications of flow cytometry
- Biosimilars

CHAPTER – 1

CELL BIOLOGY

INTRODUCTION:

Cell biology, also known as cytology, is a branch of biology that studies the structure, function, and behavior of cells. Cells are the basic structural, functional, and biological units of all living organisms, often called the "building blocks of life." Understanding cells is crucial for many fields of biology and medicine because all living organisms are composed of cells.

Historical Background

The historical background of cell biology is a fascinating journey that spans centuries of scientific inquiry and discovery. Here's a detailed exploration of key milestones and contributions in the field:

1. **Early Observations:**
   a. **Antiquity**: The earliest observations of living cells date back to ancient civilizations such as Egypt and Greece, where rudimentary microscopes were used to examine biological specimens. However, the concept of cells as the fundamental units of life did not emerge until much later.
   b. **Robert Hooke (1665):** Robert Hooke, an English scientist, is credited with the first observation of cells. In his book "Micrographia," Hooke described and illustrated cork cells, which he observed under a microscope. He coined the term "cell" based on their resemblance to the cells of a monastery.

2. **Cell Theory:**
   a. **Matthias Schleiden and Theodor Schwann (1838-1839):** The formulation of the cell theory is a cornerstone of modern cell biology. Matthias Schleiden, a botanist, and Theodor Schwann, a

zoologist, independently proposed that all living organisms are composed of cells and that cells are the basic units of structure and function in living organisms. Rudolf Virchow later added to the cell theory by proposing that cells arise only from pre-existing cells, thus completing the foundational principles of cell biology.

3. **Microscopy Advancements:**

    a. **Anton van Leeuwenhoek (17th century)**: Anton van Leeuwenhoek, a Dutch scientist, is credited with the development of the first practical microscope. His observations of microscopic organisms, including bacteria and protozoa, laid the groundwork for the field of microbiology.

    b. **Improvements in Microscopy**: Throughout the 19th and 20th centuries, advancements in microscopy techniques, such as phase contrast microscopy, fluorescence microscopy, and electron microscopy, enabled scientists to visualize cellular structures and organelles with increasing clarity and resolution.

4. **Cell Structure and Organelles:**

    a. **Organelle Discoveries**: In the late 19th and early 20th centuries, scientists such as Camillo Golgi, Santiago Ramón y Cajal, and Albert Claude made significant contributions to our understanding of cell structure and organelles. Golgi discovered the Golgi apparatus, Cajal pioneered the study of neuronal morphology, and Claude developed techniques for isolating and visualizing cell organelles using electron microscopy.

    b. **Endosymbiotic Theory**: In the 1960s, Lynn Margulis proposed the endosymbiotic theory, which suggests that eukaryotic organelles such as mitochondria and chloroplasts originated from symbiotic relationships between ancient prokaryotic cells. This theory revolutionized our understanding of cellular evolution and the origin of complex life forms.

5. **Molecular Biology and Genetics:**

   a. **Discovery of DNA:** The discovery of the structure of DNA by James Watson and Francis Crick in 1953 laid the foundation for molecular biology and revolutionized our understanding of heredity and genetic information.

   b. **Gene Expression and Regulation**: Throughout the 20th century, scientists such as Barbara McClintock, Jacques Monod, and François Jacob made groundbreaking discoveries in gene expression and regulation, elucidating the mechanisms by which cells control the transcription and translation of genetic information.

6. **Modern Techniques and Applications:**

   a. **Genetic Engineering and Biotechnology**: The development of recombinant DNA technology in the 1970s paved the way for genetic engineering and biotechnology, enabling scientists to manipulate and study genes with unprecedented precision.

   b. **Cell Culture and Tissue Engineering**: Advances in cell culture techniques and tissue engineering have enabled researchers to grow and manipulate cells outside the body, leading to applications in regenerative medicine, drug discovery, and biomedical research.

The historical background of cell biology is characterized by a rich tapestry of scientific discoveries and innovations, driven by the curiosity and ingenuity of countless scientists over the centuries. These foundational principles and advancements continue to shape our understanding of the fundamental processes of life and drive progress in biomedical research and technology.

Cell Theory

Cell theory is a fundamental principle in biology that describes the basic structural and functional unit of all living organisms, the cell. It is comprised of three main principles, which were formulated by Matthias Schleiden, Theodor Schwann, and Rudolf Virchow in the 19th century:

1. **All living organisms are composed of cells**: This principle asserts that all living things, whether they are single-celled organisms like bacteria or multicellular organisms like plants and animals, are made up of one or more cells. Cells are the building blocks of life, and the diversity of living organisms arises from variations in cell structure, function, and organization.

2. **The cell is the basic unit of structure and function in living organisms**: According to cell theory, cells are not only the structural units of living organisms but also the functional units responsible for carrying out the essential processes of life. Each cell performs specific functions necessary for the survival and reproduction of the organism as a whole. For example, in multicellular organisms, different types of cells specialize in tasks such as nutrient uptake, energy production, communication, and tissue repair.

3. **Cells arise only from pre-existing cells:** This principle, often attributed to Rudolf Virchow, states that new cells are generated through the division of pre-existing cells. This concept, known as biogenesis, contrasts with the earlier idea of spontaneous generation, which posited that living organisms could arise spontaneously from non-living matter. The principle of cell division and the continuity of life from one generation to the next are central to understanding the processes of growth, development, and reproduction in living organisms.

The formulation of cell theory marked a significant paradigm shift in biology, as it provided a unifying framework for understanding the organization and function of living organisms. Prior to the development of cell theory, the nature of cells and their role in life processes were poorly understood. The work of Schleiden, Schwann, Virchow, and other pioneering scientists laid the groundwork for modern cell biology and set the stage for further discoveries in areas such as cell structure, function, and diversity.

Cell theory continues to serve as the foundation of modern biology, guiding research and exploration into the intricate workings of cells and their roles in health, disease, and the environment. It highlights the interconnectedness of all living things and underscores the importance of cellular processes in shaping the complexity and diversity of life on Earth.

Types of Cells

Cells are the basic structural and functional units of all living organisms. They come in various types, each specialized for specific functions and roles within the organism. Here's a detailed exploration of some major types of cells:

1. **Prokaryotic Cells:**
    a. **Bacteria:** Prokaryotic cells are found in bacteria and archaea. They are characterized by the absence of a true nucleus and membrane-bound organelles. Instead, their genetic material is typically organized in a single circular chromosome located in the nucleoid region. Bacterial cells may also contain plasmids, small circular DNA molecules that can confer additional traits such as antibiotic resistance. Despite their simplicity, prokaryotic cells exhibit remarkable diversity in size, shape, and metabolic capabilities.

2. **Eukaryotic Cells:**
    a. **Animal Cells**: Animal cells are eukaryotic cells found in animals and humans. They are characterized by a true nucleus, membrane-bound organelles such as mitochondria, endoplasmic reticulum, Golgi apparatus, and lysosomes, as well as a cytoskeleton composed of microtubules, microfilaments, and intermediate

filaments. Animal cells are highly specialized and perform diverse functions such as nutrient uptake, energy production, cell signaling, and movement.

b. **Plant Cells**: Plant cells are eukaryotic cells found in plants. In addition to the organelles present in animal cells, plant cells also contain unique structures such as chloroplasts (responsible for photosynthesis), a large central vacuole (involved in storage, turgor regulation, and waste management), and a cell wall (composed of cellulose) that provides structural support and protection. Plant cells are adapted for functions such as photosynthesis, nutrient storage, and structural support.

3. **Specialized Cells:**

a. **Neurons**: Neurons are specialized cells found in the nervous system. They are responsible for transmitting electrical and chemical signals throughout the body, enabling functions such as sensory perception, motor coordination, and cognitive processing. Neurons have unique structures such as dendrites (to receive signals), axons (to transmit signals), and synaptic terminals (to communicate with other neurons or target cells).

b. **Muscle Cells**: Muscle cells, or muscle fibers, are specialized cells found in muscle tissue. They are responsible for generating force and producing movement through the contraction and relaxation of muscle fibers. Muscle cells contain specialized proteins such as actin and myosin, which interact to generate mechanical force.

c. **Epithelial Cells**: Epithelial cells form the linings of surfaces and cavities throughout the body, such as the skin, respiratory tract, gastrointestinal tract, and blood vessels. They serve as barriers to protect underlying tissues, facilitate absorption and secretion, and participate in sensory functions. Epithelial cells exhibit various shapes and arrangements depending on their location and function, such as squamous (flat), cuboidal (cube-shaped), and columnar (column-shaped) epithelia.

   d. **Immune Cells**: Immune cells are specialized cells of the immune system that protect the body from pathogens and foreign substances. They include white blood cells such as lymphocytes (B cells, T cells), neutrophils, monocytes, macrophages, dendritic cells, and natural killer (NK) cells. Immune cells play crucial roles in immune surveillance, antigen recognition, antibody production, and inflammatory responses.

These are just a few examples of the diverse types of cells found in living organisms. Each cell type is adapted for specific functions and contributes to the overall structure, function, and homeostasis of the organism. The study of cell biology aims to understand the molecular mechanisms underlying cellular structure, function, and behavior, providing insights into health, disease, and the broader processes of life.

Cell Structure

Cell structure refers to the organization and arrangement of cellular components within a cell. Cells are complex entities with a highly organized internal structure that enables them to carry out various functions necessary for life. Here's a detailed exploration of the main components of cell structure:

1. **Plasma Membrane:**

   a. The plasma membrane, also known as the cell membrane, is a phospholipid bilayer that surrounds the cell, separating its internal environment from the external environment.

   b. It regulates the passage of substances into and out of the cell, maintains cell shape and integrity, and facilitates cell communication with its surroundings through receptors and signaling molecules.

2. **Cytoplasm:**

   a. The cytoplasm refers to the semi-fluid substance that fills the interior of the cell, excluding the organelles.

   b. It consists of a watery matrix called the cytosol, which contains dissolved ions, molecules, and organelles, as well as a network of protein filaments called the cytoskeleton, which provides structural support and facilitates cell movement and shape changes.

3. **Nucleus:**

   a. The nucleus is the central organelle that houses the cell's genetic material (DNA) and controls gene expression.

   b. It is surrounded by a double membrane called the nuclear envelope, which contains nuclear pores that regulate the passage of molecules between the nucleus and the cytoplasm.

   c. Within the nucleus, DNA is organized into linear structures called chromosomes, which contain genes that encode instructions for protein synthesis and cellular functions.

4. **Organelles:**

   a. Organelles are specialized structures within the cell that perform specific functions necessary for cellular activities.

   b. **Examples of organelles include:**

      i. **Endoplasmic Reticulum (ER):** The ER is a network of membranous tubules and sacs involved in protein and lipid synthesis, as well as calcium storage and detoxification.

      ii. **Golgi Apparatus**: The Golgi apparatus is a stack of membranous sacs responsible for processing, sorting, and packaging proteins and lipids for secretion or delivery to other cellular compartments.

      iii. **Mitochondria:** Mitochondria are double-membrane organelles that serve as the site of cellular respiration, producing ATP (adenosine triphosphate) energy through oxidative phosphorylation.

    iv. **Chloroplasts**: Chloroplasts are organelles found in plant cells that carry out photosynthesis, converting light energy into chemical energy in the form of glucose.

    v. **Lysosomes:** Lysosomes are membrane-bound vesicles containing hydrolytic enzymes involved in intracellular digestion and the recycling of cellular materials.

    vi. **Perixosomes**: Peroxisomes are membrane-bound organelles that catalyze various metabolic reactions, including the breakdown of fatty acids and the detoxification of harmful substances.

5. Cytoskeleton:

    a. The cytoskeleton is a network of protein filaments that provides structural support, maintains cell shape, facilitates cell movement, and enables intracellular transport.

    b. It consists of three main types of filaments: microfilaments (composed of actin), intermediate filaments (composed of various proteins), and microtubules (composed of tubulin).

    c. Microfilaments are involved in cell contraction and cell shape changes, intermediate filaments provide mechanical strength and support, and microtubules serve as tracks for intracellular transport and facilitate cell division.

6. Cell Wall (in Plant Cells):

    a. Plant cells are surrounded by a rigid cell wall composed primarily of cellulose, hemicellulose, and pectin.

    b. The cell wall provides structural support, protection against mechanical stress, and regulates cell shape and growth.

c. In addition to the primary cell wall, some plant cells also have a secondary cell wall composed of lignin, which further strengthens and waterproofs the cell wall.

Overall, the organization and arrangement of cellular structures and organelles within a cell are essential for its functions and activities. The dynamic interactions between these components enable cells to carry out diverse processes such as metabolism, growth, division, communication, and response to environmental stimuli. Understanding cell structure is fundamental to unraveling the complexities of cellular biology and its implications for health, disease, and the broader mechanisms of life.

Cell Membrane

The cell membrane, also known as the plasma membrane, is a crucial structure that surrounds all cells, both prokaryotic and eukaryotic. It plays essential roles in maintaining cell integrity, regulating the passage of molecules into and out of the cell, and facilitating communication with the extracellular environment. Here's a detailed exploration of the cell membrane:

1. **Structure:**

    a. **Phospholipid Bilayer**: The cell membrane is primarily composed of a phospholipid bilayer. Phospholipids are amphipathic molecules, meaning they have a hydrophilic ("water-loving") head and hydrophobic ("water-fearing") tails. In the bilayer, the hydrophilic heads face outward, interacting with the aqueous environment inside and outside the cell, while the hydrophobic tails are sandwiched between the heads, creating a barrier to the passage of water-soluble molecules.

    b. **Protein**s: The phospholipid bilayer is interspersed with various proteins that serve diverse functions. Integral proteins are embedded within the lipid bilayer, while peripheral proteins are loosely associated with the membrane surface. Membrane proteins play roles in cell signaling, transport of molecules across the membrane, cell adhesion, and structural support.

c. **Cholesterol:** Cholesterol molecules are interspersed within the phospholipid bilayer, helping to stabilize the membrane structure and regulate its fluidity. Cholesterol molecules interact with phospholipids and proteins, modulating membrane permeability and flexibility.

2. **Functions:**

a. **Selective Permeability**: One of the primary functions of the cell membrane is to regulate the passage of molecules into and out of the cell. The phospholipid bilayer acts as a selective barrier, allowing only certain molecules to pass through while excluding others. Small, non-polar molecules such as oxygen and carbon dioxide can diffuse freely across the membrane, while larger or polar molecules require specific transport proteins or channels for passage.

b. **Cell Signaling**: Membrane proteins play crucial roles in cell signaling processes. Receptor proteins on the cell surface bind to signaling molecules (ligands), initiating intracellular signaling cascades that regulate cellular activities such as growth, differentiation, and gene expression. Cell signaling pathways mediated by membrane receptors are essential for coordinating cellular responses to extracellular stimuli.

c. **Cell Adhesion and Communication**: The cell membrane facilitates cell-cell adhesion and communication. Cell adhesion proteins such as integrins and cadherins mediate interactions between neighboring cells and between cells and the extracellular matrix, contributing to tissue structure and organization. Gap junctions and tight junctions are specialized structures that allow direct communication and exchange of molecules between adjacent cells.

3. **Dynamic Properties:**

    a. **Fluid Mosaic Model**: The fluid mosaic model describes the dynamic nature of the cell membrane, wherein phospholipids and proteins can move laterally within the lipid bilayer. This fluidity allows the membrane to adapt to changing environmental conditions and facilitates the diffusion of molecules across the membrane.

    b. **Membrane Fluidity**: The fluidity of the cell membrane is influenced by factors such as temperature, lipid composition, and cholesterol content. Higher temperatures increase membrane fluidity, while lower temperatures can decrease fluidity and lead to membrane solidification. Cholesterol helps to maintain optimal membrane fluidity by reducing phospholipid mobility and preventing excessive membrane stiffening or fluidization.

4. **Transport Mechanisms:**

    a. **Passive Transport**: Passive transport mechanisms, such as diffusion and facilitated diffusion, rely on the concentration gradient to drive the movement of molecules across the membrane. Diffusion occurs spontaneously, with molecules moving from areas of high concentration to areas of low concentration until equilibrium is reached. Facilitated diffusion involves the movement of molecules through membrane proteins, such as channels or carriers, to facilitate their transport across the membrane.

    b. **Active Transport**: Active transport mechanisms, such as primary active transport and secondary active transport, require energy input (in the form of ATP) to move molecules against their concentration gradient. Primary active transport involves the direct use of ATP to pump molecules across the membrane, while secondary active transport couples the movement of one molecule against its gradient with the simultaneous movement of another molecule down its gradient.

Cell Division

Cell division is a fundamental process in cell biology by which a parent cell divides to produce two or more daughter cells. It plays essential roles in growth, development, tissue repair, and reproduction in organisms. There are two main types of cell division: mitosis and meiosis. Here's a detailed explanation of each:

1. **Mitosis:**
    a. **Purpose**: Mitosis is a type of cell division that produces two genetically identical daughter cells from a single parent cell. It is involved in growth, development, tissue repair, and asexual reproduction in organisms.
    b. **Phases:**
        i. **Interphase:** The cell prepares for division by undergoing growth, DNA replication, and duplication of organelles. Interphase is divided into three stages: G1 (gap 1), S (synthesis), and G2 (gap 2).
        ii. **Prophase:** Chromatin condenses into visible chromosomes, and the nuclear envelope breaks down. Spindle fibers, composed of microtubules, form and extend from opposite poles of the cell.
        iii. **Metaphase:** Chromosomes align along the metaphase plate, an imaginary plane equidistant from the spindle poles.

    iv. **Anaphase:** Sister chromatids separate and move toward opposite poles of the cell, pulled by the spindle fibers.

    v. **Telophase**: Chromosomes decondense, and nuclear envelopes re-form around the separated chromatids at each pole, producing two distinct nuclei.

    vi. **Cytokinesis:** The cytoplasm divides, resulting in two separate daughter cells. In animal cells, cytokinesis is achieved through the formation of a cleavage furrow, while in plant cells, a cell plate forms between the daughter nuclei, eventually developing into a new cell wall.

2. **Meiosis:**

    a. **Purpose**: Meiosis is a specialized type of cell division that produces haploid gametes (sperm and eggs) from diploid germ cells. It is essential for sexual reproduction and genetic diversity.

    b. **Phases:**

        i. **Interphase:** Similar to mitotic interphase, the cell prepares for division by undergoing growth and DNA replication.

        ii. **Meiosis I:**

            1. **Prophase I:** Chromosomes condense, homologous chromosomes pair up and undergo crossing over, where segments of DNA are exchanged between non-sister chromatids.

            2. **Metaphase I**: Homologous pairs align along the metaphase plate, with one chromosome from each pair facing opposite poles.

            3. **Anaphase I:** Homologous chromosomes separate and move toward opposite poles of the cell, pulled by spindle fibers.

4. **Telophase I**: Chromosomes arrive at the poles, and nuclear envelopes may reform. Cytokinesis may occur, resulting in two haploid daughter cells.

iii. **Meiosis II:**

1. **Prophase II**: Chromosomes re-condense if necessary, and the nuclear envelope breaks down. Spindle fibers reassemble.

2. **Metaphase II:** Chromosomes align along the metaphase plate, similar to mitosis.

3. **Anaphase II:** Sister chromatids separate and move toward opposite poles of the cell.

4. **Telophase II**: Chromosomes decondense, and nuclear envelopes reform around the separated chromatids. Cytokinesis occurs, resulting in four haploid daughter cells, each with half the number of chromosomes as the parent cell.

Both mitosis and meiosis are highly regulated processes that ensure the faithful distribution of genetic material to daughter cells. Errors in cell division can lead to genetic abnormalities, developmental defects, and diseases such as cancer. Understanding the mechanisms and regulation of cell division is essential for elucidating the complexities of organismal development, evolution, and disease.

Cell Communication

Cell communication, also known as cell signaling, is the process by which cells communicate with each other to coordinate various activities within multicellular organisms. This communication is essential for the proper functioning and regulation of biological processes such as growth, development, immune response, and homeostasis. There are several types of cell communication, including direct cell-cell contact, paracrine signaling, endocrine signaling, autocrine signaling, and synaptic signaling. Let's delve into each of these in detail:

1. **Direct Cell-Cell Contact**: This type of cell communication involves physical contact between two neighboring cells. It allows for the direct exchange of signaling molecules or information through specialized junctions between cells. One prominent example of direct cell-cell contact is gap junctions, which are channels that connect the cytoplasm of adjacent cells, enabling the passage of ions, small molecules, and signaling molecules.

2. **Paracrine Signaling:** Paracrine signaling involves the release of signaling molecules, such as growth factors or neurotransmitters, by one cell to act on nearby target cells. These signaling molecules diffuse through the extracellular fluid and bind to receptors on neighboring cells, triggering a response. Paracrine signaling is crucial for local communication within tissues and organs.

3. **Endocrine Signaling**: Endocrine signaling involves the release of signaling molecules, known as hormones, into the bloodstream by specialized endocrine cells. These hormones travel through the circulatory system to target cells located in distant tissues or organs. Once they reach their target cells, hormones bind to specific receptors, initiating cellular responses. Endocrine signaling plays a vital role in long-distance communication and the regulation of various physiological processes.

4. **Autocrine Signaling**: Autocrine signaling occurs when a cell releases signaling molecules that bind to receptors on its own surface, thereby influencing its own behavior. This type of signaling allows cells to regulate their own activities in response to external stimuli or changes in their microenvironment. Autocrine signaling is often involved in processes such as cell growth, differentiation, and immune response.

5. **Synaptic Signaling**: Synaptic signaling is a specialized form of cell communication that occurs at synapses, which are junctions between nerve cells (neurons) or between neurons and target cells, such as muscle cells or other neurons. In synaptic signaling, neurotransmitters are released from the presynaptic neuron into the synaptic cleft, where they bind to receptors on the postsynaptic cell, eliciting a response. This type of signaling plays a fundamental role in neuronal communication and the regulation of nervous system function.

Overall, cell communication is a complex and highly regulated process that allows cells to coordinate their activities and respond appropriately to internal and external stimuli. Dysfunction in cell communication pathways can lead to various diseases and disorders, highlighting the importance of understanding the mechanisms underlying this fundamental biological process.

Cell Metabolism

Cell metabolism refers to the sum of all biochemical reactions that occur within a cell to maintain its function and survival. These reactions involve the conversion of nutrients into energy and building blocks for cell growth, repair, and maintenance. Cell metabolism is tightly regulated to ensure the proper balance of energy production, storage, and utilization. Let's explore the key aspects of cell metabolism in detail:

1. **Energy Metabolism:**
   a. **Glycolysis:** This is the initial stage of glucose metabolism, occurring in the cytoplasm, where glucose is converted into pyruvate, producing a small amount of ATP and NADH.
   b. **Citric Acid Cycle (Krebs Cycle):** Pyruvate generated from glycolysis enters the mitochondria, where it undergoes further oxidation to produce NADH and FADH2, which carry electrons to the electron transport chain (ETC).

c. **Electron Transport Chain (ETC):** Located in the inner mitochondrial membrane, the ETC transfers electrons from NADH and FADH2 to oxygen, generating a proton gradient across the membrane. This gradient drives ATP synthesis via oxidative phosphorylation, producing the majority of cellular ATP.

d. **Oxidative Phosphorylation**: ATP synthase utilizes the proton gradient generated by the ETC to phosphorylate ADP to ATP, providing the cell with a significant amount of energy.

2. **Anabolism (Biosynthetic Pathways):**

a. **Gluconeogenesis:** This pathway allows for the synthesis of glucose from non-carbohydrate precursors, such as pyruvate, lactate, glycerol, and certain amino acids.

b. **Glycogenesis: Glucose is polymerized into glycogen for short-term energy storage in liver** and muscle cells.

c. **Lipogenesis**: Acetyl-CoA generated from glycolysis and fatty acid synthesis is utilized to synthesize triglycerides for long-term energy storage.

d. **Protein Synthesis:** Amino acids are polymerized into proteins through the processes of transcription (DNA to mRNA) and translation (mRNA to protein) in the cytoplasm.

3. **Catabolism (Breakdown Pathways):**

a. **Glycogenolysis:** Glycogen is broken down into glucose-6-phosphate, which enters glycolysis for energy production.

b. **Glycogenolysis:** Glycogen is broken down into glucose-6-phosphate, which enters glycolysis for energy production.

c. **Fatty Acid Oxidation**: Fatty acids are broken down into acetyl-CoA through beta-oxidation in the mitochondria, which enters the citric acid cycle for ATP production.

d. **Protein Degradation**: Proteins are broken down into amino acids, which can be used for energy production or as precursors for biosynthetic pathways.

4. **Regulation of Metabolism:**

   a. **Enzyme Regulation**: Metabolic pathways are regulated by enzymes, which can be activated or inhibited by allosteric regulation, covalent modification, or changes in gene expression.

   b. **Hormonal Regulation**: Hormones such as insulin, glucagon, adrenaline, and cortisol play crucial roles in regulating metabolism by altering enzyme activity, substrate availability, and gene expression in target cells.

   c. **Cellular Signaling**: Cellular signaling pathways, such as the AMP-activated protein kinase (AMPK) pathway, respond to cellular energy levels and nutrient availability to coordinate metabolic responses and maintain cellular homeostasis.

Overall, cell metabolism is a dynamic and highly regulated process that ensures the proper balance of energy production, storage, and utilization to support cellular function and survival. Dysregulation of metabolism can lead to various diseases, including metabolic disorders, cancer, and neurodegenerative diseases, underscoring the importance of understanding the intricacies of cellular metabolism.

Applications of Cell Biology

Cell biology has numerous applications across various fields, including medicine, biotechnology, agriculture, and environmental science. Here are some detailed applications of cell biology:

1. **Medical Research and Disease Understanding:**

   a. Cell biology provides insights into the fundamental mechanisms underlying diseases such as cancer, neurodegenerative disorders, cardiovascular diseases, and autoimmune conditions.

b. Understanding cellular processes allows for the development of targeted therapies and drugs to treat diseases at the molecular level.

c. Techniques such as cell culture, microscopy, and molecular biology are used to study disease progression, identify biomarkers, and develop diagnostic tools.

2. **Drug Discovery and Development:**

a. Cell-based assays are used in drug discovery to screen potential drug candidates for efficacy and safety.

b. Cell culture systems, including 3D organoids and patient-derived cells, are employed to model disease conditions and test drug responses.

c. Cell biology techniques enable the study of drug interactions, mechanisms of action, and drug resistance in various cell types.

3. **Regenerative Medicine and Tissue Engineering:**

a. Cell biology plays a crucial role in regenerative medicine by studying stem cells and their differentiation potential for tissue repair and regeneration.

b. Techniques such as stem cell culture, tissue engineering, and gene editing are used to develop cell-based therapies for conditions such as spinal cord injuries, heart disease, and diabetes.

c. Understanding the molecular mechanisms of cell differentiation and tissue development is essential for engineering functional tissues and organs in vitro.

4. **Biotechnology and Bioprocessing:**

a. Cell biology techniques are used in biotechnology for the production of recombinant proteins, vaccines, and biofuels using genetically engineered cells.

b. Cell culture systems are utilized to scale up production and optimize bioprocesses for industrial applications.

c. Genetic engineering tools such as CRISPR-Cas9 enable the modification of cell lines to enhance protein expression, metabolic pathways, and product yields.

5. **Agricultural Biotechnology:**
   a. Cell biology is applied in agricultural biotechnology for crop improvement, genetic engineering, and plant breeding.
   b. Techniques such as tissue culture, genetic transformation, and gene editing are used to develop crops with desirable traits such as disease resistance, drought tolerance, and increased yield.
   c. Understanding plant cell biology helps in optimizing agricultural practices, improving crop productivity, and ensuring food security.

6. **Environmental Monitoring and Remediation:**
   a. Cell biology techniques are employed in environmental science for assessing the impact of pollutants, toxins, and contaminants on living organisms.
   b. Biomonitoring using cell-based assays and bioindicators helps in evaluating environmental quality and detecting ecological disturbances.
   c. Bioremediation strategies utilize microorganisms and plant cells to degrade pollutants, detoxify hazardous waste, and restore contaminated sites.

Overall, cell biology has diverse applications that contribute to advancing scientific knowledge, improving human health, enhancing food production, and protecting the environment. Continued research and innovation in cell biology hold promise for addressing current challenges and addressing emerging issues in various fields.

STRUCTURE OF CELL AND ITS ORGANELLES

Cells are the basic structural and functional units of life, and their internal components, known as organelles, carry out specific functions necessary for the cell's survival and activity. Below is a detailed look at the structure of eukaryotic cells and their organelles, along with a brief mention of prokaryotic cell structure.

Eukaryotic Cell Structure

Eukaryotic cells are characterized by the presence of a nucleus and various membrane-bound organelles. Here's a detailed description of the key components:

1. Cell Membrane (Plasma Membrane)

   a. **Structure:** A phospholipid bilayer with embedded proteins, cholesterol, and carbohydrates.

   b. **Function:** Regulates the movement of substances in and out of the cell, provides protection, and facilitates communication between cells. The fluid mosaic model describes the cell membrane as a dynamic and flexible structure.

2. Nucleus

   a. **Structure**: Surrounded by a double membrane called the nuclear envelope, which contains nuclear pores. Inside, it houses chromatin (DNA and proteins) and the nucleolus.

   b. **Function:** The control center of the cell, it stores genetic information (DNA) and coordinates activities such as growth, metabolism, and reproduction by regulating gene expression.

3. Nucleolus

   a. **Structure:** A dense region within the nucleus.

   b. **Function**: Produces ribosomal RNA (rRNA) and assembles ribosomes.

4. Cytoplasm

   a. **Structure**: A jelly-like substance composed of cytosol (fluid part), organelles, and cytoskeleton.

   b. **Function**: Provides a medium for chemical reactions and supports and suspends organelles.

5. Mitochondria

a. **Structure:** Double-membrane organelles with an inner membrane folded into cristae and an internal matrix.

b. **Function:** The powerhouse of the cell, they generate ATP through cellular respiration.

6. Ribosomes

a. **Structure**: Composed of rRNA and proteins, existing either as free ribosomes in the cytoplasm or bound to the rough endoplasmic reticulum (ER).

b. **Function**: Synthesize proteins by translating mRNA.

7. Endoplasmic Reticulum (ER)

a. **Rough ER:**

   i. **Structure:** Studded with ribosomes.

   ii. **Function:** Synthesizes and processes proteins.

b. **Smooth ER:**

   i. **Structure**: Lacks ribosomes.

   ii. **Function**: Synthesizes lipids, detoxifies toxins, and stores calcium ions.

8. Golgi Apparatus

a. **Structure**: A series of flattened membranous sacs called cisternae.

b. **Function:** Modifies, sorts, and packages proteins and lipids for transport to different destinations.

9. Lysosomes

a. **Structure**: Membrane-bound vesicles containing digestive enzymes.

b. **Function:** Break down waste materials, cellular debris, and foreign substances.

10. Peroxisomes

a. **Structure**: Membrane-bound organelles containing oxidative enzymes.

b. **Function**: Detoxify harmful substances and break down fatty acids.

11. Cytoskeleton

a. **Structure**: A network of protein filaments and tubules, including microfilaments, intermediate filaments, and microtubules.

b. **Function:** Provides structural support, facilitates cell movement, and aids in intracellular transport.

12. Centrosomes and Centrioles

a. **Structure:** The centrosome is an area in the cell where microtubules are organized; it contains a pair of centrioles in animal cells.

b. **Function**: Play a key role in cell division by organizing the mitotic spindle.

13. Vacuoles

a. **Structure**: Membrane-bound sacs, more prominent in plant cells.

b. **Function**: Store nutrients, waste products, and help maintain turgor pressure in plant cells.

14. Chloroplasts (in Plant Cells)

a. **Structure:** Double-membrane organelles containing chlorophyll and an internal system of thylakoid membranes.

b. **Function:** Conduct photosynthesis to convert light energy into chemical energy.

15. Cell Wall (in Plant Cells, Fungi, and Some Protists)

a. **Structure**: Composed of cellulose (plants), chitin (fungi), or other polysaccharides.

b. **Function:** Provides structural support and protection, and prevents excessive water uptake.

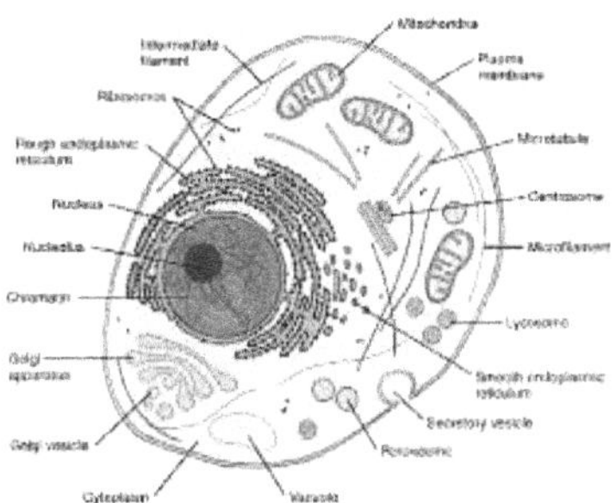

Cell structure

Prokaryotic Cell Structure

Prokaryotic cells, such as bacteria, lack a nucleus and membrane-bound organelles. Here are the main components:

1. Cell Membrane

    a. Similar in structure and function to the eukaryotic cell membrane.

2. Cell Wall

    a. Provides shape and protection, typically composed of peptidoglycan in bacteria.

3. Cytoplasm

    a. Contains all the cellular components within the cell membrane.

4. Nucleoid

    a. Region where the cell's DNA is located, not enclosed by a membrane.

5. Ribosomes

    a. Sites of protein synthesis, structurally smaller than eukaryotic ribosomes.

6. Plasmids

    a. Small, circular DNA molecules that are separate from the chromosomal DNA and can replicate independently.

7. Flagella and Pili

    a. **Flagella:** Long, whip-like structures used for movement.

    b. **Pili:** Short, hair-like structures used for attachment and conjugation.

Conclusion

Understanding the structure and function of cells and their organelles is fundamental to cell biology. This knowledge helps elucidate how cells operate, interact, and contribute to the overall functioning of organisms. It also provides insights into the mechanisms of diseases and the development of medical and biotechnological applications.

FUNCTIONS OF CELL AND ITS ORGANELLES

Cells are the fundamental units of life, and their organelles carry out specialized functions essential for the survival and proper functioning of the cell. Below is a detailed look at the functions of cells and their organelles.

Eukaryotic Cell Functions and Organelles

1. Cell Membrane (Plasma Membrane)

    a. **Function:**

        i. **Selective Permeability**: Controls the movement of substances in and out of the cell, allowing essential nutrients to enter and waste products to leave.

        ii. **Communication**: Contains receptors that receive and transmit signals from the environment and other cells.

        iii. **Protection**: Provides a barrier against harmful substances and pathogens.

        iv. **Cell Recognition**: Glycoproteins and glycolipids on the cell surface are involved in cell recognition and signaling.

2. Nucleus

    a. **Function:**

        i. **Genetic Control Center**: Houses the cell's DNA, which contains the instructions for protein synthesis and cell reproduction.

        ii. **Regulation of Gene Expression**: Controls which genes are turned on or off, influencing cell function and differentiation.

        iii. **RNA Synthesis**: Site of transcription where mRNA is synthesized from DNA.

3. **Nucleolus**

   a. **Function:**

      i. **Ribosome Production**: Synthesizes rRNA and assembles ribosomal subunits, which are then transported to the cytoplasm for protein synthesis.

4. **Cytoplasm**

   a. **Function:**

      i. **Medium for Chemical Reactions**: Provides a site for metabolic activities and biochemical reactions essential for cell survival.

      ii. **Support and Suspension**: Supports organelles and allows for their movement within the cell.

5. **Mitochondria**

   a. **Function:**

      i. **ATP Production:** Generates ATP through oxidative phosphorylation during cellular respiration, providing energy for cellular processes.

      ii. **Regulation of Metabolic** Activity: Involved in various metabolic pathways, including the citric acid cycle and fatty acid oxidation.

      iii. **Apoptosis:** Plays a role in programmed cell death by releasing cytochrome c.

6. **Ribosomes**

   a. **Function:**

      i. **Protein Synthesis**: Translate mRNA into polypeptide chains (proteins) during translation, a key process in gene expression.

7. **Endoplasmic Reticulum (ER)**

   a. **Rough ER:**

      i. **Protein Synthesis**: Synthesizes proteins destined for the cell membrane, lysosomes, or export from the cell.

ii. **Protein Folding and Quality Control**: Ensures newly synthesized proteins are correctly folded and modified.

b. Smooth ER:

i. **Lipid Synthesis**: Synthesizes lipids, including phospholipids and steroids.

ii. **Detoxification**: Metabolizes and detoxifies harmful substances and drugs.

iii. **Calcium Storage**: Stores and regulates calcium ions, which are important for muscle contraction and other cellular functions.

8. Golgi Apparatus

a. Function:

a. **Modification of Proteins and Lipids**: Modifies proteins and lipids received from the ER by adding carbohydrate groups (glycosylation) and other modifications.

b. **Sorting and Packaging**: Sorts and packages proteins and lipids into vesicles for transport to their destined locations, including the cell membrane, lysosomes, or secretion outside the cell.

c. **Formation of Lysosomes**: Involved in the formation of lysosomes.

9. Lysosomes

a. Function:

i. **Digestion**: Contain hydrolytic enzymes that break down waste materials, cellular debris, and foreign substances.

ii. **Autophagy:** Involved in the degradation and recycling of damaged organelles and macromolecules.

10. Peroxisomes

a. Function:

i. **Detoxification:** Break down toxic substances such as hydrogen peroxide using the enzyme catalase.

ii. **Fatty Acid Oxidation**: Involved in the β-oxidation of very long-chain fatty acids.

11. Cytoskeleton

a. Function:

i. **Structural Support**: Provides mechanical support to the cell, maintaining its shape.

ii. **Cell Movement**: Facilitates cell movement through structures like cilia, flagella, and actin filaments.

iii. **Intracellular Transport**: Aids in the movement of organelles, vesicles, and other cellular components within the cell.

iv. **Cell Division**: Involved in the formation of the mitotic spindle and cytokinesis.

12. Centrosomes and Centrioles

a. Function:

i. **Microtubule Organization**: Organize the microtubules in the cell and play a crucial role in the formation of the mitotic spindle during cell division.

ii. **Cell Division**: Centrioles help in the process of cytokinesis and the organization of the spindle fibers.

13. Vacuoles

a. Function:

i. **Storage:** Store nutrients, waste products, and other substances.

ii. **Turgor Pressure: In** plant cells, vacuoles maintain turgor pressure, which keeps the plant rigid and upright.

iii. **Digestion**: Similar to lysosomes, they can contain enzymes for breaking down macromolecules.

14. Chloroplasts (in Plant Cells)

a. **Function:**

    i. **Photosynthesis**: Convert light energy into chemical energy (glucose) through photosynthesis.

    ii. **Production of Oxygen**: Release oxygen as a byproduct of photosynthesis.

15. Cell Wall (in Plant Cells, Fungi, and Some Protists)

a. **Function:**

    i. **Structural Support**: Provides rigidity and strength to the cell, protecting it against mechanical stress.

    ii. **Protection**: Acts as a barrier against pathogens and physical damage.

    iii. **Regulation of Growth**: Controls the direction of cell growth and expansion.

Prokaryotic Cell Functions and Organelles

Prokaryotic cells, though simpler than eukaryotic cells, have essential functions carried out by their structures:

1. Cell Membrane

a. **Function**: Similar to eukaryotic cells, it controls the movement of substances, provides a barrier, and facilitates communication.

2. Cell Wall

a. **Function:** Provides shape, protection, and prevents osmotic lysis.

3. Cytoplasm

a. **Function:** Site for metabolic activities and biochemical reactions.

4. Nucleoid

a. **Function:** Contains the cell's genetic material (DNA) and controls cellular activities.

5. Ribosomes

- **Function**: Synthesize proteins necessary for various cellular functions.

6. Plasmids

a. **Function:** Carry extra-chromosomal DNA that often contains genes beneficial for survival, such as antibiotic resistance genes.

7. Flagella and Pili

a. **Flagella**: Enable locomotion, allowing the cell to move towards favorable environments.

b. **Pili:** Facilitate attachment to surfaces and other cells, and in some cases, allow for the transfer of genetic material (conjugation).

Conclusion

The functions of cells and their organelles are highly specialized and coordinated, ensuring the survival, growth, and reproduction of the cell. Understanding these functions provides insight into the fundamental processes of life and is crucial for advancements in medical and biotechnological fields.

GENOME ORGANIZATION

The genome of an organism encompasses all of its genetic material, including genes and non-coding sequences of DNA or RNA. The organization of the genome is crucial for understanding how genetic information is stored, accessed, and regulated within a cell. Below is a detailed look at genome organization in both prokaryotic and eukaryotic cells.

Prokaryotic Genome Organization

Prokaryotic cells, such as bacteria and archaea, have simpler genome structures compared to eukaryotic cells. Their genomes are typically organized as follows:

1. Chromosomal DNA

a. **Structure:**

i. **Single Circular Chromosome**: Prokaryotes generally have a single, circular chromosome that contains most of their genetic material.

ii. **Nucleoid Region**: The chromosome is located in the nucleoid region of the cell, which is not enclosed by a membrane.

b. **Function:**

i. **Genetic Information Storage**: Contains genes essential for the survival and reproduction of the organism.

ii. **Gene Expression and Regulation**: Genes are transcribed and translated into proteins required for cellular functions.

2. Plasmids

a. **Structure:**

i. **Small Circular DNA Molecules**: Plasmids are separate from the chromosomal DNA and can replicate independently.

ii. **Variable Copy Number**: Plasmids can exist in multiple copies within a cell.

b. **Function:**

i. **Antibiotic Resistance**: Often carry genes that confer resistance to antibiotics.

ii. **Metabolic Functions**: May contain genes for specific metabolic pathways.

iii. **Horizontal Gene Transfer**: Can be transferred between cells, facilitating genetic diversity.

3. Operons

a. **Structure:**

i. **Clusters of Genes**: Genes are organized into operons, which are groups of functionally related genes transcribed together from a single promoter.

b. **Function:**

i. **Coordinated Gene Expression**: Allows for the coordinated expression of genes involved in the same pathway or process.

ii. **Regulation**: Operons can be regulated by repressor or activator proteins in response to environmental signals.

Eukaryotic Genome Organization

Eukaryotic cells have more complex genomes, which are organized into multiple linear chromosomes contained within a nucleus. The organization includes:

1. Chromosomal DNA

    a. Structure:

        i. **Linear Chromosomes**: Eukaryotic genomes are composed of multiple linear chromosomes.

        ii. **Nucleus**: Chromosomes are enclosed within the nuclear membrane.

    b. Function:

        i. **Genetic Information Storage:** Contains the entire genetic blueprint of the organism.

        ii. **Gene Expression and Regulation**: Genes are transcribed into mRNA, which is then translated into proteins.

2. Chromatin Structure

    a. Structure:

        i. **Nucleosomes**: DNA is wrapped around histone proteins, forming nucleosomes, the basic unit of chromatin.

        ii. **Higher-Order Structures**: Nucleosomes are further organized into higher-order structures, such as solenoids and loops, to form chromatin.

    b. Function:

        i. **DNA Packaging**: Efficiently packages DNA within the nucleus.

        ii. **Regulation of Gene Expression**: Chromatin structure influences gene accessibility and expression. Euchromatin is less condensed and transcriptionally active, while heterochromatin is more condensed and transcriptionally silent.

3. Nuclear Organization

a. Structure:

i. **Nuclear Envelope**: Double membrane that encloses the nucleus, with nuclear pores allowing exchange of materials.

ii. **Nuclear Matrix**: A network of fibers providing structural support and organizing chromatin within the nucleus.

iii. **Nucleolus**: A region within the nucleus where ribosomal RNA (rRNA) synthesis and ribosome assembly occur.

b. Function:

i. **Compartmentalization**: Separates genetic material from the cytoplasm, allowing for regulation of transcription and RNA processing.

ii. **RNA Processing**: Pre-mRNA is processed into mature mRNA within the nucleus before being transported to the cytoplasm for translation.

4. Mitochondrial and Chloroplast Genomes

a. Structure:

i. **Circular DNA Molecules**: Both organelles contain their own circular DNA, similar to prokaryotic genomes.

ii. **Multiple Copies**: Multiple copies of these genomes exist within each organelle.

b. Function:

i. **Energy Production**: Mitochondrial DNA encodes proteins essential for oxidative phosphorylation.

ii. **Photosynthesis: Chloroplast** DNA encodes proteins involved in photosynthesis.

    iii. **Maternal Inheritance**: Mitochondrial and chloroplast DNA are typically inherited maternally.

5. Non-Coding DNA

    a. **Structure:**

        i. **Introns**: Non-coding sequences within genes that are removed during RNA processing.

        ii. **Regulatory Sequences**: Promoters, enhancers, and silencers that regulate gene expression.

        iii. **Repetitive DNA**: Includes satellite DNA, microsatellites, and transposable elements.

    b. **Function:**

        i. **Gene Regulation**: Non-coding DNA plays crucial roles in regulating gene expression.

        ii. **Genome Stability**: Repetitive DNA elements contribute to chromosomal structure and integrity.

Functional Implications of Genome Organization

1. Gene Expression Regulation

    a. **Epigenetic Modifications**: Chemical modifications of DNA and histones (e.g., methylation, acetylation) regulate gene expression without altering the DNA sequence.

    b. **Chromatin Remodeling:** Changes in chromatin structure influence gene accessibility and transcriptional activity.

2. Genome Replication and Segregation

    a. **DNA Replication**: Accurate replication of the genome during the S phase of the cell cycle ensures genetic continuity.

    b. **Chromosome Segregation**: Proper segregation of chromosomes during mitosis and meiosis is essential for genetic stability and variation.

3. Genomic Evolution and Diversity

a. **Mutations:** Changes in DNA sequence can introduce genetic diversity and drive evolution.

b. **Horizontal Gene Transfer**: In prokaryotes, horizontal gene transfer can rapidly spread beneficial genes, such as antibiotic resistance.

GENE EXPRESSION AND ITS REGULATION

Gene expression is the process by which information from a gene is used to synthesize functional gene products, typically proteins, but also functional RNAs in some cases. The regulation of gene expression is a complex, highly controlled process that ensures that the right genes are expressed at the right times and in the right amounts. This regulation is crucial for cellular function, differentiation, and adaptation to environmental changes.

Overview of Gene Expression

Gene expression involves several key steps:

1. **Transcription:** The process of copying a gene's DNA sequence into messenger RNA (mRNA).

2. **RNA Processing**: Modifications made to the pre-mRNA, including splicing, capping, and polyadenylation.

3. **Translation**: The process where ribosomes synthesize proteins based on the sequence of the mRNA.

4. **Post-Translational Modifications**: Modifications to the protein that affect its function and stability.

1. Transcription

Initiation:

a. **Promoters**: Specific DNA sequences where RNA polymerase binds to initiate transcription. Promoters contain core elements like the TATA box.

b. **Transcription Factors**: Proteins that bind to specific DNA sequences to regulate transcription. They can act as activators or repressors.

c. **RNA Polymerase**: The enzyme that synthesizes RNA from the DNA template.

Elongation:

a. RNA polymerase moves along the DNA, unwinding the double helix and synthesizing a complementary RNA strand.

Termination:

a. In prokaryotes, termination can occur via rho-dependent or rho-independent mechanisms.

b. In eukaryotes, termination involves cleavage of the newly synthesized RNA followed by polyadenylation.

2. RNA Processing (Eukaryotes)

Capping:

a. Addition of a 7-methylguanosine cap to the 5' end of the pre-mRNA, protecting it from degradation and aiding in ribosome binding.

Splicing:

a. Removal of introns (non-coding regions) and joining of exons (coding regions) by the spliceosome complex.

Polyadenylation:

a. Addition of a poly(A) tail to the 3' end of the mRNA, enhancing stability and export from the nucleus.

3. Translation

Initiation:

a. Ribosomes assemble around the mRNA, and the initiator tRNA binds to the start codon (AUG).

Elongation:

a. Ribosomes move along the mRNA, adding amino acids to the growing polypeptide chain based on the sequence of codons.

Termination:

a. The process ends when the ribosome reaches a stop codon (UAA, UAG, UGA), releasing the completed polypeptide.

4. Post-Translational Modifications

a. **Phosphorylation**: Addition of phosphate groups, often regulating protein activity.

b. **Glycosylation**: Addition of carbohydrate groups, important for protein folding and stability.

c. **Ubiquitination: Addition** of ubiquitin molecules, targeting proteins for degradation by the proteasome.

d. **Proteolytic Cleavage**: Removal of specific peptide segments to activate or deactivate a protein.

Regulation of Gene Expression

Gene expression is regulated at multiple levels to ensure precise control. These regulatory mechanisms can be broadly categorized as follows:

1. Regulation of Transcription

Promoter and Enhancer Elements:

a. **Promoters:** Core promoters are essential for the basic initiation of transcription, while proximal promoters help regulate the frequency of transcription initiation.

b. **Enhancers:** Distant regulatory elements that enhance transcription levels by interacting with promoters through DNA looping.

Transcription Factors:

a. Proteins that bind to specific DNA sequences to regulate transcription. They include activators, which increase transcription, and repressors, which decrease it.

Epigenetic Modifications:

a. **DNA Methylation**: Addition of methyl groups to DNA, typically reducing gene expression by hindering transcription factor binding.

b. **Histone Modifications**: Chemical modifications of histone proteins (e.g., acetylation, methylation) that affect chromatin structure and gene accessibility.

Chromatin Remodeling:

a. The alteration of chromatin structure to regulate access to DNA. Chromatin remodeling complexes can slide, eject, or restructure nucleosomes.

2. Post-Transcriptional Regulation

Alternative Splicing:

a. Producing different mRNA isoforms from the same gene by varying the combination of exons included in the final mRNA.

mRNA Stability:

a. The stability of mRNA molecules can be regulated by elements in the mRNA sequence (e.g., AU-rich elements) and by binding proteins or microRNAs (miRNAs).

RNA Interference (RNAi):

a. Small non-coding RNAs, such as miRNAs and small interfering RNAs (siRNAs), can bind to mRNA and inhibit translation or promote degradation.

3. Translational Regulation

Regulation of Initiation:

a. The initiation of translation can be regulated by initiation factors and other proteins that influence the assembly of the ribosome on the mRNA.

mRNA Localization:

a. The spatial distribution of mRNA within the cell can influence where and when proteins are synthesized.

4. Post-Translational Regulation

Protein Modifications:

a. Post-translational modifications (e.g., phosphorylation, ubiquitination) can regulate protein activity, localization, and stability.

Proteasome-Mediated Degradation:

a. Ubiquitinated proteins are targeted for degradation by the proteasome, controlling protein levels and removing damaged or misfolded proteins.

Regulatory Networks and Systems Biology

Gene expression regulation is often studied within the context of complex networks. Systems biology approaches involve:

Gene Regulatory Networks (GRNs):

a. Networks of interactions between genes, transcription factors, and other molecules that control gene expression.

Signal Transduction Pathways:

a. Pathways that transmit signals from the cell surface to the nucleus, influencing gene expression in response to external stimuli.

IMPORTANCE OF SIRNA AND MICRO RNA

Small interfering RNAs (siRNAs) and microRNAs (miRNAs) are essential components of the RNA interference (RNAi) pathway, a biological process in which RNA molecules inhibit gene expression or translation by neutralizing targeted mRNA molecules. These small RNAs play critical roles in regulating gene expression, maintaining genome stability, and defending against viral infections. Here is a detailed look at the significance of siRNAs and miRNAs in cell biology.

Small Interfering RNA (siRNA)

Origin and Biogenesis

a. **Origin**: siRNAs are typically exogenous double-stranded RNA (dsRNA) molecules, such as those derived from viruses or introduced experimentally.

b. **Biogenesis**: The enzyme Dicer processes long dsRNA into short 20-25 nucleotide siRNA duplexes. These duplexes are then loaded into the RNA-induced silencing complex (RISC).

Mechanism of Action

1. **Incorporation into RISC**: One strand of the siRNA duplex (the guide strand) is incorporated into RISC, while the other strand (the passenger strand) is degraded.
2. **Target Recognition**: The guide strand directs RISC to complementary mRNA molecules.
3. **mRNA Cleavage**: Argonaute (AGO) proteins within RISC cleave the target mRNA, leading to its degradation and thus preventing translation.

Functions and Applications

a. **Gene Silencing**: siRNAs are highly specific and efficient in knocking down the expression of target genes, making them powerful tools for studying gene function.
b. **Antiviral Defense**: siRNAs can target and degrade viral RNA, providing a defense mechanism against viral infections.
c. **Therapeutic Applications**: siRNA-based therapies are being developed to silence disease-causing genes, including treatments for genetic disorders, cancers, and viral infections.

MicroRNA (miRNA)

Origin and Biogenesis

a. **Origin:** miRNAs are endogenous, non-coding RNA molecules transcribed from miRNA genes or derived from introns of protein-coding genes.
b. **Biogenesis:**
   1. **Primary miRNA (pri-miRNA) Transcription**: miRNA genes are transcribed by RNA polymerase II, producing pri-miRNAs.

2. **Processing by Drosha**: Pri-miRNAs are processed in the nucleus by the Drosha-DGCR8 complex into precursor miRNAs (pre-miRNAs).

3. **Export and Dicer Processing**: Pre-miRNAs are exported to the cytoplasm and further processed by Dicer into mature miRNA duplexes. One strand (the guide strand) is incorporated into RISC, while the other strand is degraded.

Mechanism of Action

1. **Incorporation into RISC**: The mature miRNA is incorporated into RISC.

2. **Target Recognition:** miRNAs typically bind to complementary sequences in the 3' untranslated region (3' UTR) of target mRNAs.

3. **Translation Repression or Degradation**: Binding of miRNA to its target can result in translational repression or mRNA degradation, depending on the degree of complementarity.

Functions

a. **Gene Regulation:** miRNAs regulate gene expression post-transcriptionally, affecting various cellular processes such as development, differentiation, proliferation, and apoptosis.

b. **Developmental Timing**: miRNAs play crucial roles in controlling the timing of developmental events in multicellular organisms.

c. **Cell Differentiation**: miRNAs help establish and maintain cell identity by regulating the expression of lineage-specific genes.

d. **Stress Response:** miRNAs are involved in cellular responses to stress, including hypoxia, oxidative stress, and nutrient deprivation.

Biological Importance

Gene Expression Regulation

a. **B**oth siRNAs and miRNAs regulate gene expression at the post-transcriptional level, ensuring precise control over protein production.

b. miRNAs, in particular, can regulate multiple target mRNAs simultaneously, acting as fine-tuners of gene expression networks.

Maintenance of Genomic Stability

a. siRNAs help maintain genomic stability by silencing transposable elements and preventing their mobilization.

b. They also play a role in heterochromatin formation and maintenance, contributing to genome organization and integrity.

Immune Defense

a. siRNAs provide an innate immune defense mechanism against viral infections by targeting and degrading viral RNA.

b. miRNAs can modulate immune responses by regulating the expression of genes involved in immune cell development and function.

Development and Differentiation

a. miRNAs are crucial in developmental processes, influencing cell fate decisions, tissue patterning, and organogenesis.

b. They contribute to the maintenance of stem cell pluripotency and the regulation of differentiation pathways.

Disease Implications

a. Dysregulation of miRNAs is associated with various diseases, including cancers, cardiovascular diseases, neurodegenerative disorders, and metabolic conditions.

b. Aberrant miRNA expression can lead to uncontrolled cell proliferation, resistance to apoptosis, and metastasis in cancers.

Therapeutic Applications

RNAi-Based Therapies

a. **siRNA Therapeutics**: siRNAs are being developed as therapeutic agents to silence disease-causing genes. Examples include treatments for genetic disorders, viral infections, and cancers.

b. **miRNA Mimics and Inhibitors**: miRNA-based therapies involve using miRNA mimics to restore the function of downregulated miRNAs or using miRNA inhibitors (antagomirs) to block overexpressed miRNAs.

Drug Delivery Systems

a. Effective delivery systems, such as lipid nanoparticles and viral vectors, are being developed to deliver siRNA and miRNA-based therapeutics to target tissues and cells.

Conclusion

siRNAs and miRNAs are critical regulators of gene expression with significant roles in maintaining cellular function, development, and genome stability. Their precise control mechanisms make them valuable tools for research and therapeutic applications. Understanding their functions and mechanisms opens new avenues for treating various diseases and advancing molecular biology.

GENE MAPPING AND GENE SEQUENCING

Gene mapping and gene sequencing are fundamental techniques in molecular biology that allow researchers to identify the locations and sequences of genes within a genome. These techniques have revolutionized our understanding of genetics, enabling the study of gene function, genetic variation, and the genetic basis of diseases.

Gene Mapping

Gene mapping refers to the process of determining the specific locations of genes on a chromosome. There are two main types of gene mapping: genetic mapping and physical mapping.

Genetic Mapping

Principles:

1. Genetic mapping involves determining the relative positions of genes based on the frequency of recombination during meiosis.

2. It relies on the concept of linkage, where genes located close to each other on the same chromosome are less likely to be separated by recombination.

Methods:

1. **Linkage Analysis:**
   a. **Crossing Experiments**: Researchers cross organisms with different genotypes and analyze the offspring to determine the frequency of recombination between genes.
   b. **Genetic Markers**: Specific DNA sequences or phenotypic traits that can be used to track the inheritance of genes.

2. **Mapping Functions:**
   a. **Recombination Frequency**: The frequency with which crossing over occurs between two genes, expressed as a percentage. 1% recombination frequency equals 1 centimorgan (cM).
   b. **Map Distance**: Calculated from recombination frequencies to create a genetic map. The higher the recombination frequency, the further apart the genes are.

Applications:

1. **Identifying Disease Genes:** Genetic mapping helps in locating genes associated with hereditary diseases.
2. **Breeding Programs**: Used in agriculture and animal breeding to track desirable traits.

Physical Mapping

Principles:

1. Physical mapping determines the actual physical distance between genes or genetic markers on a chromosome, measured in base pairs (bp).

Methods:

1. **Restriction Mapping:**

a. **Restriction Enzymes**: DNA is cut into fragments using restriction enzymes, and the fragments are analyzed by gel electrophoresis to determine their sizes and relative positions.

2. **Fluorescence In Situ Hybridization (FISH):**

    a. **DNA Probes**: Fluorescently labeled DNA probes hybridize to specific chromosome regions, allowing visualization of gene locations under a fluorescence microscope.

3. **Contig Mapping:**

    a. **Clone Libraries**: Large DNA fragments are cloned into vectors to create a library. Overlapping clones are identified to assemble a contiguous sequence (contig).

4. **Radiation Hybrid Mapping:**

    a. **Radiation-Induced Breaks**: Chromosomes are fragmented using radiation, and the fragments are used to determine gene order based on their retention patterns in hybrid cell lines.

Applications:

1. **Genome Projects**: Physical maps are crucial for assembling the complete sequence of a genome.

2. **Comparative Genomics**: Helps in comparing the genomes of different species to identify conserved and divergent regions.

Gene Sequencing

Gene sequencing involves determining the precise order of nucleotides in a DNA molecule. There are several methods of gene sequencing, with next-generation sequencing (NGS) being the most advanced.

Sanger Sequencing

Principles:

Sanger sequencing, also known as the chain-termination method, was the first widely used sequencing technique.

Methods:

1. **DNA Amplification:**
   a. **Template DNA**: The DNA fragment to be sequenced is amplified using polymerase chain reaction (PCR).
2. **Chain Termination:**
   a. **Dideoxynucleotides (ddNTPs):** Incorporation of ddNTPs during DNA synthesis terminates chain elongation.
3. **Gel Electrophoresis:**
   a. **Fragment Separation**: Terminated DNA fragments of different lengths are separated by size using gel electrophoresis.
4. **Sequence Determination:**
   a. **Fluorescent Detection**: The terminal ddNTPs are labeled with fluorescent dyes, allowing the sequence to be read by detecting the fluorescence of each fragment.

Applications:

1. **Gene Identification**: Used for sequencing individual genes and small genomic regions.
2. **Mutation Detection**: Identifying mutations and single nucleotide polymorphisms (SNPs).

Next-Generation Sequencing (NGS)

Principles:

1. NGS technologies enable massively parallel sequencing, allowing the sequencing of millions of DNA fragments simultaneously.

Methods:

1. **Library Preparation:**
   a. **Fragmentation**: DNA is fragmented into short pieces.
   b. **Adapter Ligation**: Short adapter sequences are added to the ends of the DNA fragments.
2. **Amplification:**

a. **Clonal Amplification**: DNA fragments are amplified on a solid surface (e.g., beads or a flow cell) to create clusters of identical sequences.

3. **Sequencing by Synthesis:**

    a. **Real-Time Detection**: DNA polymerase incorporates nucleotides into the growing DNA strand, and each incorporation event is detected in real time by fluorescent or chemiluminescent signals.

4. **Data Analysis:**

    a. **Bioinformatics Tools**: Complex algorithms assemble the short reads into a complete sequence and analyze the data for variants, gene expression, etc.

Applications:

   a. **Whole-Genome Sequencing (WGS):** Sequencing entire genomes to study genetic variation, evolutionary biology, and personalized medicine.

   b. **Transcriptome Sequencing (RNA-Seq):** Sequencing RNA to analyze gene expression and alternative splicing.

   c. **Epigenome Sequencing**: Mapping DNA methylation and histone modifications to study epigenetic regulation.

Functional Implications of Gene Mapping and Sequencing

Understanding Genetic Diseases:

   a. Gene mapping and sequencing identify disease-causing mutations and genetic predispositions, leading to better diagnosis, treatment, and prevention strategies.

Advancing Personalized Medicine:

Sequencing individual genomes allows for tailored medical treatments based on a person's unique genetic makeup.

Exploring Evolution and Biodiversity:

Comparative genomics reveals evolutionary relationships and the genetic basis of adaptations across species.

Improving Agricultural Practices:

Identifying genes responsible for desirable traits in crops and livestock enhances selective breeding programs.

Unraveling Complex Traits:

Studying the genetic basis of complex traits, such as behavior and susceptibility to multifactorial diseases, provides insights into their underlying mechanisms.

CELL CYCLES AND ITS REGULATION

The cell cycle is a series of orderly events that lead to cell growth, DNA replication, and cell division. This process is fundamental to growth, development, and maintenance of tissues in multicellular organisms. The cell cycle is tightly regulated to ensure accuracy and to prevent uncontrolled cell proliferation, which can lead to cancer. Below is a detailed overview of the cell cycle and its regulation.

Phases of the Cell Cycle

The cell cycle consists of four main phases: G1, S, G2, and M.

1. G1 Phase (Gap 1 Phase)

a. **Cell Growth**: The cell increases in size and prepares for DNA replication.

b. **Protein Synthesis**: Essential proteins and organelles are synthesized.

c. **Checkpoint**: The G1 checkpoint ensures the cell is ready for DNA synthesis. It checks for DNA damage and ensures sufficient resources are available.

2. S Phase (Synthesis Phase)

a. **DNA Replication**: The cell replicates its DNA, so each daughter cell will have a complete set of chromosomes.

b. **Centrosome Duplication**: The centrosome, which helps in chromosome segregation, is also duplicated.

3. G2 Phase (Gap 2 Phase)

a. **Further Growth:** The cell continues to grow and produce proteins, particularly those needed for mitosis.

b. **Preparation for Mitosis**: Organelles are duplicated, and the cytoskeleton is reorganized.

c. **Checkpoint:** The G2 checkpoint ensures that DNA replication is complete and checks for DNA damage. If errors are detected, the cell cycle is halted for repairs.

4. M Phase (Mitosis Phase)

a. **Mitosis:** The cell's chromosomes are divided between two daughter nuclei. Mitosis is subdivided into prophase, prometaphase, metaphase, anaphase, and telophase.

b. **Cytokines**is: The cell's cytoplasm divides, creating two daughter cells. In animal cells, a contractile ring forms, while in plant cells, a cell plate forms to separate the daughter cells.

Regulation of the Cell Cycle

The cell cycle is regulated by a complex network of signaling pathways that ensure each phase is completed accurately before the next phase begins. Key regulatory mechanisms include:

Cyclins and Cyclin-Dependent Kinases (CDKs)

Cyclins:

1. **Role**: Cyclins are regulatory proteins whose levels fluctuate throughout the cell cycle. They activate CDKs.

2. **Types:** Different cyclins are active at different phases, such as cyclin D in G1, cyclin E in late G1 and S, cyclin A in S and G2, and cyclin B in M phase.

CDKs:

1. **Role:** CDKs are kinases that, when activated by binding to cyclins, phosphorylate target proteins to drive the cell cycle forward.

2. **Regulation**: CDK activity is tightly regulated by cyclin availability, CDK inhibitors (CKIs), and phosphorylation/dephosphorylation events.

Checkpoints

G1 Checkpoint (Restriction Point):

1. **Function**: Assesses cell size, nutrient availability, growth factors, and DNA integrity.
2. **Control**: p53 protein can induce cell cycle arrest or apoptosis in response to DNA damage.

S Phase Checkpoint:

1. **Function:** Ensures that DNA replication occurs accurately and that any damage is repaired before replication continues.

G2 Checkpoint:

1. **Function**: Verifies DNA replication completeness and checks for DNA damage.
2. **Control: ATR** and ATM kinases respond to DNA damage by activating repair pathways and halting the cell cycle.

M Checkpoint (Spindle Assembly Checkpoint):

1. **Function**: Ensures that all chromosomes are properly attached to the spindle apparatus before anaphase begins.
2. **Control:** Involves proteins like MAD2 and BUBR1, which inhibit the anaphase-promoting complex (APC) until all chromosomes are correctly attached.

Tumor Suppressors and Oncogenes

Tumor Suppressors:

1. **p53:** Activates DNA repair proteins, induces cell cycle arrest at G1/S checkpoint, and can initiate apoptosis if damage is irreparable.
2. **RB (Retinoblastoma Protein):** Inhibits cell cycle progression from G1 to S phase by binding and inactivating E2F transcription factors.

Oncogenes:

1. **Cyclin D and CDK4/6**: Overexpression can drive uncontrolled cell proliferation.

2. **MYC**: Promotes cell cycle progression by regulating cyclin and CDK expression.

DNA Damage Response and Repair

Cells possess multiple DNA repair mechanisms to maintain genomic integrity. The DNA damage response (DDR) involves:

Sensing Damage:

1. **Sensor Proteins**: Detect DNA damage and recruit repair machinery. Examples include the MRN complex (MRE11-RAD50-NBS1).

Signal Transduction:

1. **Kinases**: ATM and ATR kinases phosphorylate and activate downstream effectors like p53 and CHK1/CHK2.

Effector Responses:

1. **Cell Cycle Arrest**: Temporarily halts cell cycle progression to allow for DNA repair.

2. **DNA Repair Mechanisms**: Include nucleotide excision repair (NER), base excision repair (BER), mismatch repair (MMR), and homologous recombination (HR).

3. **Apoptosi**s: If the damage is too severe, the cell may undergo programmed cell death to prevent propagation of damaged DNA.

Cell Cycle Dysregulation and Disease

Cancer:

1. **Uncontrolled Proliferation**: Mutations in genes regulating the cell cycle (e.g., TP53, RB1, CDKs) can lead to unchecked cell division and cancer.

2. **Genomic Instability:** Defective checkpoints and DNA repair mechanisms contribute to the accumulation of mutations.

Developmental Disorders:

1. **Cell Cycle Genes**: Mutations in genes critical for cell cycle regulation can result in developmental abnormalities and diseases.

Aging:

1. **Senescence:** Cells enter a state of permanent growth arrest (senescence) in response to DNA damage or stress, contributing to aging.

CELL DEATH– EVENTS, REGULATORS

Cell death is a fundamental biological process that occurs in a highly regulated manner. It is essential for maintaining cellular homeostasis, development, and defense against diseases. There are several forms of cell death, each with distinct molecular mechanisms and regulatory pathways. The major types include apoptosis, necrosis, and autophagy.

Types of Cell Death

Apoptosis

Apoptosis is a form of programmed cell death that is crucial for development and tissue homeostasis. It is characterized by a series of controlled, energy-dependent steps that lead to the elimination of cells without triggering an inflammatory response.

Events of Apoptosis:

1. **Initiation:**
   a. **Intrinsic Pathway**: Triggered by internal signals such as DNA damage, oxidative stress, or oncogene activation. Key events include mitochondrial outer membrane permeabilization (MOMP) and release of cytochrome c.
   b. **Extrinsic Pathway**: Triggered by external signals, such as binding of ligands (e.g., FasL, TNF-α) to death receptors (e.g., Fas, TNFR).

2. **Execution:**
   a. **Caspase Activation**: Both pathways converge on the activation of caspases, a family of cysteine proteases. Initiator caspases (e.g.,

caspase-8, caspase-9) activate executioner caspases (e.g., caspase-3, caspase-7).

b. **DNA Fragmentation**: Executioner caspases cleave cellular substrates, leading to DNA fragmentation and cell dismantling.

3. **Cell Disassembly:**

a. **Formation of Apoptotic Bodies**: The cell shrinks, the nuclear envelope disassembles, and the cell membrane forms blebs, packaging cellular components into apoptotic bodies.

b. **Phagocytosis:** Apoptotic bodies are recognized and engulfed by phagocytes, preventing inflammation.

Regulators of Apoptosis:

1. **Bcl-2 Family Proteins**: Regulate the intrinsic pathway. Pro-apoptotic members (e.g., Bax, Bak) promote MOMP, while anti-apoptotic members (e.g., Bcl-2, Bcl-xL) inhibit it.

2. **Death Receptors and Ligands**: Regulate the extrinsic pathway. Examples include Fas/FasL and TNFR/TNF-α.

3. **Caspases**: Central executioners of apoptosis. Their activity is tightly regulated by inhibitors of apoptosis proteins (IAPs) and activating proteins (e.g., Apaf-1, FADD).

Necrosis

Necrosis is a form of uncontrolled cell death typically resulting from acute injury, such as trauma, infection, or ischemia. Unlike apoptosis, necrosis often triggers an inflammatory response due to the release of cellular contents into the extracellular space.

Events of Necrosis:

1. **Loss of Membrane Integrity**: The cell membrane becomes permeable, leading to swelling and rupture.

2. **Release of Cellular Contents**: Cellular components, including damage-associated molecular patterns (DAMPs), are released, causing inflammation.

3. **Energy Depletion**: Necrosis is often associated with ATP depletion, leading to the failure of ion pumps and loss of cellular homeostasis.

Regulators of Necrosis:

1. **Reactive Oxygen Species (ROS):** Elevated levels of ROS can damage cellular components and trigger necrosis.

2. **Calcium Overload**: Disruption of calcium homeostasis can activate degradative enzymes and promote cell death.

3. **Proteases:** Calpains and other proteases are activated by calcium and contribute to cellular disintegration.

Autophagy

Autophagy is a process where cells degrade and recycle their own components through the lysosomal machinery. It can serve as a survival mechanism under stress conditions but may also lead to cell death if excessively activated.

Events of Autophagy:

1. **Initiation:**

    a. **Autophagosome Formation**: Cytoplasmic components are enclosed within double-membrane vesicles called autophagosomes.

    b. **Signaling Pathways**: Key regulators include the mammalian target of rapamycin (mTOR), AMP-activated protein kinase (AMPK), and Beclin-1.

2. **Maturation and Fusion:**

    a. **Autophagosome Maturation**: Autophagosomes mature by fusing with lysosomes to form autolysosomes.

    b. **Degradation:** Lysosomal enzymes degrade the autophagosome contents, releasing basic building blocks for reuse.

3. **Regulation of Autophagy-Dependent Cell Death:**

a. **Balance with Apoptosis**: Autophagy can inhibit or promote apoptosis depending on the context. For example, it can degrade damaged mitochondria (mitophagy), reducing ROS production and preventing apoptosis.

Regulators of Autophagy:

a. **mTOR**: A key inhibitor of autophagy. When nutrients are abundant, mTOR activity is high, suppressing autophagy.

b. **AMPK:** Activates autophagy in response to low energy levels by inhibiting mTOR and activating autophagy-related genes.

c. **Beclin-1**: A crucial component of the autophagy initiation complex, regulated by interactions with Bcl-2 family proteins and other factors.

Cross-Talk Between Cell Death Pathways

Cells often integrate signals from multiple pathways to determine the mode of cell death. Key points of cross-talk include:

a. **Bcl-2 Family Proteins**: These proteins regulate both apoptosis and autophagy by controlling mitochondrial membrane permeability and interacting with Beclin-1.

b. **p53:** This tumor suppressor can induce apoptosis by upregulating pro-apoptotic genes or autophagy by activating AMPK and inhibiting mTOR.

c. **Caspase**s: While primarily involved in apoptosis, caspases can also modulate autophagy by cleaving autophagy-related proteins.

Implications of Cell Death in Health and Disease

Development:

a. Apoptosis is essential for removing excess or damaged cells during development, shaping tissues and organs.

b. Proper regulation of autophagy is crucial for cellular differentiation and homeostasis.

Cancer:

a. Dysregulation of cell death pathways can lead to uncontrolled cell proliferation and tumor development.

b. Cancer cells often evade apoptosis by mutating key regulators like p53 or overexpressing anti-apoptotic proteins like Bcl-2.

c. Therapeutic strategies aim to restore apoptosis or exploit autophagy to kill cancer cells.

Neurodegenerative Diseases:

a. Excessive apoptosis and autophagy contribute to the loss of neurons in conditions like Alzheimer's and Parkinson's diseases.

b. Understanding the balance between cell survival and death is critical for developing treatments.

Immune Response:

1. Necrosis and the release of DAMPs trigger inflammation, which is crucial for fighting infections but can cause chronic inflammatory diseases if uncontrolled.

2. Apoptosis of infected or damaged cells prevents inflammation and autoimmunity by promoting the clearance of cell debris without triggering an immune response.

INTRINSIC AND EXTRINSIC PATHWAYS OF APOPTOSIS

Sure, apoptosis, or programmed cell death, can be initiated through two main pathways: the intrinsic pathway (also known as the mitochondrial pathway) and the extrinsic pathway (also known as the death receptor pathway). Here's a detailed explanation of both:

1. **Intrinsic Pathway (Mitochondrial Pathway):**

   a. **Initiation:** The intrinsic pathway is initiated by intracellular signals such as DNA damage, growth factor deprivation, or cellular stress. These signals activate pro-apoptotic proteins within the cell.

   b. **Mitochondrial Outer Membrane Permeabilization (MOMP):** The key event in the intrinsic pathway is the permeabilization of the mitochondrial outer membrane, which allows the release of pro-apoptotic proteins from the mitochondrial intermembrane space into the cytosol. These pro-apoptotic proteins include cytochrome c, Smac/DIABLO, and apoptosis-inducing factor (AIF).

c. **Activation of Caspases**: Cytochrome c released from the mitochondria binds to Apaf-1 (apoptotic protease activating factor 1) forming the apoptosome complex. This complex then recruits and activates procaspase-9, initiating a caspase cascade. Caspase-9 activates downstream executioner caspases, such as caspase-3, -6, and -7, leading to cell dismantling.

d. **Regulation**: The intrinsic pathway is tightly regulated by the balance between pro-apoptotic proteins (such as Bax, Bak, and Bid) and anti-apoptotic proteins (such as Bcl-2, Bcl-XL). The relative levels and activities of these proteins determine whether a cell undergoes apoptosis or survives.

2. **Extrinsic Pathway (Death Receptor Pathway):**

a. **Initiation:** The extrinsic pathway is initiated by the binding of extracellular death ligands, such as Fas ligand (FasL) or tumor necrosis factor alpha (TNF-α), to death receptors on the cell surface. Common death receptors include Fas (CD95), TNF receptor 1 (TNFR1), and TRAIL receptors (DR4 and DR5).

b. **Formation of Death-Inducing Signaling Complex (DISC)**: Upon ligand binding, death receptors undergo oligomerization and recruit adaptor proteins such as FADD (Fas-associated death domain) and procaspase-8 to form the DISC.

c. **Activation of Caspases**: Within the DISC, procaspase-8 is activated and becomes caspase-8, which then initiates the caspase cascade by directly activating downstream effector caspases like caspase-3. Alternatively, caspase-8 can cleave Bid, turning it into a pro-apoptotic fragment (tBid) that can initiate the intrinsic pathway by inducing MOMP.

d. **Regulation:** The extrinsic pathway is regulated by factors that control death receptor expression and activation, as well as by cellular FLICE-like inhibitory proteins (c-FLIPs) which can inhibit caspase-8 activation and prevent apoptosis.

Both pathways ultimately converge at the activation of executioner caspases, leading to cell death by mechanisms such as DNA fragmentation, cytoskeletal breakdown, and membrane blebbing. Apoptosis plays crucial roles in various physiological processes including development, tissue homeostasis, and immune response, as well as in pathological conditions such as cancer and neurodegenerative diseases.

NECROSIS AND AUTOPHAGY

Necrosis and autophagy are two distinct cellular processes that can occur in response to various stimuli or conditions. Here's a detailed explanation of each:

Necrosis:

Necrosis is a form of cell death characterized by rapid and uncontrolled cell damage and swelling, leading to the rupture of the cell membrane and release of cellular contents into the surrounding tissue. It is typically associated with pathological conditions, such as trauma, ischemia, or inflammation.

Here's a more detailed exploration of necrosis:

1. **Mechanism:**

   a. **Ischemic Necrosis:** This type of necrosis occurs when tissues are deprived of an adequate blood supply, leading to cellular energy depletion and subsequent cell death. Ischemic necrosis can occur in various organs, such as the heart (resulting in myocardial infarction), brain (resulting in stroke), or limbs (resulting in gangrene).

b. **Chemical or Physical Injury**: Necrosis can also be induced by exposure to toxins, extreme temperatures (heat or cold), radiation, or mechanical trauma. For example, exposure to corrosive chemicals or severe burns can cause necrotic cell death in the affected tissues.

c. **Infection**: Some pathogens, such as certain bacteria and viruses, can induce necrosis through direct damage to cells or by triggering inflammatory responses. Necrotizing infections, such as necrotizing fasciitis or gangrene caused by Clostridium bacteria, are examples of infectious diseases associated with necrosis.

2. **Morphological Features:**

a. Necrotic cells often exhibit distinct morphological changes compared to apoptotic cells. These changes may include cellular swelling, loss of plasma membrane integrity, cytoplasmic vacuolization, and eventual rupture. In some cases, necrotic tissues may appear pale, swollen, and friable upon gross examination.

b. Histologically, necrosis is characterized by the presence of dead cells, cellular debris, and inflammatory infiltrates. Inflammatory responses, including infiltration of immune cells (such as neutrophils and macrophages) and tissue inflammation, typically accompany necrosis.

3. **Consequences:**

a. Necrotic cell death can have significant consequences on tissue integrity and organ function. The release of cellular contents, including damage-associated molecular patterns (DAMPs) and pro-inflammatory cytokines, can trigger immune responses and further exacerbate tissue injury and inflammation.

b. In some cases, necrosis may lead to the formation of necrotic cores within tissues, which can impair blood flow and oxygen delivery, exacerbating tissue damage and promoting further necrosis.

Overall, necrosis represents a pathological form of cell death associated with tissue damage, inflammation, and loss of organ function. Understanding the mechanisms and consequences of necrosis is essential for the development of strategies to prevent or mitigate tissue injury in various disease conditions.

Autophagy:

Autophagy is a highly regulated cellular process involved in the degradation and recycling of cellular components to maintain cellular homeostasis. It plays a crucial role in removing damaged organelles, misfolded proteins, and other cellular debris, thereby promoting cell survival and adaptation to various stress conditions. Here's a detailed explanation of autophagy:

1. **Mechanism:**

    a. **Formation of Autophagosomes**: Autophagy begins with the formation of double-membrane vesicles called autophagosomes. These autophagosomes sequester cytoplasmic material targeted for degradation, including damaged organelles and protein aggregates.

    b. **Lysosomal Fusion**: Autophagosomes then fuse with lysosomes, forming autolysosomes, where the engulfed material is degraded by lysosomal enzymes. The breakdown products, such as amino acids, fatty acids, and nucleotides, can be recycled by the cell for energy production or biosynthesis.

    c. **Regulation**: The process of autophagy is tightly regulated by a complex network of signaling pathways, including the mammalian target of rapamycin (mTOR) pathway, AMP-activated protein kinase (AMPK) pathway, and various autophagy-related genes (ATGs). These pathways integrate diverse signals, such as nutrient availability, energy status, oxidative stress, and growth factor signaling, to modulate autophagic activity accordingly.

2. **Induction:**

    a. **Nutrient Deprivation**: Autophagy is commonly induced under conditions of nutrient deprivation, such as starvation or amino acid withdrawal. In response to nutrient stress, inhibition of mTOR signaling and activation of AMPK promote autophagosome formation and autophagic flux.

    b. **Oxidative Stress**: Oxidative stress, resulting from reactive oxygen species (ROS) accumulation or exposure to toxins, can also induce autophagy as a protective response to remove damaged cellular components and maintain redox homeostasis.

    c. **Other Stimuli**: Autophagy can be triggered by various cellular stresses, including hypoxia, endoplasmic reticulum (ER) stress, intracellular pathogens, and accumulation of misfolded proteins. These stimuli activate specific signaling pathways that converge on the autophagy machinery to promote autophagosome formation and degradation of cargo.

3. **Physiological Functions:**

    a. **Cellular Homeostasis**: Autophagy plays a critical role in maintaining cellular homeostasis by removing damaged organelles (such as mitochondria, peroxisomes, and endoplasmic reticulum), protein aggregates, and intracellular pathogens.

    b. **Development and Differentiation:** Autophagy is essential for various developmental processes, including embryogenesis, tissue remodeling, and cell differentiation. It helps to eliminate unnecessary or unwanted cells during development and ensures proper tissue patterning and organogenesis.

c. **Immune Response**: Autophagy is involved in innate and adaptive immune responses by eliminating intracellular pathogens, facilitating antigen presentation, and regulating inflammatory signaling pathways.

4. **Implications:**

a. Dysregulation of autophagy has been implicated in various human diseases, including cancer, neurodegenerative disorders (such as Alzheimer's disease and Parkinson's disease), metabolic diseases (such as obesity and diabetes), and infectious diseases (such as viral infections and bacterial invasion).

b. Modulation of autophagy has emerged as a potential therapeutic strategy for these conditions. Inducing autophagy can promote cell survival and enhance clearance of toxic aggregates, while inhibiting autophagy may sensitize cancer cells to chemotherapy or promote clearance of intracellular pathogens.

Multiple-choice questions (MCQs) :

1. What is the main function of the cell membrane?

   A) DNA replication

   B) Regulation of molecule passage into and out of the cell

   C) Protein synthesis

   D) Photosynthesis

2. Which organelle is known as the powerhouse of the cell?

   A) Golgi apparatus

   B) Nucleus

   C) Mitochondria

   D) Lysosome

3. Which structure within the nucleus is responsible for rRNA synthesis and ribosome assembly?

A) Chromatin

B) Nucleolus

C) Nuclear envelope

D) Nuclear pore

4. What is the role of lysosomes in the cell?

    A) Energy production

    B) Synthesis of proteins

    C) Breaking down cellular waste

    D) DNA replication

5. The fluid mosaic model describes the structure of the:

    A) Cytoplasm

    B) Cell wall

    C) Plasma membrane

    D) Mitochondrial envelope

6. Which process describes the synthesis of RNA from DNA?

    A) Translation

    B) Transcription

    C) Replication

    D) Mitosis

7. What is the main function of ribosomes in the cell?

    A) Lipid synthesis

    B) Protein synthesis

    C) Detoxification

    D) Energy production

8. The endoplasmic reticulum is involved in:

    A) Synthesizing proteins and lipids

    B) Packaging and transporting proteins

    C) DNA replication

    D) Cell division

9. Which organelle is responsible for photosynthesis in plant cells?

A) Mitochondria

B) Chloroplast

C) Golgi apparatus

D) Lysosome

10. Cell theory states that all living organisms are made up of cells. Who proposed this theory?

A) Charles Darwin

B) Matthias Schleiden and Theodor Schwann

C) Gregor Mendel

D) Louis Pasteur

11. What does the Golgi apparatus do in the cell?

A) Breaks down lipids and carbohydrates

B) Produces ATP

C) Modifies, sorts, and packages proteins

D) Stores genetic information

12. What are peroxisomes primarily involved in?

A) Protein folding

B) Breaking down fatty acids and detoxifying substances

C) Lipid synthesis

D) Calcium storage

13. Which of the following is a function of the cytoskeleton?

A) Intracellular transport

B) Protein synthesis

C) DNA replication

D) Hormone production

14. The main function of the vacuoles in plant cells is to:

A) Produce proteins

B) Synthesize cell walls

C) Store nutrients and regulate turgor pressure

 D) Create energy

15. Which phase of the cell cycle is DNA replicated?

A) G1 phase

B) S phase

C) G2 phase

D) M phase

16. During which phase of mitosis do chromosomes align at the cell's equator?

A) Prophase

B) Metaphase

C) Anaphase

D) Telophase

17. Apoptosis is a process of:

A) Cell preservation

B) Cell division

C) Programmed cell death

D) Uncontrolled cell growth

18. What is the role of mitochondria in cells?

A) Protein synthesis

B) Lipid synthesis

C) Energy production through ATP

D) Modifying proteins

19. Which type of cell communication involves direct contact between cells?

A) Paracrine signaling

B) Endocrine signaling

C) Autocrine signaling

D) Direct cell-cell contact

20. What is the function of smooth endoplasmic reticulum?

A) Protein synthesis

B) Detoxification and lipid synthesis

C) Breaking down waste products

D) DNA replication

Short Answer Questions

1. What is the primary function of mitochondria in the cell?
2. Describe the role of the Golgi apparatus.
3. What are the main components of the cytoskeleton?
4. Explain how the plasma membrane regulates transport into and out of the cell.
5. What is the function of lysosomes?
6. How do ribosomes contribute to protein synthesis?
7. Define the process of apoptosis.
8. What is the difference between rough and smooth endoplasmic reticulum?
9. Describe the structure of a nucleolus.
10. What role do peroxisomes play in the cell?
11. Explain the significance of the cell cycle's G1 phase.
12. How does the structure of a prokaryotic cell differ from that of a eukaryotic cell?
13. What is the purpose of the cell wall in plant cells?
14. Describe the process of autophagy.
15. What are plasmids and their function in bacterial cells?
16. Explain the role of cholesterol in the cell membrane.
17. How does the extrinsic pathway of apoptosis work?
18. What is gene expression and how is it regulated?
19. Describe the process of oxidative phosphorylation.
20. What is the function of the cell membrane's carbohydrate components?

Long Answer Questions

1. Discuss the structure and function of the mitochondria and how they are involved in energy production.
2. Explain the endosymbiotic theory and its significance in the evolution of eukaryotic cells.
3. Describe the stages of the cell cycle and the importance of checkpoints.
4. How do the structures of various organelles contribute to their functions in a typical eukaryotic cell?
5. Discuss the mechanisms and functions of different types of RNA in gene expression.
6. Explain how cell signaling pathways like the MAPK pathway regulate cellular processes.
7. Describe the process of protein synthesis from transcription to translation.
8. Explain the role of autophagy in cellular homeostasis and how it can be dysregulated in disease.
9. Discuss the role of apoptosis in development and disease, detailing both intrinsic and extrinsic pathways.
10. Describe the mechanisms by which cells communicate with each other and how disruptions in these processes can lead to disease.

Answer Key:

1. B) Regulation of molecule passage into and out of the cell
2. C) Mitochondria
3. B) Nucleolus
4. C) Breaking down cellular waste
5. C) Plasma membrane
6. B) Transcription
7. B) Protein synthesis
8. A) Synthesizing proteins and lipids

9. B) Chloroplast

10.B) Matthias Schleiden and Theodor Schwann

11.C) Modifies, sorts, and packages proteins

12.B) Breaking down fatty acids and detoxifying substances

13.A) Intracellular transport

14.C) Store nutrients and regulate turgor pressure

15.B) S phase

16.B) Metaphase

17.C) Programmed cell death

18.C) Energy production through ATP

19.D) Direct cell-cell contact

20.B) Detoxification and lipid synthesis

CHAPTER – 2

CELL SIGNALLINGCELL SIGNALLING

INTRODUCTION:

Cell signaling is a complex system of communication that governs basic cellular activities and coordinates cell actions. Understanding cell signaling is crucial for comprehending how cells function, respond to their environment, and maintain homeostasis. Here's an in-depth look at cell signaling:

1. Overview of Cell Signaling

Cell signaling involves the transmission of signals from a cell's exterior to its interior, allowing cells to respond to changes in their environment. These signals can be in the form of chemical molecules, mechanical stimuli, or electromagnetic waves. The process involves several key steps:

a. **Signal reception**: A signaling molecule binds to a receptor on the cell surface or inside the cell.

b. **Signal transduction**: The signal is relayed inside the cell through a series of molecular events.

c. **Signal response**: The cell executes a specific response, such as altering gene expression or changing cell behavior.

2. Types of Cell Signaling

Cell signaling can be categorized based on the distance the signal travels:

a. **Autocrine signaling**: Cells respond to signals they produce themselves.

b. **Paracrine signaling**: Signals are released by one cell and affect nearby cells.

c. **Endocrine signaling**: Signals (hormones) are released into the bloodstream and affect distant cells.

d. **Juxtacrine signaling**: Direct contact between neighboring cells is required for signal transmission.

3. Key Components of Cell Signaling

a. **Signaling molecules (ligands):** These are the molecules that initiate the signaling process, such as hormones, neurotransmitters, and growth factors.

b. **Receptors:** These are proteins on the cell surface or within cells that bind to signaling molecules. They include:

 i. **G-protein-coupled receptors (GPCRs):** Transmembrane receptors that activate G-proteins.

 ii. **Receptor tyrosine kinases (RTKs):** Transmembrane receptors with enzymatic activity.

 iii. **Ion channel receptors**: Receptors that allow ions to pass through the cell membrane.

 iv. **Intracellular receptors**: Receptors located inside the cell that bind to hydrophobic signaling molecules like steroid hormones.

4. Signal Transduction Pathways

These pathways amplify the signal and lead to a cellular response. Key pathways include:

a. **Second Messengers**: Small molecules like cAMP, IP3, and Ca2+ that propagate the signal inside the cell.

b. **Protein Kinase Cascades**: Sequential activation of protein kinases that amplify and transmit the signal.

c. **MAPK/ERK Pathway**: Involved in cell growth and differentiation.

d. **PI3K/AKT Pathway**: Involved in cell survival and metabolism.

e. **JAK/STAT Pathway**: Involved in immune responses and cell growth.

5. Mechanisms of Signal Termination

To maintain homeostasis and prevent overstimulation, signals must be terminated. This can occur through:

a. **Degradation of signaling molecules**: Enzymatic breakdown of the ligand.

b. **Receptor desensitization**: Receptors become less responsive to the signaling molecule.

c. **Endocytosis of receptors**: Receptors are internalized and degraded.

d. **Deactivation of signal transduction proteins**: Phosphatases remove phosphate groups from proteins, deactivating them.

6. Examples of Cell Signaling Pathways

a. **Insulin signaling**: Regulates glucose uptake and metabolism.

b. **Notch signaling:** Involved in cell differentiation.

c. **Wnt signaling**: Regulates cell fate and proliferation.

d. **TGF-beta signaling**: Controls cell growth and differentiation.

7. Clinical Relevance

Dysregulation of cell signaling pathways can lead to diseases such as cancer, diabetes, and autoimmune disorders. Targeted therapies, such as tyrosine kinase inhibitors and monoclonal antibodies, have been developed to modulate these pathways in disease treatment.

INTERCELLULAR AND INTRACELLULAR SIGNALLING PATHWAYS

Cell signaling encompasses both intercellular (between cells) and intracellular (within a cell) pathways. Each type plays a critical role in ensuring proper communication and function within the body. Here's a detailed examination of these pathways:

Intercellular signalling pathways

Intercellular signaling involves the transmission of signals from one cell to another. This can occur through various mechanisms:

1. Autocrine Signaling

a. **Definition**: A cell secretes signaling molecules that bind to receptors on its own surface, affecting its own activity.

b. **Example:** Growth factors like TGF-β (transforming growth factor-beta) that regulate cell proliferation.

2. Paracrine Signaling

a. **Definition**: Signaling molecules released by a cell affect nearby target cells.

b. **Example:** Neurotransmitters such as acetylcholine released at synaptic junctions between neurons.

3. Endocrine Signaling

a. **Definition**: Hormones are released into the bloodstream by endocrine cells and travel to distant target cells.

b. **Example:** Insulin released by pancreatic beta cells regulates glucose uptake in distant tissues.

4. Juxtacrine Signaling

a. **Definition:** Direct cell-to-cell contact through membrane-bound signaling molecules.

b. **Example**: Notch signaling where the Notch receptor on one cell interacts with its ligand on an adjacent cell, playing a crucial role in cell differentiation.

5. Synaptic Signaling

a. **Definition:** Specialized form of paracrine signaling used by neurons, where neurotransmitters are released into the synaptic cleft.

b. **Example:** Dopamine signaling in the brain influencing mood and behavior.

Intracellular Signaling Pathways

Intracellular signaling refers to the cascades of molecular events within a cell that lead to a specific response following the reception of an extracellular signal. These pathways typically involve a series of steps that amplify and propagate the signal:

1. Second Messenger Systems

a. **Definition**: Small molecules generated inside the cell in response to an extracellular signal that amplify and transmit the signal.

b. **Key Second Messengers**:

    i. **cAMP (Cyclic Adenosine Monophosphate)**: Activates protein kinase A (PKA), influencing metabolism and gene expression.

    ii. **IP3 (Inositol Triphosphate)**: Triggers release of Ca2+ from the endoplasmic reticulum.

    iii. **DAG (Diacylglycerol)**: Activates protein kinase C (PKC), involved in various cellular responses.

    iv. **Ca2+ (Calcium Ions):** Act as a versatile second messenger regulating processes like muscle contraction and neurotransmitter release.

2. Protein Kinase Cascades

a. **Definition:** Sequential activation of protein kinases that phosphorylate target proteins, altering their activity.

b. **Key Pathways:**

    i. **MAPK/ERK Pathway**: Mediates cell growth and differentiation signals. Involves Ras, Raf, MEK, and ERK proteins.

    ii. **PI3K/AKT Pathway**: Regulates cell survival and metabolism. Involves PI3K activation leading to PIP3 production and subsequent activation of AKT.

    iii. **JAK/STAT Pathway**: Transduces signals from cytokines and growth factors leading to transcriptional regulation. Involves JAK kinases and STAT transcription factors.

3. Receptor Tyrosine Kinases (RTKs)

a. **Mechanism**: Binding of ligands such as growth factors leads to dimerization and autophosphorylation of RTKs, activating downstream signaling pathways.

b. **Example:** Epidermal growth factor receptor (EGFR) activation leading to cellular proliferation.

4. G-Protein-Coupled Receptors (GPCRs)

a. **Mechanism**: Ligand binding to GPCRs causes activation of heterotrimeric G-proteins, which then activate or inhibit downstream effectors such as adenylyl cyclase or phospholipase C.

b. **Example**: β-adrenergic receptors regulating cardiac function through cAMP.

5. Nuclear Receptors

a. **Mechanism**: Lipophilic ligands like steroid hormones diffuse into the cell, bind to intracellular receptors, and directly regulate gene transcription.

b. **Example:** Glucocorticoid receptor regulating genes involved in metabolism and immune response.

Integration and Crosstalk

Intracellular signaling pathways often interact, leading to complex networks of signaling cascades. This crosstalk allows for fine-tuned regulation and integration of multiple signals:

a. **Positive and Negative Feedback**: Pathways often include feedback mechanisms to regulate the intensity and duration of the signal.

b. **Pathway Crosstalk**: Signals from different pathways can converge, diverge, or cross-regulate each other, ensuring coordinated cellular responses.

Clinical Relevance

Aberrations in cell signaling pathways can lead to various diseases:

a. **Cancer:** Mutations in RTKs or downstream signaling molecules (e.g., Ras, PI3K) can lead to uncontrolled cell growth.

b. **Diabetes**: Insulin signaling pathway defects result in impaired glucose metabolism.

c. **Autoimmune Diseases**: Dysregulated JAK/STAT signaling can lead to improper immune responses.

Therapeutic interventions often target specific components of these pathways to restore normal signaling and function. For example, kinase inhibitors are used in cancer treatment to block overactive signaling pathways.

CLASSIFICATION OF RECEPTOR FAMILY AND MOLECULAR STRUCTURE LIGAND GATED ION CHANNELS

Receptors play a crucial role in cell signaling by recognizing and binding specific signaling molecules (ligands), leading to cellular responses. Receptor families can be classified based on their molecular structure and mechanism of action. Among these, ligand-gated ion channels are a unique class of receptors that mediate rapid responses to extracellular signals. Here is a detailed examination of the classification of receptor families and the molecular structure of ligand-gated ion channels.

Classification of Receptor Families

Receptor families can be broadly classified into four main categories based on their structure and signaling mechanisms:

1. G-Protein-Coupled Receptors (GPCRs)

    a. **Structure:** Seven transmembrane alpha helices.

    b. **Mechanism**: Ligand binding activates an associated G-protein, which then modulates the activity of downstream effectors (e.g., adenylyl cyclase, phospholipase C).

    c. **Examples**: β-adrenergic receptors, muscarinic acetylcholine receptors.

2. Receptor Tyrosine Kinases (RTKs)

    a. **Structure:** Single transmembrane domain with an extracellular ligand-binding domain and an intracellular kinase domain.

    b. **Mechanism:** Ligand binding induces receptor dimerization and autophosphorylation, activating downstream signaling pathways.

    c. **Examples:** Epidermal growth factor receptor (EGFR), insulin receptor.

3. Ionotropic Receptors (Ligand-Gated Ion Channels)

a. **Structure**: Typically composed of multiple subunits forming a pore through the cell membrane.

b. **Mechanism**: Ligand binding causes a conformational change that opens the ion channel, allowing specific ions to flow across the membrane, altering the cell's electrical potential.

c. **Examples**: Nicotinic acetylcholine receptor (nAChR), GABA_A receptor.

4. Nuclear Receptors

a. **Structure:** Intracellular receptors with a DNA-binding domain and a ligand-binding domain.

b. **Mechanism:** Ligand binding allows the receptor to regulate gene transcription by directly interacting with DNA.

c. **Examples**: Estrogen receptor, glucocorticoid receptor.

Molecular Structure of Ligand-Gated Ion Channels

Ligand-gated ion channels (LGICs) are a subset of ionotropic receptors that are critical for rapid synaptic transmission. They respond to specific neurotransmitters and are essential for processes such as muscle contraction, neural communication, and sensory perception.

General Structure

1. **Subunit Composition:**

    a. LGICs are typically pentameric (composed of five subunits) or tetrameric (composed of four subunits).

    b. Each subunit is a polypeptide chain with multiple transmembrane domains (usually 4 or more).

2. **Transmembrane Domains:**

    a. Each subunit has multiple (often four) transmembrane alpha-helices (M1-M4).

    b. The M2 domain usually lines the ion pore and plays a crucial role in ion selectivity and gating.

3. **Extracellular Domain:**

   a. The extracellular domain contains the ligand-binding site.

   b. Ligand binding induces a conformational change that opens the ion channel.

4. **Pore and Ion Selectivity:**

   a. The ion channel pore allows specific ions (e.g., Na+, K+, Ca2+, Cl-) to flow across the cell membrane.

   b. Ion selectivity is determined by the size and charge of the pore and specific amino acid residues within the pore region.

Examples of Ligand-Gated Ion Channels

1. **Nicotinic Acetylcholine Receptor (nAChR)**

   a. **Structure:** Pentameric receptor typically composed of α, β, γ (or ε), and δ subunits.

   b. **Function**: Mediates excitatory synaptic transmission in neuromuscular junctions by allowing Na+ and K+ ions to pass, leading to muscle contraction.

   c. **Ligand:** Acetylcholine (ACh).

2. **Gamma-Aminobutyric Acid Type A (GABA_A) Receptor**

   a. **Structure:** Pentameric receptor typically composed of α, β, and γ subunits.

   b. **Function**: Mediates inhibitory synaptic transmission in the central nervous system by allowing Cl- ions to pass, leading to hyperpolarization and inhibition of neuronal activity.

   c. **Ligand**: GABA (Gamma-Aminobutyric Acid).

3. **Glutamate Receptors (e.g., NMDA, AMPA, and Kainate Receptors)**

   a. **Structure:** Tetrameric receptors composed of various subunits (e.g., GluN1, GluN2 for NMDA receptors).

b. **Function**: Mediate excitatory synaptic transmission by allowing Na+ and Ca2+ ions to pass, playing crucial roles in synaptic plasticity and memory formation.

c. **Ligand:** Glutamate.

4. P2X Receptors

a. **Structure:** Trimeric receptors composed of three subunits.

b. **Function:** Respond to extracellular ATP by allowing Na+ and Ca2+ ions to pass, involved in processes like pain sensation and inflammation.

c. **Ligand**: ATP (Adenosine Triphosphate).

Mechanism of Action

1. **Resting State**: In the absence of a ligand, the ion channel is typically closed.

2. **Ligand Binding**: The ligand binds to the extracellular domain, causing a conformational change.

3. **Channel Opening**: This conformational change opens the ion channel pore, allowing ions to flow down their electrochemical gradient.

4. **Desensitization/Inactivation**: Prolonged exposure to the ligand can lead to desensitization, where the receptor becomes less responsive to the ligand despite its presence.

Clinical Relevance

LGICs are targets for various drugs and toxins:

1. **Anesthetics and Sedatives**: Many act on GABA_A receptors to enhance inhibitory neurotransmission.

2. **Nicotine:** Binds to nAChRs, affecting the central nervous system and leading to addiction.

3. **Antiepileptic Drugs**: Some target GABA_A receptors to increase inhibitory signaling and prevent seizures.

G-PROTEIN COUPLED RECEPTORS

G-protein coupled receptors (GPCRs) represent one of the largest and most diverse families of membrane receptors in eukaryotes. They play a crucial role in cell signaling, mediating responses to a wide variety of extracellular signals. Here is a detailed examination of GPCRs, including their structure, function, signaling mechanisms, and clinical relevance.

Structure of GPCRs

GPCRs share a common structural framework:

1. **Seven Transmembrane Helices:**
   a. GPCRs have seven alpha-helical transmembrane domains (TM1 to TM7).
   b. These helices span the cell membrane, creating an extracellular N-terminus and an intracellular C-terminus.

2. **Extracellular and Intracellular Loops:**
   a. Three extracellular loops (ECL1, ECL2, ECL3) connect the transmembrane helices and are involved in ligand binding.
   b. Three intracellular loops (ICL1, ICL2, ICL3) interact with G-proteins and other intracellular signaling molecules.

3. **Ligand-Binding Domain:**
   a. The binding site for ligands can be located within the transmembrane region, on the extracellular loops, or the N-terminal domain, depending on the receptor.

4. **Intracellular C-Terminal Tail:**
   a. The C-terminal tail interacts with intracellular proteins, including G-proteins and regulatory molecules such as kinases and arrestins.

Function of GPCRs

GPCRs mediate a wide array of physiological responses by detecting extracellular signals and activating intracellular signaling pathways. These signals include hormones, neurotransmitters, and environmental stimuli like light and odorants.

Mechanism of GPCR Signaling

The GPCR signaling mechanism involves several key steps:

1. **Ligand Binding:**

   a. A ligand (e.g., hormone, neurotransmitter) binds to the extracellular domain of the GPCR.

   b. This induces a conformational change in the receptor.

2. **G-Protein Activation:**

   a. The conformational change in the GPCR allows it to interact with a heterotrimeric G-protein (composed of α, β, and γ subunits) on the intracellular side.

   b. The G-protein binds to the receptor, causing GDP bound to the Gα subunit to be exchanged for GTP, activating the G-protein.

3. **Dissociation of G-Protein Subunits:**

   a. The binding of GTP causes the Gα subunit to dissociate from the Gβγ dimer.

   b. Both the Gα-GTP and Gβγ subunits can then interact with and regulate various downstream effectors.

4. **Signal Propagation:**

   a. The activated G-protein subunits interact with target proteins, such as adenylyl cyclase, phospholipase C, and ion channels, to propagate the signal.

   b. This leads to the production of second messengers like cAMP, IP3, DAG, and Ca2+.

5. **Termination of Signal:**

   a. The intrinsic GTPase activity of the Gα subunit hydrolyzes GTP to GDP, inactivating the G-protein.

   b. The Gα subunit re-associates with the Gβγ dimer, returning to the inactive state.

6. **Receptor Desensitization:**

a. Prolonged stimulation of GPCRs can lead to receptor desensitization, often mediated by phosphorylation of the receptor by G-protein-coupled receptor kinases (GRKs) and binding of arrestins.

b. Arrestins prevent further G-protein activation and can also mediate receptor internalization.

Types of G-Proteins and Their Effects

G-proteins are classified based on their Gα subunits, each triggering distinct signaling pathways:

1. **Gαs (Stimulatory G-protein):**

    a. Activates adenylyl cyclase, increasing the production of cAMP.

    b. **Example:** β-adrenergic receptors.

2. **Gαi/o (Inhibitory G-protein):**

    a. Inhibits adenylyl cyclase, decreasing cAMP levels.

    b. **Example:** α2-adrenergic receptors.

3. **Gαq/11:**

    a. Activates phospholipase C (PLC), leading to the production of IP3 and DAG.

    b. IP3 induces Ca2+ release from the endoplasmic reticulum, while DAG activates protein kinase C (PKC).

    c. **Example:** α1-adrenergic receptors.

4. **Gα12/13:**

    a. Regulates the Rho family of GTPases, affecting cytoskeletal dynamics and cell migration.

    b. **Example:** Thrombin receptors.

Examples of GPCR Signaling Pathways

1. **Adrenergic Receptors:**

a. **β-Adrenergic Receptors**: Respond to adrenaline/noradrenaline, activating Gαs, leading to increased cAMP and protein kinase A (PKA) activity, which enhances heart rate and muscle contraction.

b. **α1-Adrenergic Receptors**: Activate Gαq, leading to increased IP3 and DAG, which causes smooth muscle contraction.

2. **Muscarinic Acetylcholine Receptors (mAChRs):**

   a. **M2 and M4 Receptors**: Inhibit adenylyl cyclase via Gαi, decreasing cAMP levels, involved in slowing heart rate.

   b. **M1, M3, and M5 Receptors**: Activate Gαq, increasing IP3 and DAG, involved in smooth muscle contraction and glandular secretion.

3. **Rhodopsin:**

   a. Light-activated GPCR in the retina.

   b. Activates Gαt (transducin), leading to a decrease in cGMP and hyperpolarization of photoreceptor cells, which is crucial for vision.

Clinical Relevance

GPCRs are targets for a significant portion of therapeutic drugs due to their involvement in various physiological processes and diseases:

1. **Beta-Blockers:**

   a. Target β-adrenergic receptors to treat hypertension and heart disease.

2. **Antihistamines:**

   a. Block histamine H1 receptors to alleviate allergy symptoms.

3. **Antipsychotics:**

   a. Target dopamine receptors to manage schizophrenia and other psychiatric disorders.

4. **Opioids:**

   a. Bind to opioid receptors (GPCRs) to relieve pain.

5. **Antidepressants:**

   a. Many influence GPCR-mediated neurotransmitter pathways to alleviate depression.

TYROSINE KINASE RECEPTORS AND NUCLEAR RECEPTORS

Receptor Tyrosine Kinases (RTKs) are a prominent class of receptors that play vital roles in various cellular processes, including growth, differentiation, metabolism, and apoptosis. They are particularly significant in the context of cancer biology and therapy.

Structure of RTKs

1. **Extracellular Domain:**

   a. **Ligand-Binding Domain**: Responsible for binding to specific ligands such as growth factors (e.g., EGF, insulin). This domain varies greatly among different RTKs, allowing for specificity in ligand binding.

2. **Transmembrane Domain:**

   a. A single alpha-helix that anchors the receptor in the cell membrane.

3. **Intracellular Domain:**

   a. **Tyrosine Kinase Domain**: Contains enzymatic activity that phosphorylates tyrosine residues on target proteins, including the receptor itself (autophosphorylation).

   b. **Regulatory Regions**: Contain sites for autophosphorylation and interaction with downstream signaling molecules.

Mechanism of RTK Signaling

1. **Ligand Binding:**

   a. Ligand binding induces dimerization (or oligomerization) of the receptor, bringing the intracellular kinase domains into close proximity.

2. **Autophosphorylation:**

a. The kinase domains phosphorylate each other on specific tyrosine residues, activating the receptor.

3. **Recruitment of Adaptor Proteins:**

    a. Phosphorylated tyrosine residues serve as docking sites for adaptor proteins and other signaling molecules containing SH2 (Src Homology 2) or PTB (Phosphotyrosine Binding) domains.

4. **Signal Propagation:**

    a. Downstream signaling pathways are activated, including the MAPK/ERK, PI3K/AKT, and PLCγ pathways, leading to diverse cellular responses such as proliferation, survival, and differentiation.

Examples of RTK Signaling Pathways

1. **EGF Receptor (EGFR):**

    a. **Ligand:** Epidermal Growth Factor (EGF).

    b. **Pathway Activation**: EGFR activation leads to the recruitment of Grb2 and SOS, which activate the Ras/MAPK pathway, promoting cell proliferation and survival.

    c. **Clinical Relevance**: Overexpression or mutation of EGFR is associated with various cancers, and EGFR inhibitors (e.g., erlotinib) are used in cancer therapy.

2. **Insulin Receptor (IR):**

    a. **Ligand:** Insulin.

    b. **Pathway Activation**: Insulin binding activates the PI3K/AKT pathway, promoting glucose uptake and metabolism.

    c. **Clinical Relevance**: Defects in insulin receptor signaling are implicated in diabetes mellitus.

3. **VEGF Receptor (VEGFR):**

    a. **Ligand**: Vascular Endothelial Growth Factor (VEGF).

   b. **Pathway Activation**: VEGFR activation stimulates angiogenesis through the PLCγ and PI3K/AKT pathways.

   c. **Clinical Relevance**: VEGF inhibitors (e.g., bevacizumab) are used to treat cancers by inhibiting tumor angiogenesis.

Nuclear Receptors in Cell Signaling

Nuclear receptors are a class of intracellular receptors that function as transcription factors. They are involved in regulating gene expression in response to lipophilic ligands such as steroid hormones, thyroid hormones, and other small molecules.

Structure of Nuclear Receptors

1. **Ligand-Binding Domain (LBD):**
   a. Located at the C-terminal end of the receptor, this domain binds to specific ligands, inducing conformational changes necessary for receptor activation.

2. **DNA-Binding Domain (DBD):**
   a. Located centrally, this highly conserved domain contains zinc finger motifs that allow the receptor to bind to specific DNA sequences known as hormone response elements (HREs).

3. **Activation Function Domains (AF-1 and AF-2):**
   a. Located in the N-terminal (AF-1) and C-terminal (AF-2) regions, these domains are involved in the recruitment of coactivators and corepressors that modulate transcriptional activity.

Mechanism of Nuclear Receptor Signaling

1. **Ligand Binding:**
   a. The ligand diffuses across the cell membrane and binds to the nuclear receptor's LBD, inducing a conformational change that activates the receptor.

2. **Receptor Dimerization:**

a. Ligand binding often promotes the dimerization (homo- or heterodimerization) of nuclear receptors.

3. **DNA Binding:**

   a. The activated receptor dimer translocates to the nucleus (if it is not already there) and binds to specific HREs in the promoter region of target genes.

4. **Transcriptional Regulation:**

   a. The receptor complex recruits coactivators or corepressors and other components of the transcriptional machinery, modulating the transcription of target genes.

Examples of Nuclear Receptor Signaling Pathways

1. **Glucocorticoid Receptor (GR):**

   a. **Ligand:** Glucocorticoids (e.g., cortisol).

   b. **Function:** Regulates genes involved in glucose metabolism, immune response, and inflammation.

   c. **Clinical Relevance**: Glucocorticoids are used as anti-inflammatory and immunosuppressive agents in conditions such as asthma and autoimmune diseases.

2. **Estrogen Receptor (ER):**

   a. **Ligand:** Estrogens (e.g., estradiol).

   b. **Function:** Regulates genes involved in reproductive function, bone density, and cardiovascular health.

   c. **Clinical Relevance**: ER modulators (e.g., tamoxifen) are used in the treatment of estrogen receptor-positive breast cancer.

3. **Thyroid Hormone Receptor (TR):**

   a. **Ligand:** Thyroid hormones (e.g., T3, T4).

   b. **Function**: Regulates genes involved in metabolism, development, and growth.

c. **Clinical Relevance**: Dysregulation of thyroid hormone signaling can lead to conditions such as hypothyroidism and hyperthyroidism.

SECONDARY MESSENGERS: CYCLIC AMP, CYCLIC GMP, CALCIUM ION, INOSITOL 1,4,5-TRISPHOSPHATE, (IP3), NO, AND DIACYLGLYCEROL

Secondary messengers are intracellular signaling molecules released by cells in response to exposure to extracellular signaling molecules (the primary messengers). These molecules help amplify the signal and elicit a physiological response within the cell. Here, we will detail the key secondary messengers: cyclic AMP (cAMP), cyclic GMP (cGMP), calcium ions (Ca2+), inositol 1,4,5-trisphosphate (IP3), nitric oxide (NO), and diacylglycerol (DAG).

Cyclic AMP (cAMP)

Cyclic adenosine monophosphate (cAMP) is a critical secondary messenger molecule involved in cell signaling. It is synthesized from ATP by the enzyme adenylate cyclase and functions to transduce extracellular signals into intracellular responses. Here's a detailed exploration of the role of cAMP in cell signaling:

1. Synthesis and Regulation of cAMP:

a. **Adenylate Cyclase Activation**: Extracellular stimuli, such as hormones or neurotransmitters, bind to their respective receptors (e.g., G protein-coupled receptors), leading to the activation of adenylate cyclase.

b. **cAMP Production**: Activated adenylate cyclase catalyzes the conversion of ATP to cAMP, which serves as a second messenger in the signaling cascade.

c. **cAMP Degradation**: cAMP levels are tightly regulated by phosphodiesterases (PDEs), enzymes that hydrolyze cAMP to AMP, terminating the signaling cascade.

2. Signaling Pathways Mediated by cAMP:

a. **Protein Kinase A (PKA) Activation:**
   i. cAMP binds to the regulatory subunits of PKA, causing their dissociation from the catalytic subunits.
   ii. Released catalytic subunits of PKA phosphorylate serine and threonine residues on target proteins, modulating their activity and cellular functions.
   iii. PKA phosphorylates various substrates, including enzymes, ion channels, and transcription factors, to regulate processes such as metabolism, gene expression, and cell proliferation.

b. **cAMP-Regulated Ion Channels:**
   i. cAMP can directly bind to and modulate the activity of ion channels, such as cyclic nucleotide-gated (CNG) channels and hyperpolarization-activated cyclic nucleotide-gated (HCN) channels.
   ii. Activation of cAMP-regulated ion channels alters ion flux across the plasma membrane, leading to changes in membrane potential and cellular excitability.

c. **cAMP-Responsive Element-Binding Protein (CREB) Activation:**
   i. PKA-mediated phosphorylation of CREB promotes its binding to cAMP response elements (CREs) in the promoter regions of target genes.
   ii. CREB activation induces the transcription of genes involved in neuronal plasticity, cell survival, and long-term memory formation.

3. Physiological Roles of cAMP:

a. **Hormone Signaling**: cAMP mediates the effects of various hormones, including adrenaline, glucagon, and thyroid-stimulating hormone (TSH), in processes such as glycogen metabolism, lipolysis, and hormone secretion.

b. **Neuronal Signa**ling: cAMP regulates synaptic transmission, neuronal excitability, and synaptic plasticity in the central nervous system, influencing learning, memory, and behavior.

c. **Cardiac Function**: cAMP signaling modulates cardiac contractility, heart rate, and ion channel activity in cardiomyocytes, regulating cardiovascular function and blood pressure.

d. **Immune Responses**: cAMP regulates immune cell activation, cytokine production, and inflammatory responses, influencing immune cell function and inflammation.

4. Pathological Implications of Dysregulated cAMP Signaling:

a. **Endocrine Disorders**: Dysregulated cAMP signaling is implicated in endocrine disorders such as hyperthyroidism, where excessive cAMP production leads to increased thyroid hormone secretion.

b. **Neurological Disorders**: Altered cAMP signaling contributes to neurological disorders such as depression, anxiety disorders, and schizophrenia, affecting neuronal function and synaptic plasticity.

c. **Cardiovascular Diseases**: Dysregulated cAMP signaling is associated with cardiovascular diseases such as heart failure and arrhythmias, affecting cardiac contractility and ion channel function.

d. **Immune Disorders**: Aberrant cAMP signaling is linked to immune disorders such as autoimmune diseases and inflammatory disorders, influencing immune cell activation and cytokine production.

Cyclic GMP (cGMP)

Cyclic guanosine monophosphate (cGMP), similar to cyclic adenosine monophosphate (cAMP), is a critical secondary messenger molecule involved in cell signaling. It is synthesized from guanosine triphosphate (GTP) by the enzyme guanylate cyclase and regulates various physiological processes within cells. Here's a detailed exploration of the role of cGMP in cell signaling, along with comparisons to cAMP:

1. **Synthesis and Regulation of cGMP:**
   a. **Guanylate Cyclase Activation**: Guanylate cyclase can be activated by different stimuli, leading to the conversion of GTP to cGMP.
   b. **cGMP Production**: Activated guanylate cyclase synthesizes cGMP, which serves as a second messenger in the signaling cascade.
   c. **cGMP Degradation**: cGMP levels are regulated by phosphodiesterases (PDEs), which hydrolyze cGMP to GMP, thereby terminating the signaling cascade.
2. **Signaling Pathways Mediated by cGMP:**
   a. **Protein Kinase G (PKG) Activation:**
      i. cGMP binds to the regulatory domains of PKG, leading to its activation.
      ii. Activated PKG phosphorylates specific serine and threonine residues on target proteins, modulating their activity and cellular functions.
      iii. PKG regulates processes such as smooth muscle relaxation, platelet aggregation, and gene expression.
   b. **cGMP-Regulated Ion Channels:**
      i. cGMP can modulate the activity of ion channels, such as cyclic nucleotide-gated (CNG) channels and voltage-gated calcium channels (VGCCs).
      ii. Activation of cGMP-regulated ion channels alters ion flux across the plasma membrane, affecting cellular excitability and neurotransmitter release.
   c. **cGMP-Dependent Protein Kinases (cGKs):**
      i. In some cells, cGMP activates cGKs, which regulate cellular processes similar to PKGs, including smooth muscle relaxation and platelet aggregation.
3. **Physiological Roles of cGMP:**

a. **Vasodilation:** cGMP signaling mediates vasodilation by relaxing vascular smooth muscle cells, leading to decreased peripheral resistance and improved blood flow.

b. **Platelet Aggregation: cGMP inhibits platelet aggregation and thrombus formation by activating PKG**, which phosphorylates proteins involved in platelet activation and aggregation.

c. **Neuronal Signaling**: cGMP regulates synaptic transmission, neuronal excitability, and synaptic plasticity in the central nervous system, influencing learning, memory, and behavior.

d. **Vision**: cGMP plays a crucial role in phototransduction in the retina, where it regulates the opening and closing of cyclic nucleotide-gated channels in response to light stimuli.

4. Pathological Implications of Dysregulated cGMP Signaling:

a. **Cardiovascular Disorders**: Dysregulated cGMP signaling is associated with cardiovascular disorders such as hypertension, heart failure, and atherosclerosis, affecting vascular tone and blood pressure regulation.

b. **Platelet Dysfunction**: Altered cGMP signaling contributes to platelet dysfunction and thrombotic disorders, increasing the risk of myocardial infarction, stroke, and other cardiovascular events.

c. **Neurological Disorders**: Aberrant cGMP signaling is implicated in neurological disorders such as migraine, epilepsy, and neurodegenerative diseases, affecting neuronal function and synaptic transmission.

Comparison with cAMP:

a. Similarities:

  i. Both cAMP and cGMP are cyclic nucleotide second messengers synthesized by adenylate cyclase and guanylate cyclase, respectively.

  ii. They regulate cellular processes by activating protein kinases, modulating ion channels, and influencing gene expression.

b. Differences:

    i. cAMP primarily activates protein kinase A (PKA), while cGMP activates protein kinase G (PKG).

    ii. cAMP is more commonly associated with hormone signaling, while cGMP is often involved in nitric oxide (NO)-mediated signaling and ion channel regulation.

    iii. cAMP and cGMP have distinct physiological roles and signaling pathways, although there is some overlap in their functions.

Calcium Ions (Ca2+)

Calcium ions (Ca2+) are ubiquitous secondary messengers involved in numerous cellular signaling processes. Their dynamic concentration within cells is tightly regulated by various mechanisms, including influx through plasma membrane channels, release from intracellular stores, and extrusion by pumps. Here's a detailed exploration of the role of calcium ions in cell signaling:

1. Calcium Signaling Mechanisms:

a. Calcium Influx:

    i. Calcium ions enter the cell through various plasma membrane channels in response to extracellular stimuli, such as ligand binding to receptors or changes in membrane potential.

    ii. Voltage-gated calcium channels (VGCCs), ligand-gated calcium channels (e.g., NMDA receptors), and receptor-operated calcium channels (ROCCs) are examples of calcium influx pathways.

b. Calcium Release from Intracellular Stores:

    i. Calcium ions are released from intracellular stores, such as the endoplasmic reticulum (ER) or sarcoplasmic reticulum (SR), in response to signals such as IP3 or cyclic ADP-ribose (cADPR).

    ii. Inositol 1,4,5-trisphosphate (IP3) binds to IP3 receptors (IP3Rs) on the ER membrane, leading to calcium release into the cytoplasm.

c. Calcium Extrusion and Sequestration:

i.   Calcium ions are actively pumped out of the cell or sequestered into intracellular organelles (e.g., mitochondria) by calcium ATPases and calcium-binding proteins, respectively, to maintain cytosolic calcium homeostasis.

2. Calcium-Dependent Signaling Pathways:

a. Calcium-Calmodulin-Dependent Protein Kinase (CaMK) Pathway:

i.   Calcium binds to calmodulin, forming a calcium-calmodulin complex.

ii. Calcium-calmodulin complex activates CaMK, which phosphorylates target proteins involved in various cellular processes, including gene expression, metabolism, and synaptic plasticity.

b. Calcineurin-Nuclear Factor of Activated T Cells (NFAT) Pathway:

i.   Calcium activates the phosphatase calcineurin, which dephosphorylates NFAT transcription factors.

ii. Dephosphorylated NFAT translocates to the nucleus, where it regulates the expression of genes involved in immune responses, development, and cell proliferation.

c. Calcium-Dependent Ion Channels and Transporters:

i.   Calcium ions directly modulate the activity of ion channels and transporters, such as voltage-gated potassium channels (Kv channels), sodium-calcium exchangers (NCX), and calcium-activated potassium channels (KCa channels), regulating membrane excitability and ion flux.

3. Physiological Roles of Calcium Signaling:

a.   **Muscle Contraction**: Calcium signaling plays a crucial role in regulating muscle contraction by triggering the release of calcium ions from the sarcoplasmic reticulum (SR) in response to action potentials.

b. **Neuronal Signaling**: Calcium signaling regulates synaptic transmission, neurotransmitter release, and neuronal excitability, influencing processes such as learning, memory, and synaptic plasticity.

c. **Cell Proliferation and Differentiation**: Calcium signaling contributes to the regulation of cell proliferation, differentiation, and apoptosis by modulating the activity of signaling pathways involved in cell cycle progression and gene expression.

d. **Secretion and Exocytosis**: Calcium signaling mediates the exocytosis of neurotransmitters, hormones, and other signaling molecules from secretory cells, such as neurons, endocrine cells, and immune cells.

4. Pathological Implications of Dysregulated Calcium Signaling:

a. **Neurological Disorders**: Dysregulated calcium signaling is implicated in neurological disorders such as Alzheimer's disease, Parkinson's disease, and epilepsy, contributing to neuronal dysfunction and cell death.

b. **Cardiovascular Diseases**: Altered calcium signaling is associated with cardiovascular diseases such as arrhythmias, heart failure, and hypertension, affecting cardiac muscle contraction and vascular tone.

c. **Musculoskeletal Disorders**: Dysregulated calcium signaling contributes to musculoskeletal disorders such as osteoporosis, muscle weakness, and dystrophies, affecting bone remodeling and muscle function.

Inositol 1,4,5-Trisphosphate (IP3)

Inositol 1,4,5-trisphosphate (IP3) is a crucial secondary messenger molecule involved in cell signaling. It is generated through the hydrolysis of phosphatidylinositol 4,5-bisphosphate (PIP2) by phospholipase C (PLC) in response to various extracellular stimuli. IP3 acts to mobilize calcium ions (Ca2+) from intracellular stores, primarily the endoplasmic reticulum (ER), thereby regulating a multitude of cellular processes. Here's a detailed exploration of the role of IP3 in cell signaling:

1. Generation of IP3:

a. **Activation of Phospholipase C (PLC):**
   i. Extracellular stimuli, such as hormones or neurotransmitters, bind to their respective receptors, including G protein-coupled receptors (GPCRs) or receptor tyrosine kinases (RTKs).
   ii. Receptor activation triggers the activation of PLC, which cleaves PIP2 into two secondary messengers: diacylglycerol (DAG) and IP3.

2. **Signaling Pathways Mediated by IP3:**
   a. **Release of Calcium Ions (Ca2+):**
      i. IP3 binds to IP3 receptors (IP3Rs) on the ER membrane, inducing conformational changes that lead to the release of calcium ions stored within the ER lumen into the cytoplasm.
      ii. Increased cytosolic calcium concentration triggers downstream signaling events and modulates various cellular processes.

3. **Physiological Roles of IP3:**
   a. **Neuronal Signaling:**
      i. IP3-mediated calcium release regulates synaptic transmission, neuronal excitability, and synaptic plasticity in the central nervous system, influencing learning, memory, and behavior.
   b. **Muscle Contraction:**
      i. In smooth muscle cells, IP3-induced calcium release plays a crucial role in regulating muscle contraction, particularly in response to neurotransmitters or hormones.
   c. **Cell Proliferation and Differentiation:**
      i. IP3 signaling contributes to the regulation of cell proliferation, differentiation, and apoptosis by modulating calcium-dependent signaling pathways involved in cell cycle progression and gene expression.
   d. **Secretion and Exocytosis:**

i. IP3-mediated calcium release triggers the exocytosis of neurotransmitters, hormones, and other signaling molecules from secretory cells, such as neurons, endocrine cells, and immune cells.

4. Pathological Implications of Dysregulated IP3 Signaling:

a. Neurological Disorders:

i. Dysregulated IP3 signaling is implicated in neurological disorders such as Alzheimer's disease, Huntington's disease, and ischemic stroke, contributing to neuronal dysfunction and cell death.

b. Cardiovascular Diseases:

i. Altered IP3 signaling is associated with cardiovascular diseases such as arrhythmias, heart failure, and hypertension, affecting cardiac muscle contraction and vascular tone.

c. Immune Disorders:

i. Dysregulated IP3 signaling contributes to immune disorders such as autoimmune diseases and inflammatory disorders, influencing immune cell activation and cytokine production.

Nitric Oxide (NO)

Nitric oxide (NO) is a critical signaling molecule that functions as a secondary messenger in various cellular processes. It is synthesized from the amino acid L-arginine by nitric oxide synthase (NOS) enzymes and plays diverse roles in cell signaling, particularly in the cardiovascular, nervous, and immune systems. Here's a detailed exploration of the role of NO as a secondary messenger in cell signaling:

1. Generation of NO:

a. Nitric Oxide Synthase (NOS) Activation:

i. NOS enzymes catalyze the conversion of L-arginine into NO and L-citrulline in a calcium and calmodulin-dependent manner.

ii. NOS enzymes exist in three isoforms: neuronal NOS (nNOS or NOS1), inducible NOS (iNOS or NOS2), and endothelial NOS (eNOS or NOS3), each with distinct regulatory mechanisms and tissue distributions.

2. Signaling Pathways Mediated by NO:

    a. Activation of Soluble Guanylate Cyclase (sGC):

        i. NO diffuses across cell membranes and binds to the heme group of sGC, converting it from its inactive to its active form.

        ii. Activated sGC catalyzes the conversion of guanosine triphosphate (GTP) to cyclic guanosine monophosphate (cGMP), which serves as a secondary messenger in downstream signaling pathways.

    b. cGMP-Dependent Signaling Pathways:

        i. cGMP activates protein kinase G (PKG), which phosphorylates target proteins involved in various cellular processes, including smooth muscle relaxation, platelet aggregation, and gene expression.

        ii. Activation of cGMP-dependent pathways mediates many of the physiological effects of NO, particularly in the cardiovascular and nervous systems.

    c. Regulation of Ion Channels and Transporters:

        i. NO can directly modulate the activity of ion channels and transporters, including calcium channels, potassium channels, and sodium channels, influencing membrane potential and cellular excitability.

3. Physiological Roles of NO:

  a. Vasodilation:

        i. NO plays a key role in regulating vascular tone by promoting vasodilation through the activation of sGC-cGMP signaling pathways in vascular smooth muscle cells.

    ii.   NO-mediated vasodilation helps to maintain blood pressure, improve blood flow, and prevent vascular diseases such as hypertension.

b. Neuronal Signaling:

    i.   NO serves as a neurotransmitter in the central and peripheral nervous systems, where it modulates synaptic transmission, neuronal excitability, and synaptic plasticity.

    ii.   NO signaling is involved in processes such as learning, memory, and pain perception.

c. Immune Responses:

    i.   NO produced by immune cells, particularly macrophages and neutrophils, acts as a cytotoxic agent against pathogens by inducing oxidative stress and DNA damage in target cells.

    ii.   NO also regulates immune cell function, cytokine production, and inflammation in the context of innate and adaptive immunity.

4. Pathological Implications of Dysregulated NO Signaling:

a. Cardiovascular Diseases:

    i.   Dysregulated NO signaling is associated with cardiovascular diseases such as hypertension, atherosclerosis, and heart failure, leading to impaired vasodilation, endothelial dysfunction, and vascular inflammation.

b. Neurological Disorders:

    i.   Altered NO signaling is implicated in neurological disorders such as Alzheimer's disease, Parkinson's disease, and stroke, contributing to neuronal dysfunction, neuroinflammation, and neurodegeneration.

c. Inflammatory Diseases:

    i.   Dysregulated NO signaling is involved in inflammatory diseases such as rheumatoid arthritis, inflammatory bowel disease, and sepsis, contributing to excessive inflammation, tissue damage, and organ dysfunction.

Diacylglycerol (DAG)

Diacylglycerol (DAG) is another critical secondary messenger involved in cell signaling, particularly in the activation of protein kinase C (PKC) and the regulation of various cellular processes. DAG is generated through the hydrolysis of phosphatidylinositol 4,5-bisphosphate (PIP2) by phospholipase C (PLC), alongside inositol 1,4,5-trisphosphate (IP3). Here's a detailed exploration of the role of DAG in cell signaling:

1. Generation of DAG:

    a. Activation of Phospholipase C (PLC):

        i. PLC cleaves PIP2 into two secondary messengers: DAG and IP3.

        ii. This hydrolysis occurs in response to extracellular stimuli such as hormones, neurotransmitters, or growth factors binding to their receptors.

2. Signaling Pathways Mediated by DAG:

    a. Activation of Protein Kinase C (PKC):

        i. DAG acts as a crucial activator of PKC by binding to its C1 regulatory domain.

        ii. Binding of DAG to PKC, in conjunction with calcium ions (Ca2+) and phosphatidylserine, leads to the translocation of PKC from the cytosol to the plasma membrane, where it becomes activated.

    b. Phosphorylation of Target Proteins:

        i. Activated PKC phosphorylates specific serine and threonine residues on target proteins, modulating their activity and cellular functions.

        ii. PKC regulates various cellular processes, including cell growth, differentiation, apoptosis, gene expression, and neurotransmitter release.

3. Physiological Roles of DAG:

a. Cell Growth and Proliferation:

    i.   DAG-mediated activation of PKC contributes to the regulation of cell growth, proliferation, and survival by modulating signaling pathways involved in cell cycle progression and apoptosis.

b. Neuronal Signaling:

    i.   DAG/PKC signaling regulates synaptic transmission, neuronal excitability, and synaptic plasticity in the central nervous system, influencing learning, memory, and behavior.

c. Immune Responses:

    i.   DAG/PKC signaling plays a role in immune cell activation, cytokine production, and inflammatory responses, influencing immune cell function and inflammation.

d. Metabolic Regulation:

    i.   DAG/PKC signaling is involved in the regulation of metabolic processes such as glucose metabolism, lipid metabolism, and insulin signaling, affecting energy homeostasis and nutrient utilization.

4. Pathological Implications of Dysregulated DAG Signaling:

a. Cancer:

    i.   Dysregulated DAG/PKC signaling is implicated in cancer development and progression, contributing to abnormal cell proliferation, survival, angiogenesis, and metastasis.

b. Neurological Disorders:

    i.   Altered DAG/PKC signaling is associated with neurological disorders such as Alzheimer's disease, epilepsy, and schizophrenia, affecting neuronal function and synaptic plasticity.

c. Cardiovascular Diseases:

i. Dysregulated DAG/PKC signaling is linked to cardiovascular diseases such as heart failure, arrhythmias, and hypertrophy, affecting cardiac function and vascular tone.

d. Immune Disorders:

i. Aberrant DAG/PKC signaling contributes to immune disorders such as autoimmune diseases and inflammatory disorders, influencing immune cell activation and cytokine production.

DETAILED STUDY OF FOLLOWING INTRACELLULAR SIGNALLING PATHWAYS: CYCLIC AMP SIGNALING PATHWAY

The cyclic AMP (cAMP) signaling pathway is one of the most well-characterized and essential pathways in cell signaling. It plays a pivotal role in regulating numerous physiological processes, including metabolism, gene transcription, and cell growth.

Key Components of the cAMP Signaling Pathway

1. G-Protein-Coupled Receptors (GPCRs)

a. GPCRs are membrane-bound receptors that activate intracellular G-proteins in response to ligand binding. Examples include β-adrenergic receptors, which bind adrenaline.

2. Heterotrimeric G-Proteins

a. G-proteins consist of three subunits: α, β, and γ. The Gα subunit binds GDP in its inactive state and GTP when activated. The Gβγ dimer is involved in signaling but remains associated with the membrane.

3. Adenylyl Cyclase (AC)

a. An enzyme that converts ATP to cAMP upon activation by the Gαs subunit of the G-protein.

4. Cyclic AMP (cAMP)

a. A secondary messenger that activates downstream targets, primarily protein kinase A (PKA).

5. **Protein Kinase A (PKA)**

   a. A cAMP-dependent enzyme that phosphorylates various target proteins, leading to changes in their activity.

6. **Phosphodiesterases (PDEs)**

   a. Enzymes that degrade cAMP to AMP, thus terminating the signaling.

7. **CREB (cAMP Response Element-Binding Protein)**

   a. A transcription factor activated by PKA, which binds to cAMP response elements (CRE) in DNA to regulate gene expression.

Mechanism of the cAMP Signaling Pathway

1. **Ligand Binding and GPCR Activation**

   a. An extracellular ligand (e.g., adrenaline) binds to a GPCR on the cell surface, inducing a conformational change in the receptor.

2. **G-Protein Activation**

   a. The activated GPCR acts as a guanine nucleotide exchange factor (GEF) for the associated G-protein, facilitating the exchange of GDP for GTP on the Gαs subunit.

   b. Gαs-GTP dissociates from the Gβγ dimer and interacts with adenylyl cyclase.

3. **Adenylyl Cyclase Activation**

   a. The Gαs-GTP complex activates adenylyl cyclase, which catalyzes the conversion of ATP to cAMP.

4. **cAMP Production**

   a. cAMP levels increase in the cytoplasm, acting as a secondary messenger.

5. **PKA Activation**

   a. cAMP binds to the regulatory subunits of PKA, causing the release and activation of the catalytic subunits.

b. Activated PKA then phosphorylates target proteins, leading to various cellular responses.

6. Cellular Responses

a. Immediate Responses: Phosphorylation of proteins involved in metabolic pathways, ion channels, and other signaling cascades.

b. Long-Term Responses: PKA phosphorylates CREB, which binds to CREs in the promoter regions of target genes, regulating their transcription.

7. Signal Termination

a. Phosphodiesterases (PDEs) degrade cAMP to AMP, reducing its levels and thereby inactivating PKA.

b. The Gαs subunit hydrolyzes GTP to GDP, reassociating with the Gβγ dimer and returning to its inactive state.

Physiological Roles of the cAMP Signaling Pathway

1. Metabolism

a. Glycogen Breakdown: In liver and muscle cells, adrenaline activates β-adrenergic receptors, leading to increased cAMP and PKA activation. PKA phosphorylates and activates glycogen phosphorylase kinase, which then activates glycogen phosphorylase, promoting glycogen breakdown to glucose.

2. Cardiac Function

a. Heart Rate and Contractility: Adrenaline binding to β-adrenergic receptors in heart cells increases cAMP levels, activating PKA. PKA phosphorylates voltage-gated calcium channels, enhancing calcium influx and increasing heart rate and contractility.

3. Gene Expression

a. CREB Activation: In neurons and other cells, cAMP activates PKA, which phosphorylates CREB. Activated CREB binds to

CREs in DNA, regulating the transcription of genes involved in neuronal plasticity, memory formation, and survival.

4. **Hormone Regulation**
   a. Thyroid-Stimulating Hormone (TSH): TSH binding to its receptor on thyroid cells increases cAMP levels, leading to the activation of PKA and subsequent thyroid hormone production.

5. **Sensory Perception**
   a. Olfactory Receptors: Binding of odorants to olfactory receptors (a type of GPCR) increases cAMP, opening cAMP-gated ion channels and leading to depolarization and the generation of a nerve impulse.

Clinical Relevance

1. **Pharmacological Agents**
   a. **β-Blockers:** Used to treat hypertension and cardiac arrhythmias by blocking β-adrenergic receptors, thereby reducing cAMP levels and heart rate.
   b. **Phosphodiesterase Inhibitors**: Such as sildenafil (Viagra), used to treat erectile dysfunction by inhibiting PDE5, increasing cGMP levels, and promoting vasodilation.

2. **Disease States**
   a. **Heart Failure:** Altered cAMP signaling can lead to heart failure. β-adrenergic agonists and PDE inhibitors are used therapeutically to modulate this pathway.
   b. **Asthma**: β2-adrenergic agonists are used to relax bronchial smooth muscle by increasing cAMP levels.

MITOGEN-ACTIVATED PROTEIN KINASE (MAPK) SIGNALLING

The Mitogen-Activated Protein Kinase (MAPK) signaling pathway is a critical intracellular pathway that transmits extracellular signals into a variety of cellular responses, including growth, differentiation, proliferation, survival, and apoptosis. The pathway is highly conserved across eukaryotes and involves a series of protein kinases that activate each other through phosphorylation.

Key Components of the MAPK Signaling Pathway

The mitogen-activated protein kinase (MAPK) signaling pathway is a highly conserved intracellular signaling cascade involved in various cellular processes, including cell proliferation, differentiation, apoptosis, and response to extracellular stimuli. Here are the key components of the MAPK signaling pathway in detail:

1. **Receptor Tyrosine Kinases (RTKs) or G Protein-Coupled Receptors (GPCRs):**
   a. The MAPK pathway can be activated by diverse extracellular stimuli, such as growth factors, cytokines, hormones, and stress signals.
   b. RTKs and GPCRs serve as cell surface receptors that sense these extracellular signals and initiate signaling cascades.

2. **Ras Proteins:**
   a. Ras proteins (H-Ras, K-Ras, N-Ras) are small GTPases that function as molecular switches in the MAPK pathway.
   b. They are located at the inner leaflet of the plasma membrane and become activated upon stimulation of RTKs or GPCRs.
   c. Activated Ras proteins exchange GDP for GTP, leading to a conformational change that enables them to interact with downstream effector proteins.

3. **Raf Kinases (Raf-1, B-Raf, A-Raf):**
   a. Raf kinases are serine/threonine protein kinases that serve as immediate downstream effectors of activated Ras.
   b. Upon binding to GTP-bound Ras, Raf kinases undergo conformational changes and become activated.

c. Activated Raf kinases phosphorylate and activate downstream kinases in the MAPK pathway.

4. **MAP Kinase Kinases (MAPKKs or MEKs):**

   a. MAPKKs are dual-specificity protein kinases that phosphorylate and activate MAP kinases (MAPKs) in the MAPK pathway.

   b. The primary MAPKKs involved in the canonical MAPK pathway are MEK1 and MEK2.

   c. MEKs are activated by phosphorylation at specific serine and threonine residues by Raf kinases.

5. **MAP Kinases (MAPKs):**

   a. MAPKs are serine/threonine protein kinases that are phosphorylated and activated by MAPKKs.

   b. The major MAPKs in the MAPK pathway include extracellular signal-regulated kinases (ERKs), c-Jun N-terminal kinases (JNKs), and p38 MAP kinases.

   c. ERKs are primarily activated by growth factors and mitogens, while JNKs and p38 MAP kinases are activated by stress stimuli.

6. **Substrates and Transcription Factors:**

   a. Activated MAPKs phosphorylate a wide range of substrates, including cytoplasmic and nuclear proteins.

   b. MAPK-mediated phosphorylation of transcription factors, such as c-Fos, c-Jun, Elk-1 (targeted by ERKs), ATF2 (targeted by JNKs), and ATF2/CREB (targeted by p38), regulates gene expression and cellular responses.

Regulation and Feedback Mechanisms:

a. Negative Feedback Regulation:

   i. Phosphatases, such as MAPK phosphatases (MKPs), dephosphorylate and inactivate MAPKs, providing negative feedback to attenuate signaling.

ii.   Inhibition of upstream signaling components, such as Raf and Ras, by negative regulators, including kinases and scaffolding proteins, also contributes to negative feedback regulation.

b. Cross-talk with Other Signaling Pathways:

i.   The MAPK pathway can crosstalk with other signaling pathways, such as the PI3K/Akt pathway and the JAK/STAT pathway, leading to integrated cellular responses.

ii.   Cross-talk provides additional layers of regulation and enables cells to integrate multiple signals to generate specific responses.

c. Spatial and Temporal Regulation:

i.   The localization of signaling components, such as receptors, Ras, and MAPKs, in specific cellular compartments contributes to the spatial regulation of MAPK signaling.

ii.   Temporal regulation of MAPK signaling is achieved through the dynamic modulation of protein expression, post-translational modifications, and feedback mechanisms.

Understanding the intricate regulation and diverse functions of the MAPK signaling pathway is essential for elucidating its roles in cellular physiology and disease pathogenesis. Dysregulation of MAPK signaling is implicated in various diseases, including cancer, neurodegenerative disorders, and inflammatory diseases, making it an attractive target for therapeutic intervention.

Mechanism of the MAPK Signaling Pathway

The mitogen-activated protein kinase (MAPK) signaling pathway is a highly conserved intracellular signaling cascade involved in transducing extracellular stimuli into a wide range of cellular responses, including cell proliferation, differentiation, survival, and apoptosis. Here's a detailed overview of the mechanism of the MAPK signaling pathway:

1. Extracellular Stimulation:

a. The MAPK pathway is activated in response to various extracellular stimuli, including growth factors (e.g., epidermal growth factor, insulin), cytokines, hormones, and environmental stressors (e.g., UV radiation, heat shock).

b. These stimuli bind to their respective cell surface receptors, which can be receptor tyrosine kinases (RTKs) or G protein-coupled receptors (GPCRs).

2. **Activation of Ras Proteins:**

   a. Upon ligand binding, RTKs or GPCRs undergo conformational changes that lead to the activation of intracellular signaling proteins.

   b. One key mediator of MAPK pathway activation is Ras, a small GTPase protein located at the inner leaflet of the plasma membrane.

   c. Ras exists in an inactive GDP-bound form and an active GTP-bound form. Binding of the extracellular ligand to the receptor induces the exchange of GDP for GTP on Ras, resulting in Ras activation.

3. **Activation of Raf Kinases:**

   a. Activated Ras recruits and activates Raf kinases (Raf-1, B-Raf, A-Raf) to the plasma membrane.

   b. Raf kinases are serine/threonine protein kinases that serve as immediate downstream effectors of Ras.

   c. Binding of Ras-GTP induces conformational changes in Raf, leading to its activation and subsequent phosphorylation.

4. **Phosphorylation of MAP Kinase Kinases (MAPKKs or MEKs):**

   a. Activated Raf kinases phosphorylate and activate MAP kinase kinases (MAPKKs or MEKs), including MEK1 and MEK2.

b. MEKs are dual-specificity protein kinases that phosphorylate and activate MAP kinases (MAPKs) on specific threonine and tyrosine residues within the conserved Thr-Xaa-Tyr motif (where Xaa represents any amino acid).

5. **Activation of MAP Kinases (MAPKs):**

   a. Once phosphorylated and activated by MEKs, MAPKs are released from MEKs and translocate to the nucleus or other cellular compartments.

   b. The major MAPKs involved in the canonical MAPK pathway include extracellular signal-regulated kinases (ERKs), c-Jun N-terminal kinases (JNKs), and p38 MAP kinases.

   c. Each MAPK subtype phosphorylates and activates a distinct set of downstream substrates, including transcription factors and cytoplasmic proteins.

6. **Gene Transcription and Cellular Responses:**

   a. Activated MAPKs phosphorylate a wide range of substrates, including transcription factors (e.g., c-Fos, c-Jun, Elk-1), cytoplasmic proteins, and other kinases.

   b. Phosphorylation of transcription factors regulates gene expression by modulating their activity, stability, or subcellular localization.

   c. The transcriptional changes induced by MAPK signaling lead to various cellular responses, such as cell proliferation, differentiation, survival, and apoptosis.

Termination of Signaling:

1. The duration and amplitude of MAPK signaling are tightly regulated to ensure proper cellular responses and prevent aberrant activation.

2. Negative feedback mechanisms, such as the action of MAPK phosphatases (MKPs), attenuate signaling by dephosphorylating and inactivating MAPKs.

3. Downregulation of upstream signaling components, including Raf and Ras, by negative regulators further contributes to the termination of MAPK signaling.

Conclusion:

The MAPK signaling pathway is a central regulator of cellular responses to extracellular stimuli, orchestrating a diverse array of physiological processes. Dysregulation of MAPK signaling is implicated in various diseases, including cancer, neurodegenerative disorders, and inflammatory diseases. Understanding the detailed mechanism of MAPK signaling provides insights into its roles in cellular physiology and disease pathogenesis, offering opportunities for the development of targeted therapeutic interventions.

Specific MAPK Pathways

The mitogen-activated protein kinase (MAPK) signaling pathway encompasses several distinct cascades that mediate cellular responses to extracellular stimuli. Each MAPK pathway is activated by specific upstream signaling events and regulates unique cellular processes. Here's an overview of specific MAPK pathways in detail:

1. Extracellular Signal-Regulated Kinase (ERK) Pathway:

   a. **Activation:** The ERK pathway is primarily activated by growth factors, mitogens, and receptor tyrosine kinases (RTKs).

   b. **Key Components:**
      i. **Upstream**: RTKs, Ras, Raf (Raf-1, B-Raf), MEK1/2
      ii. **Downstream:** ERK1/2, various substrates including transcription factors (Elk-1, c-Fos, c-Jun), cytoplasmic proteins (kinases, phosphatases)

   c. **Mechanism:**
      i. Extracellular stimuli activate RTKs or GPCRs, leading to Ras activation.

ii. Activated Ras recruits and activates Raf kinases, which phosphorylate and activate MEK1/2.

iii. MEK1/2 phosphorylates and activates ERK1/2.

iv. Activated ERK1/2 translocates to the nucleus and phosphorylates transcription factors, leading to changes in gene expression.

v. ERK1/2 also phosphorylates cytoplasmic proteins involved in cell proliferation, survival, and differentiation.

d. **Physiological Roles**: Regulation of cell proliferation, differentiation, survival, migration, and gene expression.

2. c-Jun N-terminal Kinase (JNK) Pathway:

a. **Activation**: The JNK pathway is activated by various stress stimuli, including UV radiation, inflammatory cytokines, and osmotic stress.

b. **Key Components**:

i. **Upstream**: MAP3Ks (e.g., MEKK1-4), MKK4/7

ii. **Downstream:** JNK1/2/3, transcription factors (c-Jun, ATF2), cytoplasmic proteins (Bcl-2, p53)

c. **Mechanism:**

i. Stress stimuli activate MAP3Ks, such as MEKK1-4.

ii. Activated MAP3Ks phosphorylate and activate MKK4/7.

iii. MKK4/7 phosphorylate and activate JNK1/2/3.

iv. Activated JNKs translocate to the nucleus and phosphorylate transcription factors, such as c-Jun and ATF2.

v. Phosphorylated c-Jun forms homo- or heterodimers and regulates gene expression involved in apoptosis, inflammation, and stress responses.

d. **Physiological Roles**: Regulation of apoptosis, inflammation, cell survival, and stress responses.

3. p38 MAP Kinase Pathway:

a. **Activation**: The p38 pathway is activated by various stress stimuli, including inflammatory cytokines, UV radiation, osmotic stress, and heat shock.

b. **Key Components**:
    i. **Upstream**: MAP3Ks (e.g., ASK1, MEKK3-4), MKK3/6
    ii. **Downstream**: p38α/β/γ/δ, transcription factors (ATF2, p53, NF-κB), cytoplasmic proteins (MAPKAPK2/3)

c. **Mechanism:**
    i. Stress stimuli activate MAP3Ks, such as ASK1 and MEKK3-4.
    ii. Activated MAP3Ks phosphorylate and activate MKK3/6.
    iii. MKK3/6 phosphorylate and activate p38α/β/γ/δ.
    iv. Activated p38 MAPKs phosphorylate transcription factors, such as ATF2 and p53, and cytoplasmic proteins, such as MAPKAPK2/3.
    v. Phosphorylation of downstream targets regulates gene expression, apoptosis, inflammation, and cellular responses to stress.

d. **Physiological Roles**: Regulation of inflammation, apoptosis, cell differentiation, immune responses, and stress responses.

Regulation of MAPK Signaling

The regulation of MAPK signaling is essential for maintaining cellular homeostasis and ensuring appropriate responses to extracellular stimuli. The pathway is subject to tight control at multiple levels to prevent aberrant activation and to fine-tune the amplitude and duration of signaling. Here's a detailed overview of the regulation of MAPK signaling:

1. Regulation of MAPK Activation:

1. Receptor-Level Regulation:

a. **Desensitization**: Receptors undergo desensitization through mechanisms like receptor internalization and degradation, mediated by arrestins or ubiquitin ligases, to attenuate signaling in response to prolonged stimulation.

b. **Feedback Inhibition**: Activated MAPKs can phosphorylate and inhibit upstream signaling components, such as receptors or adaptor proteins, to dampen signaling.

2. **Ras Activation:**

    a. **Ras GTPase Activity**: Ras activity is regulated by guanine nucleotide exchange factors (GEFs) that promote GDP-GTP exchange and GTPase-activating proteins (GAPs) that accelerate GTP hydrolysis, leading to Ras inactivation.

    b. **Scaffold Proteins**: Scaffold proteins, such as KSR (kinase suppressor of Ras), facilitate the assembly of signaling complexes and enhance Ras-mediated MAPK activation.

3. **Raf Activation:**

    a. **Phosphorylation:** Raf kinases are activated by phosphorylation at specific sites, typically within their regulatory domains, by upstream activators like Ras or other signaling proteins.

    b. **Dimerization:** Raf activation often involves the formation of homo- or heterodimers, which stabilize the active conformation of Raf and promote kinase activity.

4. **MAPKK Activation:**

    a. **Phosphorylation:** MAPKKs are activated by dual-specificity MAP kinase kinases (MAPKK kinases or MAP3Ks), which phosphorylate specific serine/threonine residues within the activation loop of MAPKKs.

    b. **Scaffold Proteins**: Scaffold proteins facilitate the recruitment and activation of MAPKKs by promoting their interaction with upstream kinases and substrates.

2. **Regulation of MAPK Activity:**

1. **Phosphorylation and Dephosphorylation:**

a. **MAPK Phosphorylation**: MAPKKs phosphorylate specific threonine and tyrosine residues within the activation loop of MAPKs, leading to their activation.

b. **MAPK Dephosphorylation**: MAPK phosphatases (MKPs) dephosphorylate and inactivate MAPKs by removing phosphate groups from their activation loop, terminating signaling.

2. **Feedback Regulation:**

a. **Negative Feedback**: Active MAPKs can phosphorylate and inhibit upstream components of the pathway, such as RTKs, Ras, Raf, or MAPKKs, to attenuate signaling.

b. **Positive Feedback**: MAPK signaling can induce the expression of feedback regulators, such as scaffold proteins or phosphatases, to modulate pathway activity.

3. **Spatial and Temporal Regulation:**

1. **Subcellular Localization:**

a. **Scaffold Proteins**: Scaffold proteins localize signaling components to specific subcellular compartments, ensuring efficient signal propagation and substrate specificity.

b. **Nuclear Translocation**: Activated MAPKs can translocate to the nucleus, where they phosphorylate transcription factors and regulate gene expression.

2. **Temporal Dynamics:**

a. **Transient Activation**: MAPK signaling is often transient, with rapid activation followed by attenuation due to negative feedback and phosphatase activity.

b. **Oscillatory Behavior**: MAPK signaling can exhibit oscillatory dynamics, characterized by repeated cycles of activation and inactivation, which may contribute to cell fate decisions and developmental processes.

Physiological and Pathological Roles of MAPK Signaling

The mitogen-activated protein kinase (MAPK) signaling pathway plays crucial roles in both physiological and pathological processes by regulating diverse cellular responses to extracellular stimuli. Here's a detailed exploration of the physiological and pathological roles of MAPK signaling:

Physiological Roles:

1. **Cell Proliferation and Survival:**
   a. MAPK signaling promotes cell proliferation and survival in response to growth factors and mitogens.
   b. Physiological processes such as tissue growth, development, and wound healing rely on the regulation of cell proliferation by MAPK signaling.

2. **Cell Differentiation and Development:**
   a. MAPK signaling controls cell fate decisions and differentiation processes during embryonic development and tissue morphogenesis.
   b. Differentiation of stem cells into specialized cell types, such as neurons, muscle cells, and epithelial cells, is regulated by MAPK signaling.

3. **Immune Responses:**
   a. MAPK signaling regulates immune cell activation, cytokine production, and inflammatory responses.
   b. Physiological immune responses, including host defense against pathogens and tissue repair, depend on the precise regulation of MAPK signaling in immune cells.

4. **Neuronal Plasticity:**
   a. MAPK signaling is involved in synaptic plasticity, neuronal development, and synaptic transmission in the central nervous system.

b. Physiological processes such as learning, memory formation, and neuronal survival are modulated by MAPK signaling pathways in neurons.

5. **Metabolic Regulation:**

   a. MAPK signaling regulates metabolic processes such as glucose metabolism, lipid metabolism, and energy homeostasis.

   b. Physiological responses to nutrient availability, hormonal signals, and stress conditions are mediated by MAPK signaling in metabolic tissues.

Pathological Roles:

1. **Cancer:**

   a. Dysregulated MAPK signaling is implicated in the pathogenesis of various cancers, including melanoma, colorectal cancer, lung cancer, and pancreatic cancer.

   b. Aberrant activation of MAPK signaling promotes uncontrolled cell proliferation, survival, angiogenesis, and metastasis in cancer cells.

2. **Inflammatory Diseases:**

   a. Dysregulated MAPK signaling contributes to the pathogenesis of inflammatory diseases, such as rheumatoid arthritis, inflammatory bowel disease, and psoriasis.

   b. Excessive MAPK activation leads to increased production of pro-inflammatory cytokines, chemokines, and inflammatory mediators.

3. **Neurological Disorders:**

   a. Altered MAPK signaling is associated with neurodegenerative diseases, including Alzheimer's disease, Parkinson's disease, and Huntington's disease.

   b. Aberrant MAPK activation contributes to neuronal dysfunction, oxidative stress, neuroinflammation, and neuronal cell death in neurodegenerative disorders.

4. **Cardiovascular Diseases:**
   a. Dysregulated MAPK signaling is implicated in the pathogenesis of cardiovascular diseases, such as hypertension, atherosclerosis, and myocardial infarction.
   b. MAPK signaling regulates vascular smooth muscle cell proliferation, endothelial cell function, and cardiac hypertrophy in cardiovascular diseases.

5. **Metabolic Disorders:**
   a. Altered MAPK signaling is associated with metabolic disorders, including obesity, type 2 diabetes, and non-alcoholic fatty liver disease.
   b. Dysregulated MAPK signaling contributes to insulin resistance, inflammation, dyslipidemia, and aberrant lipid metabolism in metabolic disorders.

JANUS KINASE (JAK)/SIGNAL TRANSDUCER AND ACTIVATOR OF TRANSCRIPTION (STAT) SIGNALING PATHWAY

The Janus kinase (JAK)/signal transducer and activator of transcription (STAT) signaling pathway is a critical mechanism for transmitting signals from extracellular cytokines and growth factors to the cell nucleus, resulting in gene expression changes. This pathway is fundamental for various cellular processes, including immune function, cell growth, differentiation, and apoptosis.

Key Components of the JAK/STAT Pathway

Here's a detailed overview of the key components involved in the Janus kinase (JAK)/signal transducer and activator of transcription (STAT) signaling pathway:

1. **Cytokine Receptors:**
   a. These are cell surface receptors that bind to cytokines, growth factors, and hormones. They typically consist of multiple subunits and lack intrinsic kinase activity. Upon ligand binding, they

undergo conformational changes that lead to receptor dimerization or oligomerization.

2. **Janus Kinases (JAKs):**

   a. JAKs are cytoplasmic tyrosine kinases associated with the intracellular domains of cytokine receptors. They are activated when cytokine binding induces receptor dimerization, bringing JAKs into close proximity, allowing them to trans-phosphorylate each other and become catalytically active.

3. **Signal Transducers and Activators of Transcription (STATs):**

   a. STATs are a family of transcription factors that become activated in response to phosphorylation by JAKs. Once phosphorylated, they form homo- or heterodimers via their SH2 (Src homology 2) domains. These dimers then translocate to the nucleus, where they regulate gene expression by binding to specific DNA sequences in the promoters of target genes.

4. **Negative Regulators:**

   a. **Suppressor of Cytokine Signaling (SOCS):** SOCS proteins are negative regulators of the JAK/STAT pathway. They are induced by cytokine signaling and act as feedback inhibitors by binding to JAKs or cytokine receptors, thereby inhibiting their activity and promoting their degradation.

   b. **Protein Inhibitors of Activated STATs (PIAS):** PIAS proteins also act as negative regulators by inhibiting STAT activity. They can block the DNA binding ability of STATs or promote their sumoylation, which prevents their function.

5. **Cytokines and Growth Factors:**

   a. These extracellular signaling molecules bind to their respective receptors, leading to receptor activation and initiation of downstream signaling through the JAK/STAT pathway. Examples of cytokines and growth factors include interferons (IFNs), interleukins (ILs), growth hormone (GH), erythropoietin (EPO), and prolactin.

6. **Interferon-Stimulated Response Elements (ISREs) and Gamma-Activated Sites** (GAS):

    a. These are specific DNA sequences found in the promoters of genes regulated by the JAK/STAT pathway. STAT dimers bind to ISREs or GAS elements to initiate or enhance the transcription of target genes.

Mechanism of the JAK/STAT Signaling Pathway

The Janus kinase (JAK)/signal transducer and activator of transcription (STAT) signaling pathway is a critical mechanism for transmitting extracellular signals from cytokines, growth factors, and hormones to the nucleus, resulting in changes in gene expression. This pathway plays crucial roles in various cellular processes, including immune responses, cell growth, differentiation, and apoptosis. Here's a detailed overview of the mechanism of the JAK/STAT signaling pathway:

1. **Cytokine Binding and Receptor Activation:**

    a. The pathway is initiated by the binding of cytokines, growth factors, or hormones to their respective receptors on the cell surface. These receptors typically exist as monomers or inactive dimers in the absence of ligand binding.

2. **Receptor Dimerization and JAK Activation:**

    a. Ligand binding induces conformational changes in the receptor, leading to receptor dimerization or oligomerization. This dimerization brings the associated Janus kinases (JAKs) into close proximity, facilitating their trans-phosphorylation and activation.

3. **Phosphorylation of Receptor Tyrosine Residues:**

a. Activated JAKs phosphorylate specific tyrosine residues on the intracellular domains of the receptor. These phosphotyrosine residues serve as docking sites for downstream signaling molecules, particularly members of the STAT family.

4. **STAT Recruitment and Phosphorylation:**

   a. Phosphorylated receptor tyrosine residues recruit and activate cytoplasmic STAT proteins via their SH2 (Src homology 2) domains. The STAT proteins are then phosphorylated by the activated JAKs on specific tyrosine residues.

5. **STAT Dimerization and Nuclear Translocation:**

   a. Phosphorylated STAT proteins undergo conformational changes that promote their dimerization through reciprocal SH2 domain interactions. These STAT dimers can be homodimers or heterodimers depending on the specific STAT proteins involved.

   b. Once dimerized, the phosphorylated STAT proteins translocate from the cytoplasm to the nucleus, facilitated by nuclear localization signals (NLS) within the proteins.

6. **Gene Transcription and Regulation:**

   a. Within the nucleus, STAT dimers bind to specific DNA sequences known as gamma-activated sites (GAS) or interferon-stimulated response elements (ISREs) located in the promoters of target genes.

   b. The binding of STAT dimers to these regulatory elements initiates or enhances the transcription of target genes, leading to changes in gene expression.

   c. STAT proteins can directly activate gene transcription by recruiting co-activators or indirectly regulate gene expression by interacting with other transcription factors.

7. **Termination of Signaling:**

a. The duration and intensity of JAK/STAT signaling are tightly regulated to prevent excessive cellular responses. Negative regulators, such as suppressor of cytokine signaling (SOCS) proteins and protein inhibitors of activated STATs (PIAS), play crucial roles in terminating signaling by inhibiting JAK activity, dephosphorylating STATs, or promoting their degradation.

Specific JAK/STAT Pathways

The Janus kinase (JAK)/signal transducer and activator of transcription (STAT) signaling pathway encompasses various specific pathways that are activated by different cytokines, growth factors, and hormones. Each pathway regulates distinct cellular processes and involves specific JAKs, STATs, and target genes. Here, we'll delve into some specific JAK/STAT pathways in detail:

1. JAK1/JAK2 and STAT1/STAT2 Pathway:

a. **Activation:** This pathway is typically activated by interferons (IFNs), including IFN-α and IFN-γ.

b. **JAKs Involved**: JAK1 and JAK2 are the primary Janus kinases involved in this pathway.

c. **STATs Involved**: STAT1 and STAT2 are the primary STAT proteins activated in response to IFNs.

d. **Mechanism**:

   i. Binding of IFNs to their receptors induces receptor dimerization and activation of associated JAK1 and JAK2.

   ii. Activated JAKs phosphorylate tyrosine residues on the receptor cytoplasmic domains, creating docking sites for STAT proteins.

   iii. Phosphorylated STAT1 and STAT2 proteins bind to the receptor complex.

   iv. Upon binding, STAT1 and STAT2 are phosphorylated by JAKs.

v. Phosphorylated STAT1 and STAT2 form heterodimers, which associate with interferon regulatory factor 9 (IRF9) to form the ISGF3 complex.

vi. ISGF3 translocates to the nucleus and binds to interferon-stimulated response elements (ISREs) in the promoters of interferon-stimulated genes (ISGs).

vii. ISGF3 binding to ISREs activates the transcription of ISGs, including antiviral proteins and immunomodulatory factors.

2. JAK2 and STAT5 Pathway:

a. **Activation: This** pathway is activated by cytokines such as growth hormone (GH), erythropoietin (EPO), and prolactin.

b. **JAKs Involved**: JAK2 is the primary Janus kinase involved in this pathway.

c. **STATs Involved**: STAT5A and STAT5B are the primary STAT proteins activated in response to cytokine stimulation.

d. **Mechanism:**

i. Binding of cytokines such as GH or EPO to their respective receptors leads to receptor dimerization and activation of associated JAK2.

ii. Activated JAK2 phosphorylates tyrosine residues on the receptor cytoplasmic domains.

iii. Phosphorylated tyrosine residues serve as docking sites for STAT5 proteins.

iv. Phosphorylated STAT5 proteins bind to the receptor complex.

v. Upon binding, STAT5 proteins are phosphorylated by JAK2.

vi. Phosphorylated STAT5 proteins form homodimers or heterodimers.

vii. STAT5 dimers translocate to the nucleus and bind to specific DNA sequences in the promoters of target genes, regulating their transcription.

viii. Target genes include those involved in cell proliferation, survival, and differentiation, as well as lactation and erythropoiesis.

3. JAK1 and STAT6 Pathway:

a. **Activation:** This pathway is activated by interleukin-4 (IL-4) and interleukin-13 (IL-13).

b. **JAKs Involved**: JAK1 is the primary Janus kinase involved in this pathway.

c. **STATs Involved**: STAT6 is the primary STAT protein activated in response to IL-4 and IL-13.

d. **Mechanism:**

i. IL-4 or IL-13 binding to their respective receptors induces receptor dimerization and activation of associated JAK1.

ii. Activated JAK1 phosphorylates tyrosine residues on the receptor cytoplasmic domains.

iii. Phosphorylated tyrosine residues serve as docking sites for STAT6 proteins.

iv. Phosphorylated STAT6 proteins bind to the receptor complex.

v. Upon binding, STAT6 proteins are phosphorylated by JAK1.

vi. Phosphorylated STAT6 proteins form homodimers.

vii. STAT6 dimers translocate to the nucleus and bind to specific DNA sequences in the promoters of target genes, regulating their transcription.

viii. Target genes include those involved in Th2 cell differentiation, allergic responses, and immunomodulation.

Regulation of the JAK/STAT Pathway

The Janus kinase (JAK)/signal transducer and activator of transcription (STAT) signaling pathway is tightly regulated to ensure appropriate cellular responses to extracellular stimuli while preventing excessive activation or inappropriate signaling. Regulation of this pathway occurs at multiple levels and involves various negative and positive feedback mechanisms. Here's a detailed overview of the regulation of the JAK/STAT pathway:

Regulation of the JAK/STAT Pathway:

1. **Suppressor of Cytokine Signaling (SOCS) Proteins:**

    a. SOCS proteins are negative regulators of the JAK/STAT pathway. They are induced by cytokine signaling and act as feedback inhibitors.

    b. Mechanism:

    i. SOCS proteins inhibit JAK activity by binding to JAKs or to the activation loop of cytokine receptors, preventing further signaling.

    ii. They also compete with STATs for binding to phosphorylated tyrosine residues on receptors, blocking STAT recruitment and activation.

    iii. SOCS proteins can recruit E3 ubiquitin ligases to target JAKs or cytokine receptors for ubiquitination and degradation, further attenuating signaling.

2. **Protein Inhibitors of Activated STATs (PIAS):**

    a. PIAS proteins are negative regulators of STAT activity. They inhibit STAT function by various mechanisms.

    b. Mechanism:

    i. PIAS proteins can block the DNA binding ability of STATs by binding to their DNA-binding domains, preventing transcriptional activation.

    ii. They can promote the sumoylation of STATs, which inhibits their function by altering their activity or subcellular localization.

    iii. PIAS proteins can also recruit histone deacetylases (HDACs) to STAT-bound promoters, leading to transcriptional repression.

3. **Protein Tyrosine Phosphatases (PTPs):**

    a. PTPs are enzymes that dephosphorylate tyrosine residues on JAKs and STATs, terminating signaling.

    b. **Mechanism:**

        i. PTPs dephosphorylate activated JAKs, leading to their inactivation and dissociation from receptors.

        ii. They also dephosphorylate STAT proteins, promoting their nuclear export and inactivation.

        iii. PTPs help to terminate signaling by counteracting the action of protein tyrosine kinases (PTKs) that activate the pathway.

4. **Cytokine-Inducible SH2-Containing Protein (CIS):**

    a. CIS is a family member of the SOCS proteins and acts similarly to regulate JAK/STAT signaling.

    b. **Mechanism:**

        i. CIS competes with STATs for binding to phosphorylated tyrosine residues on receptors, inhibiting STAT recruitment and activation.

        ii. It can also target receptors for degradation, attenuating signaling.

5. **Feedback Loops:**

    a. Negative feedback loops are essential for fine-tuning the duration and intensity of JAK/STAT signaling.

    b. **Mechanism:**

i. Negative regulators like SOCS proteins and PTPs are themselves target genes of STAT-mediated transcription, creating feedback loops that help to turn off signaling.

ii. Increased expression of SOCS proteins and PTPs dampens JAK/STAT activity, preventing prolonged or excessive signaling.

6. **Crosstalk with Other Signaling Pathways:**

a. The JAK/STAT pathway can crosstalk with other signaling pathways, including the MAPK and PI3K/Akt pathways, providing additional layers of regulation.

b. **Mechanism:**

i. Cross-regulation between pathways can involve direct protein-protein interactions, phosphorylation events, or transcriptional regulation of pathway components.

ii. Crosstalk allows for integration of signals from multiple pathways and fine-tuning of cellular responses.

Physiological and Pathological Roles of the JAK/STAT Pathway

The Janus kinase (JAK)/signal transducer and activator of transcription (STAT) signaling pathway plays critical roles in various physiological processes, including immune responses, hematopoiesis, cell proliferation, differentiation, and apoptosis. Dysregulation of this pathway can contribute to the pathogenesis of numerous diseases. Here's a detailed exploration of the physiological and pathological roles of the JAK/STAT pathway:

Physiological Roles:

1. **Immune Responses:**

a. The JAK/STAT pathway is essential for mediating immune responses by regulating the development, differentiation, and function of immune cells.

b. It plays a crucial role in cytokine signaling, allowing immune cells to communicate and coordinate their activities.

c. STAT proteins regulate the expression of genes involved in immune cell proliferation, differentiation, and cytokine production.

2. **Hematopoiesis:**

   a. JAK/STAT signaling is involved in the regulation of hematopoietic stem cell maintenance, proliferation, and differentiation.

   b. Cytokines such as erythropoietin (EPO), thrombopoietin (TPO), and granulocyte colony-stimulating factor (G-CSF) signal through the JAK/STAT pathway to regulate erythropoiesis, thrombopoiesis, and myelopoiesis, respectively.

3. **Cell Proliferation and Survival:**

   a. The pathway regulates cell proliferation and survival in various cell types, including immune cells, epithelial cells, and fibroblasts.

   b. Growth factors such as growth hormone (GH) and insulin-like growth factor 1 (IGF-1) activate JAK/STAT signaling to promote cell growth and survival.

4. **Development and Differentiation:**

   a. JAK/STAT signaling is crucial for embryonic development and tissue homeostasis.

   b. It regulates the differentiation of various cell types during development, including immune cells, neurons, and muscle cells.

   c. STAT proteins control the expression of genes involved in cell fate determination, tissue patterning, and organogenesis.

5. **Inflammatory Responses:**

   a. The pathway plays a central role in mediating inflammatory responses by regulating the expression of pro-inflammatory cytokines and chemokines.

b. It controls the activation and function of immune cells, such as macrophages, dendritic cells, and T cells, in response to inflammatory stimuli.

Pathological Roles:

1. **Cancer:**

   a. Dysregulation of the JAK/STAT pathway is implicated in the pathogenesis of various cancers.

   b. Constitutive activation of JAK/STAT signaling can promote uncontrolled cell proliferation, survival, and metastasis.

   c. Mutations or aberrant expression of JAKs, STATs, or upstream regulators contribute to oncogenesis in hematological malignancies and solid tumors.

2. **Autoimmune Diseases:**

   a. Aberrant activation of the JAK/STAT pathway is associated with autoimmune diseases, such as rheumatoid arthritis, systemic lupus erythematosus, and multiple sclerosis.

   b. Dysregulated cytokine signaling and aberrant immune cell activation contribute to chronic inflammation and tissue damage in autoimmune disorders.

3. **Inflammatory Diseases:**

   a. Chronic activation of the JAK/STAT pathway contributes to the pathogenesis of inflammatory diseases, including inflammatory bowel disease, psoriasis, and asthma.

   b. Excessive production of pro-inflammatory cytokines leads to sustained inflammation and tissue injury in affected organs.

4. **Hematological Disorders:**

   a. Mutations in JAK2 and other components of the JAK/STAT pathway are associated with hematological disorders, including myeloproliferative neoplasms and lymphoproliferative disorders.

b. Dysregulated JAK/STAT signaling disrupts hematopoietic cell homeostasis, leading to abnormal proliferation and differentiation of blood cells.

5. **Neurological Disorders:**

   a. Abnormal JAK/STAT signaling has been implicated in the pathogenesis of neurological disorders, such as Alzheimer's disease, Parkinson's disease, and multiple sclerosis.

   b. Dysregulated cytokine signaling and neuroinflammation contribute to neuronal dysfunction and neurodegeneration in these disorders.

Therapeutic Targeting of the JAK/STAT Pathway

Therapeutic targeting of the Janus kinase (JAK)/signal transducer and activator of transcription (STAT) pathway has emerged as a promising strategy for the treatment of various diseases, including cancer, autoimmune disorders, and inflammatory diseases. Here's a detailed exploration of the therapeutic approaches targeting the JAK/STAT pathway:

Therapeutic Targeting Strategies:

1. **JAK Inhibitors:**

   a. Small molecule inhibitors that selectively target JAKs have been developed as therapeutic agents.

   b. These inhibitors competitively bind to the ATP-binding pocket of JAKs, preventing their phosphorylation and activation.

   c. By inhibiting JAK activity, these inhibitors block downstream STAT activation and cytokine signaling.

   d. **Examples of JAK inhibitors approved for clinical use include:**

      i. **Ruxolitinib:** Approved for the treatment of myeloproliferative neoplasms, such as polycythemia vera and myelofibrosis.

      ii. **Tofacitinib:** Approved for the treatment of rheumatoid arthritis, psoriatic arthritis, and ulcerative colitis.

    iii. **Baricitinib:** Approved for the treatment of rheumatoid arthritis and atopic dermatitis.

    iv. **Upadacitinib:** Approved for the treatment of rheumatoid arthritis.

2. **STAT Inhibitors:**

   a. Direct inhibition of STAT proteins is challenging due to their lack of enzymatic activity and the absence of well-defined binding pockets.

   b. However, strategies to disrupt STAT-DNA interactions or interfere with protein-protein interactions involved in STAT signaling are being explored.

   c. Peptide inhibitors and small molecules that target STAT dimerization or DNA binding have shown potential in preclinical studies but have yet to reach clinical application.

3. **Cytokine Inhibitors:**

   a. Since cytokines are upstream regulators of the JAK/STAT pathway, blocking their activity can indirectly inhibit JAK/STAT signaling.

   b. Monoclonal antibodies or soluble receptors that neutralize cytokines have been developed as therapeutic agents.

   c. **Examples include:**

    i. Anti-TNF antibodies (e.g., adalimumab, infliximab) for the treatment of autoimmune diseases such as rheumatoid arthritis and inflammatory bowel disease.

    ii. Anti-IL-6 antibodies (e.g., tocilizumab) for the treatment of rheumatoid arthritis and cytokine release syndrome.

    iii. Anti-IL-23 antibodies (e.g., ustekinumab) for the treatment of psoriasis and inflammatory bowel disease.

4. **Combination Therapies:**

a. Combining JAK inhibitors with other targeted therapies or immunomodulatory agents has shown promise for enhancing therapeutic efficacy and overcoming resistance.

b. Combination therapies may target multiple nodes within the JAK/STAT pathway or synergistically inhibit complementary signaling pathways.

c. Clinical trials evaluating the efficacy of combination therapies in various diseases, including cancer and autoimmune disorders, are ongoing.

5. Biosimilars and Next-Generation Inhibitors:

a. Development of biosimilars of existing JAK inhibitors aims to increase treatment accessibility and reduce costs.

b. Next-generation JAK inhibitors with improved selectivity, pharmacokinetics, and safety profiles are also under development to address limitations of current therapies, such as off-target effects and adverse events.

MCQ Questions Based on the Context

1. What type of signaling involves cells responding to their own secreted molecules?

   A) Juxtacrine

   B) Endocrine

   C) Autocrine

   D) Paracrine

2. Which receptor type involves ligand binding that typically causes ion channels to open or close?

   A) G-Protein-Coupled Receptors (GPCRs)

   B) Nuclear Receptors

   C) Receptor Tyrosine Kinases (RTKs)

D) Ionotropic Receptors

3. Which pathway is involved in cell survival and metabolism and includes PI3K activation?

    A) JAK/STAT Pathway

    B) MAPK/ERK Pathway

    C) PI3K/AKT Pathway

    D) Calcium signaling pathway

4. Which molecule acts as a second messenger in Calcium signaling?

    A) cAMP

    B) DAG

    C) IP3

    D) ATP

5. How does the MAPK/ERK pathway primarily get activated?

    A) Through G-protein coupled receptors

    B) By cytokine receptors

    C) Via receptor tyrosine kinases

    D) Through nuclear receptors

6. What is the role of phosphodiesterases in cell signaling?

    A) Amplify the signal

    B) Bind to receptors

    C) Degrade cAMP

    D) Phosphorylate proteins

7. Which of the following is NOT a component of the JAK/STAT signaling pathway? A) JAK kinases

    B) SOCS proteins

    C) Adenylyl cyclase

    D) STAT transcription factors

8. In which signaling does Notch participate by direct cell-to-cell contact?

    A) Endocrine

B) Paracrine

C) Autocrine

D) Juxtacrine

9. What type of receptors are involved in the detection of light and odors?

    A) Ionotropic receptors

    B) GPCRs

    C) RTKs

    D) Nuclear receptors

10. Which pathway uses cyclic AMP as a second messenger?

    A) PI3K/AKT

    B) Calcium signaling

    C) cAMP signaling pathway

    D) IP3 signaling pathway

11. What is the primary mechanism of action for receptor tyrosine kinases?

    A) G-protein activation

    B) Dimerization and autophosphorylation

    C) Ligand-gated ion channel opening

    D) DNA binding

12. Which signaling molecule is involved in neurotransmission and muscle contraction, primarily by allowing Na+ and K+ ions to pass?

    A) Glutamate

    B) GABA

    C) Acetylcholine

    D) Dopamine

13. Which pathway involves the transcription factor CREB?

    A) MAPK/ERK

    B) cAMP

    C) Calcium signaling

    D) JAK/STAT

14. What is the typical composition of ligand-gated ion channels?

A) Single polypeptide

B) Two subunits

C) Four subunits

D) Five subunits

15. Which kinase is directly activated by cyclic AMP?

A) Protein kinase C

B) Protein kinase A

C) Protein kinase G

D) MAP Kinase

16. Which of the following is not a characteristic function of G-protein coupled receptors (GPCRs)?

A) Activating ion channels

B) Direct phosphorylation of proteins

C) Influencing cell metabolism

D) Detecting extracellular molecules

17. What role do nuclear receptors play in the cell?

A) Phosphorylate other proteins

B) Act as transcription factors

C) Act as second messengers

D) Open ion channels

18. What is primarily responsible for the inactivation of G-proteins?

A) Hydrolysis of GTP to GDP

B) Phosphorylation by kinases

C) Binding of secondary messengers

D) Ligand dissociation from the receptor

19. What is a key feature of autocrine signaling?

A) It involves signals from distant cells.

B) It involves signals that affect the secreting cell itself.

C) It requires hormonal signaling.

D) It relies solely on nuclear receptors.

20. Which type of cell signaling is characterized by the release of hormones into the bloodstream to affect distant cells?

A) Juxtacrine signaling

B) Autocrine signaling

C) Paracrine signaling

D) Endocrine signaling

Short Answer Type Questions

1. What are G-protein-coupled receptors (GPCRs) and how do they function?

2. Describe the role of second messengers in cell signaling.

3. What is the significance of the PI3K/AKT pathway in cell survival and metabolism?

4. Explain the function of receptor tyrosine kinases (RTKs) in cell signaling.

5. How do ionotropic receptors function and what role do they play in neurotransmission?

6. What is autocrine signaling and give an example?

7. Discuss the role of calcium ions as secondary messengers.

8. How is the JAK/STAT pathway activated?

9. Describe the role of MAPK/ERK pathway in cell differentiation.

10. What is receptor desensitization and how does it occur?

11. Explain the clinical relevance of targeting cell signaling pathways in disease treatment.

12. What are the physiological roles of cyclic AMP (cAMP) in cell signaling?

13. Describe the process of signal transduction in cell signaling.

14. How do nuclear receptors function differently from membrane-bound receptors?

15. What are protein kinase cascades and their significance in signaling pathways?

16. Explain how synaptic signaling works in neurons.

17. What mechanisms are involved in the termination of cell signaling?

18. Describe the role of phosphodiesterases in the regulation of signal pathways.

19. How do ligand-gated ion channels facilitate cellular responses to external signals?

20. What is the significance of the TGF-beta signaling pathway in cell regulation?

Long Answer Type Questions

1. Discuss the molecular mechanisms involved in the activation and regulation of the G-protein-coupled receptor (GPCR) signaling pathway and its impact on human health.

2. Explain the role and regulation of calcium signaling in cardiac function and how dysregulation can lead to disease states.

3. Describe the detailed mechanism of action of receptor tyrosine kinases and their role in cancer development.

4. Analyze the JAK/STAT signaling pathway, including its activation, function, and importance in immune system regulation.

5. Discuss the role of cyclic AMP (cAMP) in neuronal signaling and its implications for learning and memory.

6. Provide a detailed description of the MAPK/ERK signaling pathway, its components, and its role in cell growth and differentiation.

7. Elaborate on the physiological and pathological roles of the PI3K/AKT pathway, with particular emphasis on its implications in cancer therapy.

8. Explain how ionotropic receptors are structured and function in the nervous system, and discuss their role in neurological diseases.

9. Describe the mechanism by which nuclear receptors influence gene expression and their impact on metabolism and reproductive health.

10. Discuss the therapeutic targeting of cell signaling pathways, focusing on the use of kinase inhibitors in treating diseases such as cancer and rheumatoid arthritis.

Answer Key

1. C) Autocrine
2. D) Ionotropic Receptors
3. C) PI3K/AKT Pathway
4. C) IP3
5. C) Via receptor tyrosine kinases
6. C) Degrade cAMP
7. C) Adenylyl cyclase
8. D) Juxtacrine
9. B) GPCRs
10. C) cAMP signaling pathway
11. B) Dimerization and autophosphorylation
12. C) Acetylcholine
13. B) cAMP
14. D) Five subunits
15. B) Protein kinase A
16. B) Direct phosphorylation of proteins
17. B) Act as transcription factors
18. A) Hydrolysis of GTP to GDP
19. B) It involves signals that affect the secreting cell itself.
20. D) Endocrine signaling

CHAPTER – 3

GENOMIC AND PROTEOMIC TOOLS

INTRODUCTION:

Genomic and proteomic tools are essential in modern biological research, allowing scientists to study the genetic and protein components of organisms in great detail. These tools enable the understanding of complex biological processes, the identification of disease mechanisms, and the development of new therapeutic strategies. Below is an in-depth introduction to both genomic and proteomic tools.

Genomic Tools

1. DNA Sequencing:

   a. **Sanger Sequencing**: The first widely used method for DNA sequencing, which uses chain-terminating dideoxynucleotides. It is accurate but relatively low-throughput.

   b. **Next-Generation Sequencing (NGS):** Includes technologies like Illumina sequencing, which allow massive parallel sequencing, providing high-throughput and cost-effective sequencing of entire genomes or targeted regions.

   c. **Third-Generation Sequencing**: Methods like PacBio and Oxford Nanopore sequencing, which offer longer read lengths and can sequence single molecules in real-time, aiding in the analysis of complex genomic regions.

2. Polymerase Chain Reaction (PCR):

   a. **Conventional PCR:** Amplifies specific DNA sequences, making them easier to study.

   b. **Quantitative PCR (qPCR):** Allows quantification of DNA, useful for measuring gene expression levels.

c. **Digital PCR**: Provides highly precise quantification of nucleic acids, beneficial in detecting low-abundance targets.

3. CRISPR-Cas9:

a. A genome editing tool that allows precise modifications to DNA sequences. It is widely used for gene knockout, knock-in, and gene regulation studies.

4. Microarrays:

a. Used for analyzing gene expression profiles by hybridizing labeled DNA or RNA to probes on a solid surface. Microarrays can monitor the expression of thousands of genes simultaneously.

5. Genome-Wide Association Studies (GWAS):

a. Identify genetic variations associated with specific diseases or traits by scanning the genomes of many individuals.

6. Bioinformatics Tools:

a. **Sequence Alignment Tools**: BLAST, ClustalW, and others for comparing DNA sequences.

b. **Genome Assembly Tools**: SPAdes, Velvet, etc., for assembling short reads into longer genomic sequences.

c. **Annotation Tools**: Tools like Ensembl and UCSC Genome Browser for identifying gene locations and functions.

Proteomic Tools

1. Mass Spectrometry (MS):

a. **Tandem MS (MS/MS):** Used for protein identification and quantification by analyzing the mass-to-charge ratio of ionized protein fragments.

b. **Matrix-Assisted Laser Desorption/Ionization (MALDI):** Ionizes proteins with minimal fragmentation, suitable for analyzing large biomolecules.

c. **Electrospray Ionization (ESI):** Produces ions from liquid samples, used in conjunction with liquid chromatography (LC-MS).

2. Two-Dimensional Gel Electrophoresis (2D-GE):

a. Separates proteins based on isoelectric point and molecular weight, allowing analysis of complex protein mixtures.

3. Western Blotting:

a. Detects specific proteins in a sample using antibodies, providing information on protein size and abundance.

4. Protein Microarrays:

a. Analyze protein-protein interactions, protein-DNA interactions, and other functions on a large scale.

5. X-ray Crystallography:

a. Determines the 3D structure of proteins by analyzing the diffraction patterns of X-rays passing through crystallized proteins.

6. Nuclear Magnetic Resonance (NMR) Spectroscopy:

a. Provides information on the structure, dynamics, and interactions of proteins in solution.

7. Surface Plasmon Resonance (SPR):

a. Measures the binding interactions between proteins and other molecules in real-time without the need for labels.

8. Bioinformatics Tools:

a. **Protein Sequence Databases**: UniProt, PDB for storing protein sequences and structures.

b. **Protein Identification Tools**: Mascot, SEQUEST, and others used in conjunction with MS data.

c. **Structural Prediction Tools**: SWISS-MODEL, Phyre2 for predicting protein 3D structures based on sequence.

Integration of Genomics and Proteomics

1. Systems Biology:

a. Combines genomic, proteomic, and other omics data to understand the complex interactions within biological systems.

2. Personalized Medicine:

- Uses genomic and proteomic information to tailor medical treatments to individual patients, enhancing therapeutic efficacy and minimizing side effects.

3. Functional Genomics and Proteomics:

a. Studies the relationship between genes and their protein products, focusing on how genetic variations affect protein function and contribute to diseases.

PRINCIPLES AND APPLICATIONS OF GENOMIC AND PROTEOMIC TOOLS

DNA Sequencing:

a. Principles:

i. **Sanger Sequencing**: Uses chain-terminating dideoxynucleotides to terminate DNA synthesis at specific bases, allowing determination of the DNA sequence.

ii. **Next-Generation Sequencing (NGS):** Involves fragmenting DNA, attaching adapters, and amplifying DNA on a solid surface, followed by sequencing by synthesis or ligation. High-throughput and parallel processing capabilities enable rapid sequencing of large genomes.

iii. **Third-Generation Sequencing**: Utilizes real-time sequencing of single molecules without the need for amplification, providing longer read lengths and the ability to analyze complex regions of the genome.

b. Applications:

i. **Whole Genome Sequencing (WGS):** Used to identify genetic variations, mutations, and structural variants across the entire genome.

ii. **Exome Sequencing**: Focuses on sequencing the coding regions of the genome to identify disease-causing mutations.

iii. **Targeted Sequencing**: Sequences specific regions of interest, useful in clinical diagnostics and research.

2. Polymerase Chain Reaction (PCR):

a. Principles:

i. Amplifies specific DNA sequences using temperature cycles and DNA polymerase. Consists of denaturation, annealing, and extension steps.

ii. **qPCR:** Uses fluorescent dyes or probes to quantify DNA in real-time.

iii. **Digital PCR**: Partitioning the sample into thousands of reactions allows absolute quantification of DNA molecules.

b. Applications:

i. **Diagnostic Testing**: Detection of pathogens, genetic disorders, and cancer markers.

ii. **Gene Expression Analysis**: Measuring mRNA levels to study gene expression patterns.

iii. **Cloning and Genetic Manipulation**: Amplifying DNA for cloning or gene editing purposes.

3. CRISPR-Cas9:

a. Principles:

i. Utilizes RNA-guided endonuclease Cas9 to introduce double-strand breaks at specific genomic locations, allowing for precise genome editing.

ii. Guide RNA (gRNA) directs Cas9 to the target DNA sequence.

b. Applications:

    i.   **Gene Knockout/Knock-in**: Creating gene knockouts to study gene function or introducing specific mutations.

    ii.   **Gene Therapy**: Correcting genetic defects in somatic cells.

    iii.   **Functional Genomics**: High-throughput screening of gene functions and interactions.

4. Microarrays:

a. Principles:

    i.   Involves hybridizing labeled DNA or RNA to probes on a solid surface, allowing simultaneous analysis of thousands of sequences.

    ii.   Fluorescence intensity indicates the level of hybridization, correlating with gene expression or genetic variation.

b. Applications:

    i.   **Gene Expression Profiling**: Comparing gene expression levels between different conditions or tissues.

    ii.   **Genotyping**: Identifying single nucleotide polymorphisms (SNPs) and other genetic variations.

    iii.   **Comparative Genomic Hybridization (CGH):** Detecting copy number variations across the genome.

5. Genome-Wide Association Studies (GWAS):

a. Principles:

    i.   Scans the genomes of many individuals to identify genetic variants associated with specific traits or diseases.

    ii.   Involves statistical analysis to correlate genetic markers with phenotypic traits.

b. Applications:

    i.   **Disease Gene Identification**: Discovering genetic risk factors for complex diseases like diabetes, cancer, and cardiovascular diseases.

ii. **Personalized Medicine**: Informing treatment decisions based on individual genetic profiles.

iii. **Population Genetics**: Studying genetic diversity and evolutionary history.

Principles and Applications of Proteomic Tools

1. Mass Spectrometry (MS):

  a. Principles:

    i. Ionizes protein fragments and measures their mass-to-charge ratio. Tandem MS (MS/MS) involves multiple rounds of mass analysis for detailed peptide sequencing.

    ii. MALDI: Uses a laser to ionize proteins, suitable for large biomolecules.

    iii. **ESI:** Ionizes proteins from a liquid phase, often coupled with liquid chromatography (LC-MS) for separation.

  b. Applications:

    i. **Protein Identification**: Determining the amino acid sequence of proteins and identifying post-translational modifications.

    ii. **Quantitative Proteomics**: Measuring protein abundance and comparing protein expression levels between samples (e.g., label-free quantification, SILAC, TMT).

    iii. **Biomarker Discovery**: Identifying protein markers for diseases, which can be used in diagnostics and therapeutic monitoring.

2. Two-Dimensional Gel Electrophoresis (2D-GE):

  a. Principles:

    i. Separates proteins first by isoelectric point (isoelectric focusing) and then by molecular weight (SDS-PAGE), allowing resolution of complex protein mixtures.

  b. Applications:

i. **Protein Profiling**: Comparing protein expression patterns under different conditions (e.g., healthy vs. diseased tissues).

ii. **Protein Purification**: Isolating specific proteins for further analysis.

3. Western Blotting:

a. Principles:

i. Transfers proteins separated by gel electrophoresis to a membrane, where they are probed with specific antibodies to detect target proteins.

b. Applications:

i. **Protein Detection**: Confirming the presence and size of specific proteins in a sample.

ii. **Post-Translational Modifications**: Analyzing modifications such as phosphorylation or glycosylation.

4. Protein Microarrays:

a. Principles:

i. Immobilizes proteins on a solid surface to study interactions with other proteins, nucleic acids, or small molecules.

b. Applications:

i. **Interaction Studies**: Mapping protein-protein, protein-DNA, or protein-drug interactions.

ii. **Functional Proteomics**: Identifying protein functions and signaling pathways.

5. X-ray Crystallography:

a. Principles:

i. Determines the 3D structure of proteins by analyzing the diffraction patterns of X-rays passing through crystallized proteins.

b. Applications:

i. **Structural Biology**: Understanding protein function and mechanism at the atomic level.

ii. **Drug Design:** Designing small molecules that specifically target protein structures.

6. Nuclear Magnetic Resonance (NMR) Spectroscopy:

a. Principles:

i. Uses the magnetic properties of atomic nuclei to determine the structure, dynamics, and interactions of proteins in solution.

b. Applications:

i. **Structural Analysis**: Investigating the 3D structure of proteins that cannot be crystallized.

ii. **Dynamics and Interactions**: Studying protein folding, conformational changes, and interactions with other molecules.

7. Surface Plasmon Resonance (SPR):

a. Principles:

i. Measures changes in refractive index near a sensor surface to detect binding interactions between biomolecules in real-time.

b. Applications:

i. **Kinetic Studies**: Determining the binding kinetics and affinity of protein interactions.

ii. **Drug Discovery**: Screening for potential drug candidates by measuring their binding to target proteins.

Integration of Genomics and Proteomics

1. Systems Biology:

a. Principles:

i. Combines data from genomics, proteomics, transcriptomics, and other omics to create comprehensive models of biological systems.

b. Applications:

i. **Pathway Analysis**: Understanding the interactions and regulatory networks underlying biological processes and diseases.

ii. **Predictive Modeling**: Simulating cellular behavior and predicting responses to perturbations (e.g., drug treatments).

2. Personalized Medicine:

a. Principles:

i. Uses individual genetic and proteomic profiles to tailor medical treatments.

b. Applications:

i. **Therapeutic Targeting**: Identifying specific molecular targets for personalized therapies.

ii. **Risk Assessment**: Predicting an individual's risk of developing certain diseases based on genetic markers.

3. Functional Genomics and Proteomics:

a. Principles:

i. Studies the relationship between genes and their protein products to understand gene function and regulation.

b. Applications:

i. **Gene Function Analysis**: Investigating how genetic variations affect protein function and contribute to phenotypes.

ii. **Disease Mechanisms**: Identifying molecular mechanisms underlying diseases, which can lead to new therapeutic strategies.

Genomic and proteomic tools, when used together, provide a powerful approach to understanding biological systems, identifying disease mechanisms, and developing personalized treatments.

DNA ELECTROPHORESIS

DNA electrophoresis is a fundamental technique used to separate DNA fragments based on size and charge. This method is essential in both genomic and proteomic research for analyzing DNA fragments, RNA molecules, and even proteins when coupled with other techniques. Below is a detailed look at DNA electrophoresis, including its principles, types, procedures, and applications.

Principles of DNA Electrophoresis

DNA electrophoresis is based on the principle that DNA molecules are negatively charged due to their phosphate backbone. When an electric field is applied, DNA fragments migrate towards the positive electrode. The rate of migration is inversely proportional to the size of the DNA fragments, allowing for separation by size.

Types of DNA Electrophoresis

1. **Agarose Gel Electrophoresis:**
   a. **Principles:**
      i. Uses an agarose matrix, which forms a gel when dissolved in a buffer and cooled.
      ii. Pores in the agarose gel act as a molecular sieve, allowing smaller DNA fragments to migrate faster than larger ones.
   b. **Procedure:**
      i. Prepare the agarose gel by dissolving agarose powder in an appropriate buffer and pouring it into a casting tray with a comb to form wells.
      ii. Load DNA samples mixed with a loading dye into the wells.
      iii. Apply an electric field across the gel.
      iv. Visualize the DNA fragments using a DNA-binding dye such as ethidium bromide or SYBR Safe under UV or blue light.
   c. **Applications:**
      i. Routine analysis of PCR products.
      ii. Restriction fragment length polymorphism (RFLP) analysis.
      iii. DNA fingerprinting and genotyping.

iv. Quality control of DNA samples before sequencing.

2. **Polyacrylamide Gel Electrophoresis (PAGE):**

   a. **Principles:**

      i. Uses a polyacrylamide matrix, which provides higher resolution than agarose and is suitable for separating small DNA fragments and single-stranded DNA.

   b. **Procedure:**

      i. Prepare the polyacrylamide gel by polymerizing acrylamide and bis-acrylamide in a buffer.

      ii. Load DNA samples into the wells and apply an electric field.

      iii. Stain and visualize the DNA bands using appropriate dyes.

   c. **Applications:**

      i. DNA sequencing (e.g., Sanger sequencing).

      ii. Analysis of short DNA fragments and oligonucleotides.

      iii. Protein electrophoresis when coupled with SDS-PAGE.

3. **Capillary Electrophoresis:**

   a. **Principles:**

      i. Uses a thin capillary tube filled with a gel or polymer solution.

      ii. High voltage is applied, and DNA fragments are separated based on their size and charge-to-mass ratio.

   b. **Procedure:**

      i. Inject DNA samples into the capillary tube.

      ii. Apply an electric field and detect the DNA fragments as they pass through a detector.

   c. **Applications:**

      i. High-throughput DNA sequencing (e.g., automated Sanger sequencing).

ii. Fragment analysis for microsatellite genotyping and forensic analysis.

iii. Quantification of nucleic acids.

Procedure of Agarose Gel Electrophoresis (Detailed Example)

1. **Gel Preparation:**

   a. Dissolve agarose powder in an appropriate buffer (e.g., TAE or TBE) by heating until clear.

   b. Cool slightly and pour into a gel casting tray with a comb to create wells.

   c. Allow the gel to solidify at room temperature.

2. **Sample Preparation:**

   a. Mix DNA samples with a loading dye that contains a density agent (e.g., glycerol) and tracking dyes (e.g., bromophenol blue, xylene cyanol).

3. **Running the Gel:**

   a. Place the gel in an electrophoresis chamber and cover with running buffer.

   b. Load DNA samples into the wells using a micropipette.

   c. Connect the chamber to a power supply and apply an electric field (e.g., 80-120 volts for 30-60 minutes).

4. **Visualization:**

   a. After electrophoresis, stain the gel with a DNA-binding dye (e.g., ethidium bromide) by immersing it in the staining solution.

   b. Visualize the DNA bands using a UV transilluminator or blue light imager.

Applications of DNA Electrophoresis

1. **Genomic Applications:**

   a. **PCR Product Analysis**: Confirming the presence and size of amplified DNA fragments.

b. **Restriction Digestion Analysis**: Identifying and characterizing DNA fragments produced by restriction enzyme digestion.

c. **DNA Mapping**: Constructing physical maps of genomes by analyzing the sizes of DNA fragments.

d. **Genotyping**: Identifying genetic variations, such as single nucleotide polymorphisms (SNPs) and short tandem repeats (STRs).

2. **Proteomic Applications:**

a. **Nucleic Acid-Protein Interactions**: Analyzing interactions between DNA/RNA and proteins using techniques such as electrophoretic mobility shift assays (EMSAs).

b. **RNA Analysis**: Separating and analyzing RNA molecules, including mRNA, rRNA, and tRNA.

Advantages and Limitations

Advantages:

a. Simple and cost-effective.

b. Suitable for routine analysis of DNA fragments.

c. Provides good resolution for a wide range of DNA sizes.

Limitations:

a. Limited resolution for very small DNA fragments compared to polyacrylamide gels.

b. Ethidium bromide is a hazardous chemical and requires careful handling and disposal.

c. Analysis can be time-consuming and requires visualization equipment such as UV transilluminators.

Recent Advances

1. Automated Systems:

a. Automated electrophoresis systems, such as Agilent's Bioanalyzer and TapeStation, provide high-throughput and reproducible DNA fragment analysis.

2. Integration with Other Techniques:

a. Combining electrophoresis with techniques like mass spectrometry and next-generation sequencing for comprehensive analysis of nucleic acids and proteins.

3. Improved Staining Methods:

a. Development of safer and more sensitive DNA stains, such as SYBR Safe and GelRed, which reduce the hazards associated with traditional stains like ethidium bromide.

DNA electrophoresis remains a cornerstone technique in genomic and proteomic research, enabling the separation and analysis of nucleic acids with high precision and accuracy. Its applications span from basic research to clinical diagnostics, making it an indispensable tool in molecular biology.

PCR (REVERSE TRANSCRIPTION AND REAL TIME)

Polymerase Chain Reaction (PCR) is a versatile technique used to amplify specific DNA sequences, making them easier to analyze and study. Variants of PCR, such as Reverse Transcription PCR (RT-PCR) and Real-Time PCR (qPCR), have expanded its applications in genomics and proteomics. Below, we explore these PCR methods in detail, including their principles, procedures, and applications.

1. Reverse Transcription PCR (RT-PCR)

Principles:

a. RT-PCR is used to amplify RNA by first converting it into complementary DNA (cDNA) using the enzyme reverse transcriptase.

b. This cDNA then serves as the template for PCR amplification.

Procedure:

1. RNA Extraction:

a. Isolate RNA from cells or tissues using RNA extraction kits or methods like TRIzol extraction.

2. **Reverse Transcription:**

   a. Mix RNA with reverse transcriptase, primers (random hexamers, oligo(dT), or gene-specific primers), dNTPs, and a buffer.

   b. Incubate the reaction mixture to synthesize cDNA.

3. **PCR Amplification:**

   a. Use the synthesized cDNA as a template in a conventional PCR reaction.

   b. Mix with DNA polymerase, primers specific to the target gene, dNTPs, and a buffer.

   c. Perform thermal cycling (denaturation, annealing, and extension).

Applications:

a. **Gene Expression Analysis:**

   i. Measure the expression levels of specific genes by quantifying mRNA.

b. **Detection of RNA Viruses:**

   i. Diagnose viral infections like SARS-CoV-2, HIV, and influenza.

c. **Cloning and Sequencing:**

   i. Clone cDNA for sequencing or functional studies.

2. Real-Time PCR (qPCR)

Principles:

a. qPCR quantifies DNA in real-time during the PCR process by using fluorescent dyes or probes that emit fluorescence when bound to double-stranded DNA.

b. The increase in fluorescence correlates with the amount of DNA produced during each cycle.

Types of Detection Chemistries:

a. **SYBR Green**: Binds to double-stranded DNA and emits fluorescence upon binding. It is a nonspecific dye that binds to any double-stranded DNA.

b. **TaqMan Probes**: Use sequence-specific probes labeled with a fluorescent reporter dye and a quencher. The probe is degraded during amplification, separating the reporter from the quencher and resulting in increased fluorescence.

Procedure:

1. **Preparation:**

   a. Mix DNA or cDNA template with qPCR master mix, which includes DNA polymerase, primers, dNTPs, fluorescent dye/probe, and buffer.

2. **Thermal Cycling:**

   a. Similar to conventional PCR, but fluorescence is measured at the end of each cycle.

   b. Denaturation, annealing, and extension phases are carried out with fluorescence detection at the end of the extension phase.

3. **Data Analysis:**

   a. Analyze the fluorescence data to determine the threshold cycle (Ct) value, which is inversely proportional to the initial amount of target nucleic acid.

Applications:

a. **Quantification of Gene Expression:**

   i. Measure the expression levels of genes with high sensitivity and specificity.

b. **Genetic Variation Analysis:**

   i. Detect and quantify single nucleotide polymorphisms (SNPs) and other genetic variations.

c. **Pathogen Detection:**

     i.   Diagnose infectious diseases by quantifying pathogen DNA/RNA.

d. Validation of RNAi and CRISPR Experiments:

     i.   Assess the efficiency of gene knockdown or editing.

Integration with Genomic and Proteomic Tools

Genomic Applications:

a. Genotyping and Mutation Detection:

     i.   Identify genetic variations and mutations associated with diseases.

b. Epigenetic Studies:

     i.   Measure DNA methylation levels using methylation-specific PCR (MSP).

c. Copy Number Variation (CNV) Analysis:

     i.   Quantify gene copy number variations associated with genetic disorders.

Proteomic Applications:

a. Gene-Protein Correlation Studies:

     i.   Analyze the correlation between mRNA levels (measured by RT-qPCR) and protein levels (measured by proteomic techniques like Western blotting or mass spectrometry).

b. Functional Genomics:

     i.   Study the functional consequences of genetic variations on protein expression and function.

Advantages and Limitations

Advantages:

a. High Sensitivity and Specificity:

     i.   Detect and quantify low-abundance nucleic acids.

b. Quantitative Data:

     i.   Provides quantitative measurements of nucleic acid levels.

c. Real-Time Monitoring:

i. Allows real-time monitoring of the amplification process, reducing the risk of contamination.

Limitations:

a. RNA Quality:

i. RT-PCR requires high-quality RNA, which can be degraded easily.

b. Primer Design:

i. Specific and efficient primer design is critical for successful amplification.

c. Cost:

i. Real-time PCR instruments and reagents can be expensive.

Recent Advances

Digital PCR (dPCR):

a. Provides absolute quantification of nucleic acids without the need for standard curves.

b. Partitions the sample into thousands of individual reactions, allowing for precise quantification.

High-Throughput qPCR:

a. Automated systems enable high-throughput analysis of large numbers of samples, improving efficiency in clinical diagnostics and large-scale studies.

Multiplex qPCR:

a. Allows simultaneous amplification and quantification of multiple targets in a single reaction, saving time and reagents.

Integration with Next-Generation Sequencing (NGS):

a. Combining qPCR with NGS for validating and quantifying sequencing results, enhancing the accuracy and reliability of genomic studies.

PCR, RT-PCR, and qPCR are indispensable tools in genomics and proteomics, enabling the amplification, detection, and quantification of nucleic acids with high precision and accuracy. These techniques are fundamental for gene expression analysis, pathogen detection, genetic variation studies, and many other applications in biomedical research and diagnostics.

GENE SEQUENCING

Gene sequencing is a fundamental technology in genomics and proteomics, enabling the detailed analysis of genetic material. It provides the sequence of nucleotides in DNA, allowing researchers to identify genes, understand genetic variations, and study gene function and regulation. This section delves into the principles, technologies, procedures, applications, and advancements in gene sequencing.

Principles of Gene Sequencing

Gene sequencing determines the precise order of nucleotides within a DNA molecule. The fundamental principles involve:

1. **Template Preparation**: Isolating DNA to serve as the template for sequencing.
2. **Sequencing Reaction**: Using chemical or enzymatic methods to generate readable sequence data.
3. **Detection:** Identifying the sequence of nucleotides, often through fluorescence or other labeling techniques.
4. **Data Analysis**: Interpreting sequence data using bioinformatics tools.

Major Gene Sequencing Technologies

1. **Sanger Sequencing:**
    a. **Principles:**
        i. Uses chain-terminating dideoxynucleotides (ddNTPs) to produce DNA fragments of varying lengths during DNA replication.
        ii. Incorporation of ddNTPs terminates DNA strand elongation, allowing determination of the nucleotide sequence.
    b. **Procedure:**
        i. DNA is denatured into single strands.

ii. Primers, DNA polymerase, dNTPs, and fluorescently labeled ddNTPs are added.

iii. DNA synthesis is carried out, producing fragments terminated at each possible nucleotide.

iv. Fragments are separated by capillary electrophoresis and detected based on the fluorescent labels.

c. Applications:

i. Sequencing single genes or small regions of the genome.

ii. Mutation detection and validation.

iii. Cloning and verification of constructs.

2. **Next-Generation Sequencing (NGS):**

a. Principles:

i. Involves massively parallel sequencing of millions of DNA fragments simultaneously.

ii. Various platforms use different methods, such as sequencing by synthesis, sequencing by ligation, and ion semiconductor sequencing.

b. Procedure:

i. DNA is fragmented and adapters are ligated to both ends.

ii. Fragments are amplified and immobilized on a solid surface or in solution.

iii. Sequencing by synthesis involves incorporation of fluorescently labeled nucleotides, with each incorporation event recorded.

c. Applications:

i. Whole genome sequencing (WGS) and whole exome sequencing (WES).

ii. Transcriptome sequencing (RNA-Seq).

iii. Epigenetic studies (e.g., methyl-seq, ChIP-seq).

iv. High-throughput genotyping and variant detection.

3. **Third-Generation Sequencing (Single-Molecule Sequencing):**

   a. **Principles:**

      i. Sequences single molecules of DNA in real-time without the need for amplification.

      ii. Technologies include PacBio Single Molecule Real-Time (SMRT) sequencing and Oxford Nanopore sequencing.

   b. **Procedure:**

      i. **PacBio SMRT**: DNA is synthesized in real-time with fluorescently labeled nucleotides.

      ii. **Oxford Nanopore:** DNA is passed through a nanopore, and changes in ionic current are measured to determine the sequence.

   c. **Applications:**

      i. Sequencing long reads for resolving complex genomic regions.

      ii. Structural variation analysis.

      iii. Metagenomics and microbial genomics.

      iv. Direct RNA sequencing.

Procedure of Next-Generation Sequencing (NGS)

1. **Sample Preparation:**

   a. Extract DNA from the sample.

   b. Fragment DNA to an appropriate size (e.g., 200-600 bp).

   c. Ligate adapters to both ends of the DNA fragments.

2. **Library Preparation:**

   a. PCR amplify the library to enrich for adapter-ligated fragments.

   b. Quantify and validate the library quality.

3. **Sequencing:**

   a. Load the library onto the sequencing platform.

b. Perform sequencing by synthesis, where fluorescently labeled nucleotides are incorporated and imaged.

c. Generate raw sequence data (reads).

4. **Data Analysis:**

a. Align reads to a reference genome.

b. Identify variants (SNPs, indels, structural variations).

c. Annotate and interpret genetic variations.

Applications of Gene Sequencing

1. **Genomic Applications:**

a. **Whole Genome Sequencing (WGS):** Provides a comprehensive view of the entire genome, useful for studying genetic variations, evolutionary biology, and disease mechanisms.

b. **Whole Exome Sequencing (WES):** Focuses on the coding regions of the genome, identifying mutations associated with diseases.

c. **Targeted Sequencing:** Sequences specific genes or regions of interest, useful in diagnostics and research.

2. **Transcriptomic Applications:**

a. **RNA-Seq:** Measures gene expression levels and identifies transcript variants, fusion genes, and alternative splicing events.

b. **Single-Cell RNA-Seq:** Analyzes gene expression at the single-cell level, revealing cellular heterogeneity and uncovering rare cell types.

3. **Epigenomic Applications:**

a. **Methyl-Seq:** Analyzes DNA methylation patterns, which play a role in gene regulation and disease.

b. **ChIP-Seq: Identifies** DNA-protein interactions, revealing binding sites of transcription factors and histone modifications.

4. **Microbiome Studies:**

a. **16S rRNA Sequencing**: Profiles microbial communities by sequencing the 16S ribosomal RNA gene.

b. **Metagenomics**: Studies the genetic material recovered directly from environmental samples, providing insights into microbial diversity and function.

5. **Clinical Applications:**

a. **Cancer Genomics**: Identifies somatic mutations, copy number variations, and structural variations in tumors.

b. **Pharmacogenomic**s: Analyzes how genetic variations affect individual responses to drugs.

c. **Genetic Diagnostics**: Detects genetic disorders and carrier status for inherited diseases.

Integration with Proteomic Tools

1. **Proteogenomics:**

a. Combines genomic and proteomic data to improve gene annotation and discover novel proteins and isoforms.

b. Uses mass spectrometry to validate protein-coding regions predicted by genomic data.

2. **Functional Genomics:**

a. Studies the relationship between genotype and phenotype, often integrating transcriptomic and proteomic data to understand gene function and regulation.

3. **Systems Biology:**

a. Integrates multi-omics data (genomics, transcriptomics, proteomics, metabolomics) to model complex biological systems and understand disease mechanisms.

Recent Advances in Gene Sequencing

1. **Long-Read Sequencing:**

a. Advances in technologies like PacBio and Oxford Nanopore enable sequencing of long DNA fragments, improving the resolution of complex regions and structural variants.

2. **Single-Cell Sequencing:**

   a. Techniques for sequencing DNA and RNA from individual cells reveal cellular diversity and provide insights into development, disease progression, and immune responses.

3. **CRISPR-Based Sequencing:**

   a. CRISPR technology enhances targeted sequencing, enabling precise editing and analysis of specific genomic regions.

4. **AI and Machine Learning:**

   a. Integration of artificial intelligence and machine learning improves sequence data analysis, variant interpretation, and predictive modeling.

5. **Portable Sequencers:**

   a. Development of portable sequencing devices like the Oxford Nanopore MinION allows for on-site sequencing and real-time data analysis.

Gene sequencing has revolutionized our understanding of biology and disease, providing detailed insights into genetic variation, gene function, and molecular mechanisms. Its integration with proteomic tools and continuous technological advancements promises to further enhance its applications in research, diagnostics, and personalized medicine.

MICRO ARRAY TECHNIQUE

Microarray technology is a powerful tool used to analyze the expression of many genes simultaneously, identify genetic variations, and study protein interactions. This technique involves the hybridization of nucleic acids or proteins to a solid surface containing probes, allowing researchers to measure gene expression levels, detect single nucleotide polymorphisms (SNPs), and analyze protein expression and interactions. Below is a detailed overview of the microarray technique, including its principles, procedures, applications, advantages, and limitations.

Principles of Microarray Technology

Microarray technology is based on the principle of hybridization, where complementary strands of nucleic acids or specific protein interactions are used to detect and quantify target molecules. The key components include:

1. **Probes**: Short, single-stranded DNA, RNA, or protein sequences immobilized on a solid surface.
2. **Targets:** Labeled nucleic acids or proteins from the sample that bind to complementary probes.
3. **Detection**: Fluorescent or chemiluminescent labels that enable visualization and quantification of hybridized targets.

Types of Microarrays

1. **DNA Microarrays:**
   a. Used to measure gene expression levels, detect SNPs, and analyze genomic content.
   b. **cDNA Microarrays**: Contain complementary DNA (cDNA) sequences derived from mRNA.
   c. **Oligonucleotide Microarrays**: Contain synthetic oligonucleotides representing specific genes or genetic variations.

2. **Protein Microarrays:**
   a. Used to study protein expression, interactions, and functions.
   b. **Analytical Protein Microarrays**: Contain antibodies or other binding proteins to detect specific proteins in a sample.
   c. **Functional Protein Microarrays**: Contain purified proteins to study interactions, enzyme activities, and other functional properties.

Procedure of DNA Microarray Analysis

1. **Sample Preparation:**
   a. Extract total RNA from the sample.
   b. Convert RNA into cDNA using reverse transcription and label with fluorescent dyes (e.g., Cy3 and Cy5).

2. **Hybridization:**
   a. Hybridize the labeled cDNA to the microarray slide containing immobilized probes.
   b. Incubate the slide under controlled conditions to allow specific binding between target cDNA and probes.

3. **Washing and Detection:**
   a. Wash the slide to remove unbound and non-specifically bound cDNA.
   b. Scan the slide using a microarray scanner to detect and quantify the fluorescence signals.

4. **Data Analysis:**
   a. Analyze the fluorescence intensity data using software to determine the expression levels of genes.
   b. Perform normalization and statistical analysis to identify differentially expressed genes and interpret biological significance.

Applications of Microarray Technology

1. **Genomic Applications:**
   a. **Gene Expression Profiling**: Measure the expression levels of thousands of genes simultaneously to study biological processes, disease mechanisms, and response to treatments.
   b. **SNP Genotyping:** Identify genetic variations associated with diseases and traits.
   c. **Comparative Genomic Hybridization (CGH):** Detect chromosomal abnormalities and copy number variations (CNVs).

2. **Proteomic Applications:**

a. **Protein Expression Profiling**: Measure the expression levels of multiple proteins in different conditions.

b. **Protein-Protein Interactions**: Study interactions between proteins using functional protein microarrays.

c. **Antibody Profiling:** Identify specific antibodies in serum for diagnostics and therapeutic purposes.

3. **Clinical Applications:**

a. **Disease Diagnosis**: Identify gene expression signatures and biomarkers associated with specific diseases, such as cancer.

b. **Pharmacogenomics:** Study genetic variations affecting drug response and tailor personalized treatments.

c. **Pathogen Detection:** Detect and identify pathogens in clinical samples using specific probes.

Advantages and Limitations of Microarray Technology

Advantages:

1. **High Throughput**: Analyze thousands of genes or proteins simultaneously in a single experiment.

2. **Quantitative Analysis**: Measure relative expression levels and identify differentially expressed genes or proteins.

3. **Versatility:** Applicable to various biological molecules, including DNA, RNA, and proteins.

Limitations:

1. **Static Nature**: Provides a snapshot of gene or protein expression at a single time point, lacking dynamic information.

2. **Limited Sensitivity**: May not detect low-abundance targets or rare variants with high accuracy.

3. **Cross-Hybridization**: Non-specific binding can lead to background noise and false positives.

4. **High Cost:** Requires specialized equipment and reagents, making it expensive for large-scale studies.

Recent Advances in Microarray Technology

1. **Next-Generation Microarrays:**

   a. Development of high-density microarrays with improved sensitivity and specificity.

   b. Incorporation of advanced materials and fabrication techniques to enhance performance.

2. **Integration with Next-Generation Sequencing (NGS):**

   a. Combining microarray data with NGS to validate findings and provide complementary insights.

   b. Use of sequencing-based approaches for high-resolution analysis of gene expression and genetic variations.

3. **Multiplexed Assays:**

   a. Development of multiplexed microarrays capable of analyzing multiple types of biomolecules simultaneously.

   b. Application in studying complex biological networks and interactions.

4. **Single-Cell Analysis:**

   a. Adaptation of microarray technology for single-cell analysis to study cellular heterogeneity and rare cell populations.

   b. Integration with microfluidics and other technologies for high-throughput single-cell profiling.

5. **Clinical and Diagnostic Applications:**

   a. Use of microarrays in clinical diagnostics for early disease detection, prognosis, and monitoring treatment responses.

   b. Development of point-of-care microarray devices for rapid and on-site testing.

Microarray technology remains a cornerstone in genomics and proteomics, providing valuable insights into gene and protein expression, genetic variations, and molecular interactions. Continuous advancements and integration with other technologies are enhancing its capabilities and expanding its applications in research, diagnostics, and personalized medicine.

SDS PAGE

Sodium Dodecyl Sulfate Polyacrylamide Gel Electrophoresis (SDS-PAGE) is a fundamental technique used in proteomics to separate proteins based on their molecular weight. This technique is essential for protein analysis, purification, and characterization. Here, we explore the principles, procedures, applications, and recent advancements of SDS-PAGE in detail.

Principles of SDS-PAGE

SDS-PAGE separates proteins primarily based on their size (molecular weight), regardless of their native charge or shape. This is achieved through the use of sodium dodecyl sulfate (SDS), a detergent that denatures proteins and gives them a uniform negative charge.

Key Components:

1. **SDS (Sodium Dodecyl Sulfate):** An anionic detergent that binds to proteins, causing them to unfold and linearize. SDS imparts a negative charge proportional to the length of the polypeptide chain, allowing proteins to be separated based on size.

2. **Polyacrylamide Gel:** A cross-linked polymer that forms a mesh-like matrix through which proteins migrate. The concentration of acrylamide determines the pore size, influencing the resolution of protein separation.

3. **Electrophoresis:** The application of an electric field to move negatively charged proteins through the polyacrylamide gel towards the positive electrode.

Procedure of SDS-PAGE

1. **Sample Preparation:**

a. Extract proteins from cells or tissues.

b. Mix protein samples with SDS, a reducing agent (e.g., β-mercaptoethanol or DTT), and a loading buffer containing glycerol and tracking dye (e.g., bromophenol blue).

c. Heat the mixture to denature proteins and ensure complete SDS binding.

2. **Gel Preparation:**

a. Prepare a polyacrylamide gel consisting of a separating (resolving) gel and a stacking gel.

b. The separating gel (lower part) has a higher acrylamide concentration and resolves proteins based on size.

c. The stacking gel (upper part) has a lower acrylamide concentration and helps concentrate proteins into sharp bands.

3. **Electrophoresis:**

a. Load protein samples and molecular weight markers (protein standards) into the wells of the stacking gel.

b. Apply an electric field to move proteins through the gel.

c. Proteins migrate according to their size, with smaller proteins moving faster through the gel matrix.

4. **Staining and Visualization:**

a. After electrophoresis, stain the gel with Coomassie Brilliant Blue, silver stain, or other protein-specific stains to visualize protein bands.

b. Destain the gel to remove excess stain, leaving only the stained protein bands.

5. **Data Analysis:**

a. Compare the migration distance of sample proteins to the molecular weight markers to estimate the molecular weight of the proteins.

b. Analyze band intensity and pattern to study protein expression, purity, and other properties.

Applications of SDS-PAGE

1. **Protein Identification and Characterization:**

   a. Determine the molecular weight of proteins and compare them with known standards.

   b. Characterize protein modifications, such as glycosylation or phosphorylation, by changes in molecular weight.

2. **Protein Purification:**

   a. Assess the purity of protein samples during purification processes.

   b. Monitor the presence of contaminants or degradation products.

3. **Comparative Proteomics:**

   a. Compare protein expression levels between different samples, such as healthy vs. diseased tissues.

   b. Analyze changes in protein expression in response to treatments or environmental conditions.

4. **Quality Control in Biotechnology:**

   a. Ensure the consistency and purity of recombinant proteins and biopharmaceutical products.

   b. Verify the molecular weight and integrity of proteins in quality control assays.

5. **Western Blotting:**

   a. Combine SDS-PAGE with Western blotting to identify specific proteins using antibodies.

   b. Detect post-translational modifications and study protein-protein interactions.

Advantages and Limitations of SDS-PAGE

Advantages:

1. **High Resolution**: Effectively separates proteins with different molecular weights.

2. **Versatility:** Applicable to a wide range of proteins and experimental conditions.

3. **Quantitative:** Allows for semi-quantitative analysis of protein expression levels.

4. **Compatibility**: Compatible with downstream techniques like Western blotting, mass spectrometry, and protein sequencing.

Limitations:

1. **Denaturing Conditions**: SDS-PAGE denatures proteins, making it unsuitable for studying native protein structures and interactions.

2. **Limited Sensitivity**: Standard staining methods may not detect low-abundance proteins.

3. **Complex Samples**: High-complexity samples may result in overlapping bands, complicating analysis.

4. **Size Limitations**: Very large or very small proteins may not resolve well on standard gels.

Recent Advances in SDS-PAGE

1. **Fluorescent Staining:**
   a. Development of fluorescent dyes for protein staining increases sensitivity and enables multiplexing.
   b. Allows for quantitative analysis using fluorescence imaging systems.

2. **2D SDS-PAGE:**
   a. Combines isoelectric focusing (IEF) with SDS-PAGE to separate proteins based on isoelectric point (pI) and molecular weight.
   b. Provides higher resolution and better separation of complex protein mixtures.

3. **Automated Systems:**

a. Automated electrophoresis systems streamline the SDS-PAGE process, improving reproducibility and throughput.

b. Integration with robotic sample handling and imaging systems for high-throughput analysis.

4. Microfluidic SDS-PAGE:

a. Miniaturized SDS-PAGE systems using microfluidic technology enable faster and more efficient protein separation.

b. Requires smaller sample volumes and offers rapid analysis with high resolution.

5. Mass Spectrometry Integration:

a. Coupling SDS-PAGE with mass spectrometry (MS) for in-gel digestion and protein identification.

b. Enhances proteomic analysis by providing detailed information on protein identity, modifications, and interactions.

6. Enhanced Detection Methods:

a. Advanced detection methods, such as chemiluminescent and infrared imaging, improve sensitivity and dynamic range.

b. Enable precise quantification of protein bands and detection of low-abundance proteins.

Integration with Genomic and Proteomic Tools

1. Proteomics:

a. SDS-PAGE is a critical step in sample preparation for proteomic analyses, including mass spectrometry-based proteomics.

b. Allows for the separation and isolation of proteins for subsequent identification and characterization.

2. Genomics:

a. Used to verify the expression of recombinant proteins encoded by cloned genes.

b. Analyze protein products of gene expression studies, including those involving CRISPR and RNAi technologies.

3. **Functional Genomics:**

   a. Study the functional consequences of genetic variations by analyzing protein expression and modifications.

   b. Investigate protein interactions and pathways associated with specific genes.

4. **Systems Biology:**

   a. Integrate SDS-PAGE data with transcriptomic and metabolomic data to understand complex biological systems.

   b. Provide insights into the regulation of gene expression and protein function.

SDS-PAGE is a versatile and widely used technique in both genomic and proteomic research, providing essential information on protein size, purity, and expression levels. Advances in staining methods, automation, and integration with other technologies continue to enhance its utility and application in various fields of biological and medical research.

ELISA AND WESTERN BLOTTING

ELISA (Enzyme-Linked Immunosorbent Assay) and Western Blotting are two fundamental techniques used extensively in genomics and proteomics for the detection, quantification, and analysis of proteins. Here is a detailed overview of each technique and their roles in genomic and proteomic research:

ELISA (Enzyme-Linked Immunosorbent Assay)

Principle

ELISA is a plate-based assay technique designed for detecting and quantifying soluble substances such as peptides, proteins, antibodies, and hormones. The assay uses specific antibodies to capture and detect the target antigen.

Types of ELISA

1. **Direct ELISA**: Involves the direct attachment of the antigen to the plate and detection with an enzyme-labeled antibody.

2. **Indirect ELISA**: Involves an unlabeled primary antibody and a labeled secondary antibody that binds to the primary antibody.

3. **Sandwich ELISA**: Uses two different antibodies specific to different epitopes of the same antigen (capture and detection antibodies).

4. **Competitive ELISA**: Involves the competition between the sample antigen and a reference antigen for binding to a limited amount of antibody.

Steps

1. **Coating:** The wells of a microplate are coated with the capture antibody.

2. **Blocking:** Blocking buffer is added to block non-specific binding sites.

3. **Sample Addition**: The sample containing the target antigen is added to the wells.

4. **Detection**: An enzyme-linked antibody specific to the target antigen is added.

5. **Substrate Addition**: A substrate is added that the enzyme converts to a detectable signal (usually a color change).

6. **Detection and Quantification**: The signal intensity is measured using a plate reader.

Applications

i. Quantifying cytokines, hormones, and growth factors.

ii. Detecting specific antibodies or antigens in diagnostics.

iii. Assessing the concentration of proteins in cell lysates or tissue extracts.

iv. Verifying the presence of biomolecules in research and clinical samples.

Western Blotting

Principle

Western Blotting (or Immunoblotting) is used to detect specific proteins in a complex mixture of proteins extracted from cells or tissues. It combines gel electrophoresis and antigen-antibody interactions for protein identification.

Steps

1. **Sample Preparation**: Proteins are extracted from cells or tissues and prepared in a buffer.
2. **Gel Electrophoresis**: Proteins are separated based on their size using SDS-PAGE (Sodium Dodecyl Sulfate-Polyacrylamide Gel Electrophoresis).
3. **Transfer:** The separated proteins are transferred from the gel to a membrane (usually nitrocellulose or PVDF).
4. **Blocking**: The membrane is blocked with a blocking buffer to prevent non-specific binding.
5. **Incubation with Primary Antibody**: The membrane is incubated with a primary antibody specific to the target protein.
6. **Incubation with Secondary Antibody**: A secondary antibody, conjugated to an enzyme or a fluorescent tag, binds to the primary antibody.
7. **Detection**: The enzyme-linked secondary antibody catalyzes a reaction with a substrate to produce a detectable signal (chemiluminescence, colorimetric, or fluorescence).
8. **Visualization**: The signal is visualized using an appropriate imaging system, such as a chemiluminescent detector or a fluorescent scanner.

Applications

i. Confirming the expression of specific proteins.
ii. Analyzing post-translational modifications like phosphorylation or glycosylation.
iii. Comparing protein levels between different samples or conditions.
iv. Identifying protein-protein interactions.

Role in Genomics and Proteomics

Genomics

While primarily a field focused on DNA and RNA, genomics benefits from these techniques in understanding gene expression at the protein level. For example:

i. Validating gene knockouts or knockdowns by verifying the reduction or absence of the corresponding protein using Western Blotting.

ii. Measuring protein products of genes of interest in different genetic backgrounds or conditions using ELISA.

Proteomics

In proteomics, the study of the entire set of proteins produced by an organism, these techniques are crucial:

i. Quantifying specific proteins in complex mixtures to study protein abundance and dynamics (ELISA).

ii. Identifying and characterizing proteins, including modifications and interactions (Western Blotting).

iii. Validating mass spectrometry results by confirming the presence and size of proteins of interest (Western Blotting).

iv. Screening large numbers of samples for specific proteins in biomarker discovery and validation (ELISA).

Both ELISA and Western Blotting are indispensable tools in molecular biology, providing precise and reliable methods for protein analysis, crucial for advancing research in genomics and proteomics.

RECOMBINANT DNA TECHNOLOGY AND GENE THERAPY

Recombinant DNA technology and gene therapy are integral to advancing both genomic and proteomic research. They allow for the manipulation of genetic material and the correction of genetic disorders, respectively, and are essential tools in modern molecular biology.

Recombinant DNA Technology

Principle

Recombinant DNA (rDNA) technology involves combining DNA from different sources to create a new genetic sequence. This technology enables the insertion of specific genes into plasmids or other vectors to be expressed in host cells.

Steps

1. **Isolation of DNA**: Extraction of DNA from cells.
2. **Cutting DNA:** Using restriction enzymes to cut DNA at specific sequences.
3. **Ligating DNA**: Using DNA ligase to join DNA fragments, creating recombinant DNA.
4. **Transformation**: Introducing the recombinant DNA into host cells (bacteria, yeast, plant, or animal cells).
5. **Selection and Screening**: Identifying host cells that have successfully taken up the recombinant DNA using selectable markers (antibiotic resistance genes) and screening techniques (PCR, colony hybridization).

Applications

1. **Protein Production**: Expression of recombinant proteins, such as insulin, growth hormones, and monoclonal antibodies.
2. **Genetic Engineering**: Creating genetically modified organisms (GMOs) for agriculture, such as pest-resistant plants.
3. **Gene Function Studies**: Investigating gene function by overexpressing or knocking down genes in model organisms.
4. **Vaccines**: Developing recombinant vaccines (e.g., hepatitis B vaccine).

Role in Genomics

i. **Gene Cloning**: Cloning genes of interest for sequencing and functional studies.
ii. **CRISPR/Cas9**: Utilizing rDNA technology to create guide RNAs for genome editing.

iii. **Functional Genomics**: Overexpressing or silencing genes to study their roles in cellular processes.

Role in Proteomics

i. **Recombinant Protein Expression**: Producing large quantities of proteins for structural and functional analysis.

ii. **Protein Engineering**: Creating proteins with novel functions or improved characteristics.

iii. **Protein-Protein Interaction Studies**: Expressing tagged recombinant proteins to study interactions in pull-down assays or co-immunoprecipitation.

Gene Therapy

Principle

Gene therapy involves the introduction, removal, or alteration of genetic material within a patient's cells to treat or prevent disease. It aims to correct defective genes responsible for disease development.

Types of Gene Therapy

1. **Somatic Gene Therapy**: Targets non-reproductive cells; changes are not passed to offspring.

2. **Germline Gene Therapy**: Targets reproductive cells; changes can be inherited.

Delivery Methods

1. **Viral Vectors**: Modified viruses (adenovirus, lentivirus, AAV) used to deliver therapeutic genes into host cells.

2. **Non-Viral Methods**: Direct delivery of DNA via methods such as electroporation, liposomes, or nanoparticles.

Steps

1. **Identification of Target Gene**: Identifying the gene responsible for the disorder.

2. **Gene Cloning and Modification**: Cloning the therapeutic gene and modifying it to be delivered by a vector.

3. **Vector Construction**: Inserting the therapeutic gene into a viral or non-viral vector.

4. **Delivery to Target Cells**: Administering the vector to the patient (in vivo) or extracting and modifying cells outside the body before reintroducing them (ex vivo).

5. **Expression and Monitoring**: Ensuring the therapeutic gene is expressed and monitoring the patient's response.

Applications

i. **Monogenic Disorders**: Treating diseases caused by a single defective gene, such as cystic fibrosis, hemophilia, and muscular dystrophy.

ii. **Cancer Therapy**: Introducing genes that can trigger immune responses against cancer cells or directly induce cancer cell death.

iii. **Cardiovascular Diseases**: Delivering genes that promote the regeneration of heart tissue.

Role in Genomics

i. **CRISPR/Cas9 Gene Editing**: Correcting genetic mutations at the DNA level.

ii. **Gene Therapy Clinical** Trials: Applying knowledge from genomic research to develop and test new therapies.

iii. **Functional Genomics**: Using gene therapy techniques to study the effects of gene modification in vivo.

Role in Proteomics

i. **Protein Replacement**: Delivering genes encoding functional proteins to replace defective ones in genetic disorders.

ii. **Regulation of Protein Expression**: Modulating the expression of proteins involved in disease pathways.

iii. **Biomarker Discovery**: Analyzing changes in the proteome following gene therapy to identify biomarkers for treatment efficacy and safety.

Integration in Genomic and Proteomic Research

Recombinant DNA technology and gene therapy are complementary to genomic and proteomic studies, providing the means to manipulate genes and proteins. This synergy enables:

- **Functional Analysis**: Understanding gene function and regulation by observing the effects of gene overexpression, knockdown, or correction.

- **Therapeutic Development**: Creating novel treatments based on genetic and proteomic insights, particularly for genetic disorders and cancer.

- **Personalized Medicine**: Tailoring therapies to individual genetic and proteomic profiles for more effective treatments.

BASIC PRINCIPLES OF RECOMBINANT DNA TECHNOLOGY-RESTRICTION ENZYMES

Recombinant DNA technology relies heavily on the use of restriction enzymes, also known as restriction endonucleases. These enzymes play a crucial role in cutting DNA at specific sequences, allowing for the manipulation of genetic material. Here's an in-depth look at the basic principles of recombinant DNA technology, with a focus on restriction enzymes, in genomic and proteomic tools:

1. Principles of Recombinant DNA Technology

Recombinant DNA technology involves the manipulation of DNA molecules to create new combinations of genetic material. The basic principles include:

i. **Isolation of DNA**: DNA is extracted from cells or tissues using various extraction methods.

ii. **Cutting DNA**: Specific DNA sequences are cleaved at precise locations using restriction enzymes.

iii. **Joining DNA Fragments**: Cleaved DNA fragments are ligated together using DNA ligase.

iv. **Introduction of Recombinant DNA**: The recombinant DNA is introduced into host cells, where it can be replicated and expressed.

2. Restriction Enzymes

a. Functionality

i. Restriction enzymes are enzymes that recognize specific DNA sequences (restriction sites) and cleave the DNA at or near these sites.

ii. They are found naturally in bacteria, where they act as a defense mechanism against invading viruses (bacteriophages) by cutting their DNA.

b. Specificity

i. Each restriction enzyme recognizes a specific DNA sequence, typically 4 to 8 base pairs in length.

ii. Some enzymes create blunt ends when they cut, while others generate staggered ends called sticky ends.

c. Nomenclature

i. Restriction enzymes are named based on the bacteria from which they were isolated. For example, EcoRI is derived from *Escherichia coli* strain RY13.

ii. The letter(s) after the bacterial genus name indicate the specific strain, while the Roman numeral denotes the order of discovery.

d. Types

i. **Type I:** Cuts DNA at random sites away from the recognition sequence.

ii. **Type II:** Cuts DNA at specific sequences within or near the recognition site. These are commonly used in recombinant DNA technology.

iii. **Type III**: Cuts DNA a short distance from the recognition site.

e. Application in Genomic and Proteomic Tools

i.   **Gene Cloning**: Restriction enzymes are used to cut both the vector DNA (e.g., plasmids) and the DNA fragment of interest. This creates compatible ends for ligation.

ii. **Polymerase Chain Reaction (PCR):** Some restriction enzymes are used in PCR to digest unwanted DNA from PCR products in a process called digestion or to linearize plasmids for subsequent cloning steps.

iii. **Site-Directed Mutagenesis**: Restriction enzymes can be used to introduce specific mutations into DNA sequences.

iv. **Proteomics:** In proteomics, restriction enzymes are used in techniques such as protein mapping and peptide fingerprinting to generate smaller peptide fragments for analysis.

f. Considerations

i.   **Buffer Compatibility**: Each restriction enzyme has specific buffer requirements for optimal activity.

ii. **Recognition Sequence**: Choosing the appropriate restriction enzyme depends on the DNA sequence to be cleaved and the desired fragment sizes.

iii. **Methylation Sensitivity**: Some restriction enzymes are sensitive to DNA methylation, which can affect their activity.

VARIOUS TYPES OF VECTORS

Vectors play a crucial role in genomic and proteomic research by facilitating the manipulation, cloning, and expression of DNA or RNA molecules in host cells. Here, I'll provide an in-depth overview of various types of vectors used in these fields:

1. Plasmid Vectors

a. Definition

i.   Circular DNA molecules found in bacteria, capable of replicating independently from the host genome.

ii. Commonly used in gene cloning, protein expression, and molecular biology research.

b. Features

i. **Origin of Replication**: Contains a region that allows replication in the host cell.

ii. **Selectable Marker**: Gene conferring antibiotic resistance or another selectable phenotype.

iii. **Multiple Cloning Site (MCS):** Region containing multiple unique restriction sites for inserting DNA fragments.

iv. **Reporter Genes**: Genes encoding proteins that allow visualization or selection of transformed cells.

c. Applications

i. **Gene Cloning:** Inserting DNA fragments into plasmids for replication and amplification.

ii. **Expression Vectors**: Expressing foreign genes in host cells to produce proteins of interest.

iii. **Reporter Assays**: Studying gene expression, protein-protein interactions, or promoter activity.

2. Bacterial Artificial Chromosomes (BACs) and Phage Lambda Vectors

a. Definition

i. **BACs:** Large DNA vectors capable of carrying large inserts (100-300 kb) derived from bacterial chromosomes.

ii. **Lambda Vectors**: Derived from bacteriophage lambda, capable of carrying larger inserts than plasmids (up to 20 kb).

b. Features

i. **Large Insert Capacity**: Suitable for cloning large genomic fragments or gene clusters.

ii. **Stable Maintenance**: Replicate as a low-copy plasmid in bacteria.

iii. **Selectable Markers**: Allow for the selection of transformed cells.

c. Applications

    i.   **Genomic Libraries**: Cloning large genomic fragments for genome sequencing or mapping.

    ii. **Functional Genomics**: Studying gene regulation, gene expression, and gene function in model organisms.

3. Viral Vectors

a. Definition

    i.   Derived from viruses, engineered to carry and deliver genetic material into host cells.

    ii. Efficiently infect a wide range of cell types, enabling gene delivery and expression.

b. Types

    i.   **Adenoviral Vectors**: Derived from adenoviruses, commonly used for transient gene expression.

    ii. **Lentiviral Vectors**: Derived from lentiviruses, can integrate into the host genome for stable gene expression.

    iii. **Adeno-Associated Viral (AAV) Vectors**: Derived from adeno-associated viruses, efficiently transduce dividing and non-dividing cells.

c. Features

    i.   **High Transduction Efficiency**: Infect host cells and deliver genetic material with high efficiency.

    ii. **Cell Type Specificity**: Can be engineered for cell type-specific targeting.

    iii. **Transient or Stable Expression**: Depending on the vector type, can enable transient or stable gene expression.

d. Applications

    i.   **Gene Therapy**: Delivering therapeutic genes for the treatment of genetic disorders or cancer.

    ii. **Gene Editing**: Delivering CRISPR/Cas9 components for genome editing.

    iii. **Vaccine Development**: Delivering antigen genes for vaccine production.

APPLICATIONS OF RECOMBINANT DNA TECHNOLOGY

Recombinant DNA technology has revolutionized genomic and proteomic research by enabling the manipulation, analysis, and expression of DNA and RNA molecules. Here, I'll provide a detailed overview of the applications of recombinant DNA technology in both genomic and proteomic tools:

Applications of Recombinant DNA Technology in Genomic Tools:

1. **Gene Cloning and Molecular Cloning:**
   a. **Isolation of Genes:** Recombinant DNA technology allows the isolation and amplification of specific genes of interest from genomic DNA or cDNA libraries.
   b. **Construction of Recombinant DNA Molecules**: Cloning vectors, such as plasmids and bacterial artificial chromosomes (BACs), are used to clone and manipulate DNA fragments.
   c. **Gene Expression Studies**: Recombinant DNA technology enables the study of gene expression patterns, regulation, and function by cloning genes into expression vectors.

2. **Genomic Sequencing and Mapping:**
   a. **Whole Genome Sequencing**: Recombinant DNA technology is essential for sequencing entire genomes, allowing the identification of genes, regulatory elements, and genetic variation.
   b. **Physical Mapping**: Recombinant DNA technology facilitates the mapping of genes and genetic markers to specific locations on chromosomes using techniques like fluorescence in situ hybridization (FISH) and Southern blotting.

3. **Functional Genomics:**
   a. **Gene Knockout and Knockdown**: Recombinant DNA technology, including CRISPR/Cas9-mediated genome editing, is used to disrupt or modify specific genes to study their functions.

b. **Gene Overexpression**: Recombinant DNA technology allows the overexpression of genes to investigate their effects on cellular processes.

4. **Comparative Genomics:**

   a. **Comparative Genome Analysis**: Recombinant DNA technology is used to compare the genomes of different species to study evolutionary relationships, identify conserved sequences, and understand genome evolution.

Applications of Recombinant DNA Technology in Proteomic Tools:

1. **Recombinant Protein Expression:**

   a. Recombinant DNA technology enables the expression of recombinant proteins in host cells, such as bacteria, yeast, or mammalian cells, for biochemical and structural studies.

   b. Various expression systems, including bacterial expression systems (e.g., E. coli), yeast expression systems (e.g., Pichia pastoris), and mammalian expression systems (e.g., HEK293 cells), are used to produce recombinant proteins.

2. **Protein Engineering:**

   a. Recombinant DNA technology is used to engineer proteins with altered or improved properties, such as stability, activity, or specificity.

   b. Techniques such as site-directed mutagenesis, DNA shuffling, and directed evolution are employed to generate protein variants with desired characteristics.

3. **Protein-Protein Interaction Studies:**

   a. Recombinant DNA technology is used to express tagged proteins for protein-protein interaction studies.

b. Techniques like co-immunoprecipitation, yeast two-hybrid screening, and protein microarrays enable the identification and characterization of protein interactions.

4. **Proteomics and Biomarker Discovery:**

   a. Recombinant DNA technology plays a crucial role in proteomics research by providing methods for protein expression, purification, and analysis.

   b. Recombinant proteins are used as standards, controls, and reagents in mass spectrometry-based proteomics and other analytical techniques.

   c. Recombinant antibodies, such as monoclonal antibodies and antibody fragments, are generated for biomarker discovery and diagnostic applications.

GENE THERAPY

Gene therapy is a revolutionary approach in both genomic and proteomic research, aimed at treating genetic disorders, cancer, and other diseases by delivering therapeutic genes or nucleic acids into target cells. Here's a detailed overview of gene therapy and its applications in genomic and proteomic tools:

1. Principles of Gene Therapy:

   a. **Delivery of Therapeutic Genes**: Gene therapy involves the introduction of therapeutic genes, such as functional copies of defective genes or genes encoding therapeutic proteins, into target cells to correct or modulate specific biological processes.

   b. **Methods of Delivery:** Gene delivery can be achieved using viral vectors (e.g., adenoviruses, lentiviruses, adeno-associated viruses) or non-viral vectors (e.g., liposomes, nanoparticles) that carry the therapeutic genes into target cells.

c. **Integration or Expression**: Therapeutic genes can be integrated into the host genome for stable expression or delivered transiently for temporary expression, depending on the therapeutic goals.

2. Applications of Gene Therapy in Genomic Tools:

a. **Treatment of Genetic Disorders**: Gene therapy holds promise for treating monogenic disorders caused by mutations in single genes, such as cystic fibrosis, hemophilia, and muscular dystrophy. Therapeutic genes can be delivered to correct the underlying genetic defects or provide functional copies of defective genes.

b. **Gene Editing**: CRISPR/Cas9-mediated gene editing is a powerful tool used in gene therapy to precisely modify the genome by correcting or disrupting disease-causing mutations. It enables targeted modifications of specific DNA sequences to restore normal gene function.

c. **Functional Genomics**: Gene therapy can be used to study gene function and regulation by modulating gene expression levels or introducing specific genetic modifications in cells or model organisms.

3. Applications of Gene Therapy in Proteomic Tools:

a. **Protein Replacement Therapy**: Gene therapy can deliver therapeutic genes encoding functional proteins to replace or supplement deficient or malfunctioning proteins in patients with protein deficiencies or metabolic disorders.

b. **Immunotherapy:** Gene therapy is used to engineer immune cells, such as T cells, with chimeric antigen receptors (CARs) or other immune-modulatory genes to enhance their anti-tumor activity and target specific cancer cells in adoptive cell therapy approaches.

c. **Protein Expression and Secretion**: Gene therapy vectors can deliver genes encoding therapeutic proteins or antibodies for sustained expression and secretion in vivo, providing long-term therapeutic benefits.

4. Challenges and Considerations:

a. **Safety:** Gene therapy approaches must ensure the safety of gene delivery vectors and minimize the risk of adverse effects, such as immune responses, insertional mutagenesis, or off-target effects.

b. **Efficacy:** Optimization of gene delivery methods, vector design, and therapeutic gene expression levels is crucial to achieving therapeutic efficacy in clinical applications.

c. **Ethical and Regulatory Considerations**: Gene therapy raises ethical and regulatory challenges related to patient consent, privacy, equitable access to treatment, and oversight of clinical trials and gene editing technologies.

Various types of gene transfer techniques

Gene therapy relies on various techniques for transferring therapeutic genes into target cells, allowing for the correction of genetic defects, modulation of gene expression, or delivery of therapeutic proteins. Here are several types of gene transfer techniques used in gene therapy, explained in detail:

1. Viral Gene Transfer Techniques:

a. Retroviral Vectors:

i. **Mechanism**: Retroviruses are used as vectors to deliver therapeutic genes into target cells. They integrate their genetic material into the host genome, allowing for stable, long-term expression.

ii. **Applications:** Used for treating diseases such as severe combined immunodeficiency (SCID) and certain types of cancer.

iii. **Limitations:** Limited cargo capacity, potential for insertional mutagenesis, and immune responses against viral vectors.

b. Adenoviral Vectors:

i. **Mechanism**: Adenoviruses are non-integrating viral vectors that efficiently infect a wide range of dividing and non-dividing cells. They deliver therapeutic genes but do not integrate into the host genome.

ii.   **Applications**: Used for transient gene expression, vaccination, and cancer therapy.

iii.   **Limitations:** Transient expression, potential immunogenicity, and pre-existing immunity in some individuals.

c. Adeno-Associated Viral (AAV) Vectors:

i.   **Mechanism**: AAV vectors are small, non-pathogenic viruses that can deliver therapeutic genes into host cells. They can integrate into the host genome or persist episomally, allowing for stable, long-term expression.

ii.   **Applications**: Widely used in gene therapy for treating genetic disorders, such as inherited retinal diseases and muscular dystrophy.

iii.   **Limitations**: Limited cargo capacity and pre-existing immunity in some individuals.

2. Non-viral Gene Transfer Techniques:

a. Lipid-based Vectors:

i.   **Mechanism**: Liposomes or lipid nanoparticles are used to encapsulate and deliver therapeutic DNA or RNA into target cells.

ii.   **Applications**: Used for gene delivery in vitro and in vivo, including gene editing and vaccination.

iii.   **Limitations:** Lower transfection efficiency compared to viral vectors, potential cytotoxicity, and immune responses.

b. Electroporation:

i.   **Mechanism**: High-voltage electric pulses are applied to cells to create transient pores in the cell membrane, allowing DNA or RNA molecules to enter the cells.

ii.   **Applications**: Used for transient gene expression, gene editing, and cell-based therapies.

iii.   **Limitations**: Cell damage or death due to high-voltage pulses, limited cell types amenable to electroporation.

c. Particle Bombardment (Gene Gun):

i. **Mechanism:** Gold or tungsten particles coated with DNA are propelled into target cells using a high-pressure gene gun.

ii. **Applications**: Used for gene delivery into cells, tissues, or organs in vitro and in vivo.

iii. **Limitations**: Potential tissue damage, inefficient gene transfer to some cell types.

3. Other Gene Transfer Techniques:

a. CRISPR/Cas9 Delivery:

i. **Mechanism:** CRISPR/Cas9 components, including guide RNAs and Cas9 protein, are delivered into cells using viral or non-viral vectors to induce targeted genome editing.

ii. **Application**s: Used for precise genome editing, gene knockout, and gene correction in gene therapy and functional genomics.

iii. **Limitations**: Off-target effects, efficiency of delivery, and potential immunogenicity.

b. Ex vivo and In vivo Approaches:

i. **Ex vivo Gene Therapy**: Therapeutic genes are introduced into cells outside the body (e.g., stem cells or T cells) and then transplanted back into the patient.

ii. **In vivo Gene Therapy**: Therapeutic genes are directly delivered into target tissues or organs in the patient's body.

Clinical applications of gene therapy

Gene therapy holds tremendous promise for treating a wide range of genetic disorders, cancer, and other diseases by delivering therapeutic genes, RNA molecules, or gene-editing tools into target cells. Here's a detailed overview of the clinical applications of gene therapy in both genomic and proteomic tools:

1. Treatment of Genetic Disorders:

a. Monogenic Disorders:

i. **Cystic Fibrosis**: Gene therapy aims to deliver functional copies of the cystic fibrosis transmembrane conductance regulator (CFTR) gene into airway epithelial cells to restore chloride ion transport.

ii. **Hemophilia:** Gene therapy involves delivering the gene encoding clotting factors (e.g., Factor VIII or Factor IX) into liver cells to restore normal blood clotting function.

iii. **Muscular Dystrophy**: Gene therapy targets the delivery of dystrophin or other therapeutic genes into muscle cells to improve muscle function and reduce muscle degeneration.

b. Inherited Retinal Diseases:

i. **Leber Congenital Amaurosis (LCA):** Gene therapy aims to deliver functional copies of the RPE65 gene into retinal cells to restore vision in patients with LCA caused by RPE65 mutations.

ii. **Retinitis Pigmentosa**: Gene therapy targets the delivery of therapeutic genes (e.g., RPGR or MERTK) into retinal cells to slow down or halt retinal degeneration.

2. Cancer Therapy:

a. Immunotherapy:

i. **CAR-T Cell Therapy**: Gene therapy is used to engineer patients' T cells to express chimeric antigen receptors (CARs) targeting specific tumor antigens, enabling enhanced targeting and killing of cancer cells.

ii. **Tumor Suppressor Gene Therapy**: Therapeutic genes encoding tumor suppressors (e.g., p53) are delivered into cancer cells to induce apoptosis or inhibit tumor growth.

b. Oncolytic Virotherapy:

i. **Herpes Simplex Virus (HSV) Vectors**: Gene therapy involves the use of oncolytic HSV vectors engineered to selectively replicate in and kill cancer cells while sparing normal cells.

ii.   **Adenovirus-based Vectors**: Adenoviral vectors are modified to deliver therapeutic genes or oncolytic agents into cancer cells, leading to tumor cell death.

3. Cardiovascular Diseases:

a. Gene Therapy for Heart Failure:

i.   Therapeutic genes encoding growth factors (e.g., VEGF, FGF) or anti-apoptotic factors are delivered into heart muscle cells to promote angiogenesis, improve cardiac function, and reduce apoptosis in patients with heart failure.

b. Inherited Cardiovascular Disorders:

i.   Gene therapy aims to deliver therapeutic genes (e.g., dystrophin or α-galactosidase A) into cardiac or vascular cells to treat inherited disorders such as Duchenne muscular dystrophy or Fabry disease.

4. Neurological Disorders:

a. Neurodegenerative Diseases:

i.   **Parkinson's Disease**: Gene therapy involves delivering genes encoding neurotrophic factors (e.g., GDNF) or enzymes (e.g., aromatic L-amino acid decarboxylase) into the brain to promote neuronal survival and function.

ii.   **Spinal Muscular Atrophy (SMA):** Gene therapy aims to deliver functional copies of the SMN1 gene into motor neurons to restore SMN protein levels and improve motor function in patients with SMA.

b. Neurological Disorders with Gene Mutations:

i.   Gene therapy targets the delivery of therapeutic genes or RNA molecules to correct or modulate gene expression in neurons affected by genetic mutations associated with disorders such as Huntington's disease or ALS.

Recent advances in gene therapy

Recent advances in gene therapy have propelled the field forward, leading to novel strategies, improved safety profiles, and enhanced therapeutic outcomes.

Here's a detailed overview of some of the recent advances in gene therapy, focusing on genomic and proteomic tools:

1. Next-Generation Viral Vectors:

a. Improved Transduction Efficiency:

i. Engineering of viral vectors, such as adeno-associated viruses (AAVs), has led to enhanced transduction efficiency, allowing for more effective delivery of therapeutic genes into target cells and tissues.

ii. Novel AAV variants with improved tropism and tissue-specific targeting have been developed, enabling precise gene delivery to specific cell types.

b. Capsid Engineering:

i. Rational design and directed evolution approaches have been used to engineer viral capsids with altered antigenicity, reduced immunogenicity, and enhanced stability, improving the safety and efficacy of viral vectors.

2. Non-viral Gene Delivery Systems:

a. Advances in Lipid Nanoparticles (LNPs):

i. LNPs have emerged as promising non-viral vectors for delivering nucleic acids, including mRNA and gene editing tools, into target cells.

ii. Optimization of LNP formulations, including lipid composition and surface modifications, has led to improved delivery efficiency, stability, and safety profiles.

b. Nanoparticle-based Delivery Systems:

i. Development of nanoparticle-based delivery systems, such as polymer nanoparticles and inorganic nanoparticles, has expanded the repertoire of non-viral gene delivery platforms, offering opportunities for targeted and controlled gene delivery.

3. Gene Editing Technologies:

a. CRISPR/Cas Systems:

i. Continuous advancements in CRISPR/Cas genome editing technologies have enabled precise and efficient gene editing for correcting disease-causing mutations, modulating gene expression, and engineering cellular pathways.

ii. Novel CRISPR/Cas variants, such as base editors and prime editors, have expanded the scope of genome editing applications, allowing for precise nucleotide substitutions and targeted insertions/deletions.

b. Delivery of CRISPR Components:

i. Development of viral and non-viral delivery systems for CRISPR components, including Cas proteins and guide RNAs, has facilitated efficient genome editing in a wide range of cell types and tissues.

ii. Strategies for in vivo delivery of CRISPR components, such as AAV-mediated delivery and nanoparticle-based systems, are being optimized for therapeutic applications in gene therapy.

4. Advances in Proteomic Tools:

a. High-throughput Screening Platforms:

i. High-throughput screening platforms, such as CRISPR-based genetic screens and protein interaction assays, enable large-scale functional genomics and proteomics studies, providing insights into gene function, protein-protein interactions, and cellular pathways.

b. Single-cell Proteomics:

i. Recent advancements in single-cell proteomics technologies, including mass spectrometry-based methods and single-cell antibody profiling techniques, allow for the comprehensive analysis of protein expression and post-translational modifications at the single-cell level, revealing cellular heterogeneity and dynamics.

5. Therapeutic Applications:

a. Gene Therapy for Neurological Disorders:

i. Advances in viral vector design and delivery strategies have enabled progress in gene therapy for neurological disorders, including spinal muscular atrophy (SMA), Huntington's disease, and amyotrophic lateral sclerosis (ALS).

b. Cancer Immunotherapy:

i. Gene therapy-based approaches, such as CAR-T cell therapy and tumor-targeted viral vectors, are being increasingly explored for cancer immunotherapy, offering potential curative treatments for hematological malignancies and solid tumors.

Multiple-choice questions based:

1. What does CRISPR-Cas9 technology primarily allow researchers to do?
   A) Modify protein structures
   B) Sequence entire genomes
   C) Edit genes precisely
   D) Enhance protein interactions

2. Which sequencing method uses real-time sequencing of single molecules?
   A) Sanger Sequencing
   B) Next-Generation Sequencing (NGS)
   C) Third-Generation Sequencing
   D) Polymerase Chain Reaction (PCR)

3. What does quantitative PCR (qPCR) enable scientists to do?
   A) Visualize DNA fragments
   B) Amplify entire genomes
   C) Quantify DNA sequences in real-time
   D) Modify specific DNA sequences

4. Which tool is used to study protein-protein interactions on a large scale?
   A) X-ray Crystallography

B) Protein Microarrays

C) Nuclear Magnetic Resonance (NMR) Spectroscopy

D) Mass Spectrometry

5. What is the main advantage of using Third-Generation Sequencing technologies like PacBio and Oxford Nanopore?

A) They are cost-effective

B) They provide longer read lengths

C) They require no sample preparation

D) They use smaller samples

6. Which method involves hybridizing labeled DNA or RNA to probes on a solid surface?

A) Microarrays

B) CRISPR-Cas9

C) Western Blotting

D) PCR

7. What is the main principle behind DNA electrophoresis?

A) DNA fragments are visualized using a DNA-binding dye

B) DNA molecules migrate towards an electric field

C) DNA samples are amplified

D) DNA fragments are separated based on their molecular weight

8. What is an application of Genome-Wide Association Studies (GWAS)?

A) Editing genes

B) Identifying genetic variations linked to diseases

C) Protein quantification

D) Gene cloning

9. Which proteomic tool is used for determining the 3D structure of proteins?

A) Mass Spectrometry

B) X-ray Crystallography

C) Western Blotting

D) Two-Dimensional Gel Electrophoresis

10. What does Surface Plasmon Resonance (SPR) measure?

A) Protein size

B) Gene expression levels

C) Binding interactions between proteins

D) The effect of mutations on protein function

11. What is the primary purpose of using a gene gun in gene therapy?

A) To remove genetic mutations

B) To deliver DNA coated particles into cells

C) To sequence DNA fragments

D) To edit genes using CRISPR

12. Which of the following is a non-viral gene transfer technique?

A) Adenoviral Vectors

B) Retroviral Vectors

C) Lipid-based Vectors

D) Lentiviral Vectors

13. What type of gene therapy targets reproductive cells?

A) Somatic Gene Therapy

B) Germline Gene Therapy

C) Adenovirus Gene Therapy

D) Retrovirus Gene Therapy

14. Which technique uses enzymes to generate a detectable signal in ELISA?

A) Electrophoresis

B) CRISPR editing

C) Enzyme-linked detection

D) Fluorescence detection

15. In SDS-PAGE, what does SDS do to the proteins?

A) Phosphorylates them

B) Denatures and imparts a negative charge

C) Crystallizes them

D) Makes them react with antibodies

16. What is one main use of fluorescent in situ hybridization (FISH)?

A) Measuring protein concentrations

B) Gene editing

C) Mapping genes on chromosomes

D) Amplifying DNA fragments

17. What feature do Bacterial Artificial Chromosomes (BACs) have that makes them suitable for cloning large genomic fragments?

A) Small size

B) High copy number

C) Large insert capacity

D) Protein expression capability

18. Which tool uses light or UV to visualize separated DNA fragments?

A) CRISPR-Cas9

B) DNA electrophoresis

C) Microarrays

D) Real-time PCR

19. Which is a direct application of Mass Spectrometry in proteomics?

A) Gene editing

B) Sequencing genomes

C) Protein identification

D) Mapping genetic variations

20. Which recombinant DNA technology involves introducing a therapeutic gene to correct defective genes?

A) Gene Cloning

B) Gene Therapy

C) DNA Microarrays

D) PCR

Short Answer Type Questions

1. What are the main advantages of Next-Generation Sequencing (NGS) over Sanger Sequencing?

2. How does quantitative PCR (qPCR) differ from conventional PCR?

3. Describe the basic principle of CRISPR-Cas9 technology.

4. What is the role of microarrays in genomic research?

5. Explain the importance of Genome-Wide Association Studies (GWAS).

6. How does Mass Spectrometry (MS) contribute to proteomic research?

7. Describe the process of Two-Dimensional Gel Electrophoresis (2D-GE).

8. What is Western Blotting used for in proteomics?

9. How does X-ray Crystallography help in understanding protein structures?

10. What is Surface Plasmon Resonance (SPR) and what does it measure?

11. Explain the significance of bioinformatics tools in genomic research.

12. How do DNA microarrays work?

13. What is the purpose of Sanger Sequencing in DNA analysis?

14. How does digital PCR enhance DNA quantification?

15. Describe the role of protein microarrays in studying protein interactions.

16. What is the principle of Nuclear Magnetic Resonance (NMR) Spectroscopy in studying proteins?

17. How does the gene gun method contribute to gene therapy?

18. Explain the difference between germline and somatic gene therapy.

19. What is enzyme-linked detection used for in ELISA?

20. Describe how SDS-PAGE separates proteins.

Long Answer Type Questions

1. Discuss the principles and applications of Next-Generation Sequencing (NGS) in detail.

2. Explain how CRISPR-Cas9 has revolutionized genomic research and give examples of its applications.

3. Describe the workflow of proteomic analysis using Mass Spectrometry, including sample preparation and data analysis.

4. Explain the integration of genomic and proteomic data in personalized medicine and how it impacts therapeutic approaches.

5. Discuss the advancements in Third-Generation Sequencing technologies like PacBio and Oxford Nanopore, and their impact on genomic research.

6. Outline the process and applications of Two-Dimensional Gel Electrophoresis in proteomic research.

7. Discuss the role of bioinformatics in managing and analyzing data from high-throughput sequencing and proteomic experiments.

8. Describe the applications and limitations of Western Blotting in the detection and analysis of proteins.

9. Provide a detailed explanation of how Surface Plasmon Resonance (SPR) is used in drug discovery and protein interaction studies.

10. Discuss the principles, advantages, and challenges of using gene therapy for treating genetic disorders.

Answer Key:

1. C (Edit genes precisely)

2. C (Third-Generation Sequencing)

3. C (Quantify DNA sequences in real-time)

4. B (Protein Microarrays)

5. B (They provide longer read lengths)

6. A (Microarrays)

7. D (DNA fragments are separated based on their molecular weight)

8. B (Identifying genetic variations linked to diseases)

9. B (X-ray Crystallography)

10.C (Binding interactions between proteins)

11.B (To deliver DNA coated particles into cells)

12.C (Lipid-based Vectors)

13.B (Germline Gene Therapy)

14.C (Enzyme-linked detection)

15.B (Denatures and imparts a negative charge)

16.C (Mapping genes on chromosomes)

17.C (Large insert capacity)

18.B (DNA electrophoresis)

19.C (Protein identification)

20.B (Gene Therapy)

CHAPTER – 4

PHARMACOGENOMICS

INTRODUCTION:

Definition and Overview

Pharmacogenomics is the study of how an individual's genetic makeup influences their response to drugs. This field combines pharmacology (the science of drugs) and genomics (the study of genes and their functions) to develop effective, safe medications and doses tailored to a person's genetic profile.

Historical Context

The concept that genetic differences can affect drug response dates back to the mid-20th century. Early observations of adverse drug reactions in certain individuals led to the hypothesis that genetic variability might underlie these differences. The completion of the Human Genome Project in 2003 accelerated research in this field, providing the necessary tools to explore the relationship between genes and drug response in depth.

Mechanisms and Pathways

Pharmacogenomics focuses on several key areas where genetic variations can influence drug response:

1. **Drug Metabolism**: Enzymes involved in the metabolism of drugs can vary significantly between individuals. For example, the cytochrome P450 family of enzymes, particularly CYP2D6, CYP2C9, and CYP2C19, are well-studied for their role in drug metabolism.

2. **Drug Transporters**: Variations in genes encoding drug transporters can affect the absorption, distribution, and elimination of drugs. The ABC and SLC families of transporters are examples where genetic differences can alter drug efficacy and toxicity.

3. **Drug Targets**: Genetic polymorphisms in drug targets, such as receptors or enzymes, can influence the effectiveness of a drug. For instance, variations in the VKORC1 gene affect sensitivity to warfarin, an anticoagulant.

4. **Drug Receptors:** Genetic variations in receptors that drugs bind to can influence how well a drug works. For instance, polymorphisms in the beta-adrenergic receptors can affect the response to beta-blockers used in treating hypertension.

Applications

Pharmacogenomics has several important applications in clinical practice:

1. **Personalized Medicine**: Tailoring drug therapy based on an individual's genetic profile to maximize efficacy and minimize adverse effects.

2. **Drug Development**: Identifying genetic factors that influence drug response can help in the development of new drugs and in the design of clinical trials.

3. **Disease Susceptibility**: Understanding genetic predispositions to certain diseases can aid in preventative strategies and early interventions.

Techniques and Technologies

Several technologies are employed in pharmacogenomic research and clinical application:

1. **Genotyping**: Identifying specific genetic variants in an individual's DNA.

2. **Sequencing:** Determining the entire DNA sequence to uncover genetic differences.

3. **Bioinformatics:** Using computational tools to analyze and interpret genetic data in relation to drug response.

Challenges and Limitations

Despite its potential, pharmacogenomics faces several challenges:

1. **Complexity of Genetic Interactions**: Drug response is often influenced by multiple genes and their interactions with environmental factors.

2. **Ethical and Legal Issues**: Concerns about genetic privacy, discrimination, and the use of genetic information.
3. **Clinical Implementation**: Integrating pharmacogenomic data into routine clinical practice requires education, infrastructure, and guidelines for healthcare providers.

Future Directions

The future of pharmacogenomics is promising, with ongoing research aimed at:

1. **Expanding Genetic Databases**: Increasing the diversity and size of genetic databases to better understand drug responses across different populations.
2. **Advancing Technologies**: Improving sequencing technologies and bioinformatics tools for more accurate and comprehensive analysis.
3. **Integrative Approaches**: Combining pharmacogenomics with other omics (e.g., proteomics, metabolomics) for a more holistic understanding of drug response.

GENE MAPPING AND CLONING OF DISEASE GENE

Introduction

Gene mapping and cloning are fundamental techniques in pharmacogenomics, aiding in the identification and characterization of genes associated with disease susceptibility and drug response. These techniques help uncover the genetic underpinnings of various conditions and facilitate the development of personalized therapeutic strategies.

Gene Mapping

1. Definition and Purpose

Gene mapping involves identifying the specific locations of genes on chromosomes. It is crucial for linking particular genetic variations with disease traits or drug responses. This process helps in understanding the genetic architecture of complex traits and in identifying candidate genes for further study.

2. Techniques in Gene Mapping

Several methods are used to map genes, each with its own strengths and applications:

a. Linkage Analysis

i. **Concept:** Linkage analysis looks for co-segregation of genetic markers with disease traits within families. It relies on the principle that genes close to each other on a chromosome tend to be inherited together.

ii. **Applications:** Useful for identifying genes associated with Mendelian (single-gene) disorders.

b. Association Studies

i. **Concept:** Association studies compare the frequency of genetic variants in individuals with a disease (cases) versus those without the disease (controls). This method identifies genetic variants that are statistically associated with the disease.

ii. **Types:** Genome-Wide Association Studies (GWAS) are a common approach, scanning the entire genome for variants associated with a trait.

iii. **Applications:** Effective for complex diseases influenced by multiple genes, such as diabetes, heart disease, and drug response traits.

c. Fine Mapping

i. **Concept:** Once a region associated with a disease is identified, fine mapping narrows down the specific genetic variants responsible. This involves higher-resolution analysis of the region.

ii. **Applications:** Used to pinpoint causal variants within a broader associated region identified by linkage or GWAS.

3. Tools and Technologies

i. **Microsatellites and SNPs:** Microsatellites (short tandem repeats) and single nucleotide polymorphisms (SNPs) are commonly used genetic markers in mapping studies.

ii. **High-Throughput Sequencing**: Next-generation sequencing technologies allow for rapid and comprehensive analysis of large genomic regions.

iii. **Bioinformatics**: Computational tools are essential for managing and analyzing the large datasets generated in mapping studies.

Gene Cloning

1. Definition and Purpose

Gene cloning involves isolating and making multiple copies of a gene of interest. This is essential for studying the gene's function, its role in disease, and its potential as a therapeutic target.

2. Techniques in Gene Cloning

a. Traditional Cloning

i. **Concept**: Traditional cloning methods involve inserting a DNA fragment containing the gene of interest into a vector (such as a plasmid), which is then introduced into a host cell (usually bacteria) for replication.

ii. **Steps:**

    a. **Isolation of DNA**: Extracting the DNA containing the gene of interest.

    b. **Digestion with Restriction Enzymes**: Cutting the DNA into fragments.

    c. **Ligation**: Inserting the DNA fragment into a plasmid vector.

    d. **Transformation**: Introducing the recombinant plasmid into bacteria.

    e. **Selection and Screening**: Identifying bacteria that have taken up the plasmid.

b. PCR-Based Cloning

i. **Concept:** Polymerase Chain Reaction (PCR) amplifies the gene of interest, which can then be inserted into a vector.

ii. **Advantages:** Faster and more precise than traditional cloning.

c. Advanced Cloning Techniques

i. **Gibson Assembly**: An isothermal method that allows the seamless joining of multiple DNA fragments in a single reaction.

ii. **CRISPR/Cas9:** A genome editing tool that can be used to insert or modify genes within their native genomic context.

3. Applications in Pharmacogenomics

i. **Functional Studies**: Cloned genes can be expressed in model systems (e.g., cell lines, animals) to study their function and role in drug response.

ii. **Drug Target Validation**: Cloning and characterizing genes involved in drug metabolism and response helps in identifying and validating new drug targets.

iii. **Gene Therapy**: Cloned therapeutic genes can be used to develop gene therapies for genetic disorders.

Integrative Approaches

Combining Gene Mapping and Cloning

1. **From Mapping to Cloning**: Once gene mapping identifies a candidate region, gene cloning can be used to isolate and study the specific genes within that region.

2. **Functional Genomics**: Integrating gene mapping and cloning with functional genomics helps elucidate the biological pathways involved in drug response and disease.

Role of Bioinformatics

1. **Data Analysis:** Bioinformatics tools are essential for analyzing gene mapping data and for designing cloning strategies.

2. **Genomic Databases**: Resources such as the Human Genome Project and various SNP databases provide valuable reference information for mapping and cloning efforts.

Challenges and Future Directions

Challenges

1. **Complexity of Traits**: Many drug responses and diseases are influenced by multiple genes and environmental factors, complicating mapping and cloning efforts.

2. **Technical Limitations**: Despite advances, there are still technical challenges in cloning large or complex genes.

Future Directions

1. **Precision Medicine**: Continued advancements in gene mapping and cloning will enhance personalized medicine, tailoring treatments based on individual genetic profiles.

2. **Integration with Other Omics**: Combining genomics with proteomics, metabolomics, and other omics data will provide a more comprehensive understanding of drug response and disease mechanisms.

GENETIC VARIATION AND ITS ROLE IN HEALTH/ PHARMACOLOGY

Introduction

Genetic variation plays a crucial role in determining individual responses to drugs and susceptibility to diseases. Pharmacogenomics leverages these variations to develop personalized medical treatments, aiming to maximize therapeutic efficacy while minimizing adverse effects.

Types of Genetic Variation

1. **Single Nucleotide Polymorphisms (SNPs):**
   a. **Definition**: SNPs are single base pair changes in the DNA sequence. They are the most common type of genetic variation, occurring approximately every 300 nucleotides.
   b. **Impact**: SNPs can affect gene function in various ways, such as altering protein structure, influencing gene expression, or affecting splicing.

2. **Insertions and Deletions (Indels):**
   a. **Definition**: Indels are the addition or loss of small DNA segments.

b. **Impact**: Indels can disrupt gene function by causing frameshift mutations or altering protein-coding sequences.

3. **Copy Number Variations (CNVs):**

   a. **Definition**: CNVs are large segments of the genome that are duplicated or deleted.

   b. **Impact**: CNVs can lead to dosage imbalances of genes, affecting gene expression and phenotypic traits.

4. **Structural Variations:**

   a. **Definition:** These include larger chromosomal changes such as inversions, translocations, and large-scale duplications or deletions.

   b. **Impact**: Structural variations can disrupt gene function or regulatory regions, leading to altered gene expression and disease susceptibility.

5. **Epigenetic Modifications:**

   a. **Definition**: Changes in gene expression that do not involve alterations in the DNA sequence, such as DNA methylation and histone modification.

   b. **Impact:** Epigenetic modifications can influence how genes are expressed and are often influenced by environmental factors.

Role of Genetic Variation in Health

1. **Disease Susceptibility:**

   a. Genetic variations can predispose individuals to certain diseases. For example, BRCA1 and BRCA2 gene mutations are strongly associated with an increased risk of breast and ovarian cancers.

2. **Disease Progression:**

   a. Variations can influence the progression and severity of diseases. For instance, specific alleles of the ApoE gene are linked to the risk and progression of Alzheimer's disease.

3. **Response to Environmental Factors:**

a. Genetic differences can modulate how individuals respond to environmental exposures, such as toxins, pathogens, and lifestyle factors.

Role of Genetic Variation in Pharmacology

1. **Drug Metabolism:**

   a. **Cytochrome P450 Enzymes**: Genetic polymorphisms in CYP450 enzymes (e.g., CYP2D6, CYP2C9, CYP2C19) significantly influence drug metabolism. Variants can classify individuals as poor, intermediate, extensive, or ultra-rapid metabolizers, affecting drug efficacy and toxicity.

   b. **Examples:**

      i. **CYP2D6**: Variants affect the metabolism of drugs like codeine, antidepressants, and antipsychotics. Poor metabolizers may experience reduced efficacy or increased toxicity.

      ii. **CYP2C19:** Variants influence the metabolism of proton pump inhibitors and antiplatelet drugs like clopidogrel. Poor metabolizers of clopidogrel have a higher risk of cardiovascular events.

2. **Drug Transport:**

   a. **Transporter Proteins**: Genetic variations in transporter genes (e.g., ABCB1, SLCO1B1) can alter drug absorption, distribution, and elimination.

   b. **Examples**:

      i. **ABCB1 (P-glycoprotein):** Variants can affect the efflux of drugs from cells, impacting drug bioavailability and resistance.

ii. **SLCO1B1**: Variants are associated with altered statin pharmacokinetics, influencing the risk of statin-induced myopathy.

3. **Drug Targets:**

   a. **Receptors and Enzymes: Genetic differences in drug targets can affect drug** binding and efficacy.

   b. **Examples:**

      i. **VKORC1**: Variants affect sensitivity to warfarin, necessitating dose adjustments to avoid adverse effects.

      ii. **Beta-Adrenergic Receptors**: Variants in ADRB1 and ADRB2 genes can influence responses to beta-blockers used in hypertension and heart failure.

4. **Adverse Drug Reactions (ADRs):**

   a. Genetic predispositions can increase the risk of adverse drug reactions. For instance, HLA-B*5701 is associated with hypersensitivity to the antiretroviral drug abacavir.

Clinical Applications of Pharmacogenomics

1. **Personalized Medicine:**

   a. Tailoring drug therapy based on genetic profiles can optimize treatment outcomes. For example, genetic testing for CYP2C9 and VKORC1 variants guides warfarin dosing.

2. **Predictive Testing:**

   a. Identifying individuals at risk for adverse drug reactions or non-response to therapies can enhance patient safety and treatment efficacy.

3. **Drug Development:**

   a. Understanding genetic influences on drug response can inform the development of new drugs and the design of clinical trials, leading to more effective and safer therapies.

4. **Diagnostic Tools:**

   a. Pharmacogenomic testing panels are increasingly used in clinical practice to guide drug selection and dosing for various conditions.

Challenges and Future Directions

1. **Complexity of Genetic Interactions:**

   a. Drug response is often influenced by multiple genes and their interactions with environmental factors, making it challenging to predict outcomes based solely on genetic information.

2. **Ethical and Legal Considerations:**

   a. Issues related to genetic privacy, discrimination, and consent must be carefully managed to ensure ethical implementation of pharmacogenomics.

3. **Integration into Clinical Practice:**

   a. Widespread adoption of pharmacogenomics requires education and infrastructure to support genetic testing and data interpretation in clinical settings.

4. **Expanding Research:**

   a. Ongoing research is needed to discover new genetic variants associated with drug response and to validate their clinical relevance across diverse populations.

POLYMORPHISMS

Introduction

Polymorphisms are variations in the DNA sequence that occur commonly within a population. In pharmacogenomics, polymorphisms are critically important because they can influence how individuals metabolize medications, respond to treatments, and experience adverse drug reactions. Understanding these genetic differences is key to developing personalized medicine approaches that optimize therapeutic outcomes and minimize risks.

Types of Polymorphisms

1. **Single Nucleotide Polymorphisms (SNPs):**
   a. **Definition:** A SNP is a variation at a single position in the DNA sequence among individuals. SNPs are the most common type of genetic variation.
   b. **Impact:** SNPs can occur in coding regions (affecting protein function), non-coding regions (affecting gene regulation), or within introns (affecting splicing).
2. **Insertion/Deletion Polymorphisms (Indels):**
   a. **Definition:** Indels are variations where small segments of DNA are inserted or deleted from the genome.
   b. **Impact:** Indels can cause frameshift mutations, affecting the protein-coding sequence, or disrupt regulatory elements.
3. **Copy Number Variations (CNVs):**
   a. **Definition**: CNVs are large segments of DNA that are duplicated or deleted.
   b. **Impact:** CNVs can result in gene dosage changes, potentially leading to altered gene expression and phenotypic effects.
4. **Variable Number Tandem Repeats (VNTRs):**
   a. **Definition**: VNTRs are short sequences of DNA that are repeated in tandem. The number of repeats can vary between individuals.
   b. **Impact**: VNTRs can affect gene expression and protein function, depending on their location and size.

Role of Polymorphisms in Pharmacogenomics

1. **Drug Metabolism:**
   a. Polymorphisms in genes encoding drug-metabolizing enzymes can significantly impact the metabolism of medications, influencing their efficacy and safety.
2. **Examples:**

a. **CYP2D6:** Polymorphisms in CYP2D6 can categorize individuals as poor, intermediate, extensive, or ultra-rapid metabolizers. Poor metabolizers may experience toxicity with standard doses of drugs like codeine, while ultra-rapid metabolizers may not achieve therapeutic effects.

b. **CYP2C9:** Variants in CYP2C9 affect the metabolism of drugs like warfarin and phenytoin. Patients with certain polymorphisms may require lower doses to avoid adverse effects.

3. **Drug Transport:**

    a. Polymorphisms in genes encoding drug transporters can influence the absorption, distribution, and elimination of drugs.

4. **Examples:**

    a. **ABCB1**: Also known as P-glycoprotein, polymorphisms in this gene can affect the efflux of drugs from cells, impacting drug bioavailability and resistance.

    b. **SLCO1B1**: Variants in this gene affect the transport of statins. The SLCO1B1*5 allele, for example, is associated with an increased risk of statin-induced myopathy.

5. **Drug Targets:**

    a. Polymorphisms in genes encoding drug targets, such as receptors and enzymes, can alter drug binding and efficacy.

6. **Examples:**

    a. **VKORC1:** Polymorphisms in VKORC1 affect sensitivity to warfarin, influencing the dose required to achieve therapeutic anticoagulation.

    b. **ADRB1:** Variants in the beta-1 adrenergic receptor gene (ADRB1) can influence the response to beta-blockers used in the treatment of hypertension and heart failure.

7. **Adverse Drug Reactions (ADRs):**

a. Genetic predispositions due to polymorphisms can increase the risk of ADRs, leading to severe and potentially life-threatening conditions.

8. **Examples:**

    a. **HLA-B*5701**: This allele is associated with hypersensitivity to the antiretroviral drug abacavir. Screening for HLA-B*5701 before starting treatment can prevent severe reactions.

    b. **TPMT**: Polymorphisms in the thiopurine S-methyltransferase (TPMT) gene affect the metabolism of thiopurine drugs used in leukemia and autoimmune diseases. TPMT deficiency can lead to severe myelosuppression.

Clinical Applications of Pharmacogenomics

1. **Personalized Medicine:**

    a. Using genetic information to tailor drug therapy based on an individual's genetic profile can optimize treatment efficacy and safety.

2. **Example:**

    a. **Warfarin:** Dosing algorithms incorporating CYP2C9 and VKORC1 genotypes help determine the appropriate starting dose, reducing the risk of bleeding or thromboembolism.

3. **Predictive Testing:**

    a. Genetic testing can identify individuals at risk for adverse drug reactions or non-response to certain therapies, guiding drug selection and dosing.

4. **Example:**

    a. **Clopidogrel:** Testing for CYP2C19 polymorphisms can identify patients who are poor metabolizers and may benefit from alternative antiplatelet therapy.

5. **Drug Development:**

a. Understanding genetic variations that influence drug response can inform the development of new drugs and the design of clinical trials, leading to more effective and safer therapies.

6. **Example:**

a. **Cancer Therapy**: Targeted therapies, such as those against specific mutations in the EGFR gene in non-small cell lung cancer, are developed based on the understanding of genetic variations in tumors.

Challenges and Future Directions

1. **Complexity of Genetic Interactions:**

a. Drug response is often influenced by multiple genes and their interactions with environmental factors, making it challenging to predict outcomes based solely on genetic information.

2. **Ethical and Legal Considerations:**

a. Issues related to genetic privacy, discrimination, and consent must be carefully managed to ensure ethical implementation of pharmacogenomics.

3. **Integration into Clinical Practice:**

a. Widespread adoption of pharmacogenomics requires education and infrastructure to support genetic testing and data interpretation in clinical settings.

4. **Expanding Research:**

a. Ongoing research is needed to discover new genetic variants associated with drug response and to validate their clinical relevance across diverse populations.

AFFECTING DRUG METABOLISM GENETIC VARIATION IN DRUG TRANSPORTERS

Introduction

Drug transporters are proteins that move drugs and other compounds across cellular membranes. Genetic variations in these transporters can significantly influence the pharmacokinetics (absorption, distribution, metabolism, and excretion) of drugs, affecting their efficacy and safety. Understanding these variations is crucial in pharmacogenomics for developing personalized medicine strategies.

Major Drug Transporters

1. **ATP-Binding Cassette (ABC) Transporters:**
   a. **Role:** ABC transporters use energy from ATP hydrolysis to transport various molecules across membranes.
   b. **Examples**: ABCB1 (P-glycoprotein), ABCC1-6 (Multidrug resistance-associated proteins), ABCG2 (Breast cancer resistance protein).

2. **Solute Carrier (SLC) Transporters:**
   a. **Role**: SLC transporters facilitate the movement of ions and organic molecules across membranes through various mechanisms, including facilitated diffusion and secondary active transport.
   b. **Examples**: SLCO1B1 (Organic anion transporting polypeptide 1B1), SLC22A1 (Organic cation transporter 1), SLC6A4 (Serotonin transporter).

Genetic Variations in Drug Transporters

ABCB1 (P-glycoprotein)

1. **Function:** Efflux transporter that pumps drugs out of cells, affecting drug absorption and distribution, particularly at the blood-brain barrier, intestinal epithelium, and liver.

2. **Genetic Variations**:
   a. **SNPs:** Common SNPs include C3435T, G2677T/A, and C1236T. These variants can alter the expression and function of P-glycoprotein.

b. **Impact:** Variations can affect drug bioavailability and resistance. For example, the C3435T polymorphism is associated with altered plasma levels of various drugs, such as digoxin and antiretrovirals.

SLCO1B1 (OATP1B1)

1. **Function:** Uptake transporter primarily expressed in the liver, involved in the hepatic uptake of statins, bilirubin, and other drugs.
2. **Genetic Variations:**
   a. **SNPs:** Common variants include *SLCO1B15 (521T>C) and SLCO1B115* (388A>G and 521T>C).
   b. **Impact:** The SLCO1B1*5 allele is associated with reduced transporter activity, leading to higher plasma levels of statins and an increased risk of statin-induced myopathy.

ABCG2 (BCRP)

1. **Function**: Efflux transporter that protects tissues by limiting drug penetration into cells, expressed in the intestine, liver, placenta, and blood-brain barrier.
2. **Genetic Variations:**
   a. **SNPs:** The Q141K (421C>A) polymorphism is a well-studied variant associated with reduced transporter function.
   b. **Impact:** Variations can influence the pharmacokinetics of drugs such as sulfasalazine, statins, and certain anticancer agents, potentially leading to altered efficacy and toxicity.

SLC22A1 (OCT1)

1. **Function**: Uptake transporter expressed in the liver, involved in the hepatic uptake of metformin and other cationic drugs.
2. **Genetic Variations:**
   a. **SNPs:** Variants such as R61C, G401S, and 420del can affect transporter function.

b. **Impact**: Genetic variations can influence the therapeutic response to metformin, affecting glucose-lowering efficacy in diabetic patients.

SLC6A4 (Serotonin Transporter)

1. **Function**: Uptake transporter that regulates serotonin levels in the synaptic cleft, influencing mood and behavior.

2. **Genetic Variations**:

   a. **SNPs:** The 5-HTTLPR polymorphism involves a variable number of tandem repeats (VNTR) in the promoter region, affecting transporter expression.

   b. **Impact:** Variants can influence the response to antidepressants such as selective serotonin reuptake inhibitors (SSRIs), with implications for efficacy and side effects.

Clinical Implications of Genetic Variations in Drug Transporters

1. **Drug Efficacy:**

   a. Variations in drug transporters can lead to differences in drug absorption and distribution, influencing therapeutic outcomes. For example, reduced function of SLCO1B1 can result in higher plasma levels of statins, enhancing their cholesterol-lowering effect but also increasing the risk of adverse effects.

2. **Drug Safety:**

   a. Genetic variations can predispose individuals to adverse drug reactions. For instance, individuals with the ABCG2 Q141K variant may experience increased toxicity with certain chemotherapy drugs due to impaired drug efflux.

3. **Dosing Adjustments:**

   a. Understanding transporter genetics can inform dose adjustments to achieve optimal therapeutic levels. For example, patients with reduced-function alleles of SLC22A1 may require lower doses of metformin to avoid side effects while maintaining efficacy.

4. **Personalized Medicine:**

   a. Pharmacogenomic testing for transporter polymorphisms can guide personalized treatment plans. For example, screening for SLCO1B1 variants before initiating statin therapy can help identify patients at risk for myopathy and guide the choice of alternative therapies or dosing strategies.

Examples of Pharmacogenomic Applications

1. **Statins and SLCO1B1:**

   a. Genetic testing for SLCO1B1 variants can identify patients at risk for statin-induced myopathy, allowing for personalized statin therapy to minimize adverse effects.

2. **Antidepressants and SLC6A4:**

   a. Testing for the 5-HTTLPR polymorphism can help predict patient response to SSRIs, aiding in the selection of the most effective antidepressant with the fewest side effects.

3. **Chemotherapy and ABCG2:**

   a. Screening for ABCG2 polymorphisms can help tailor chemotherapy regimens to reduce toxicity while maintaining efficacy, particularly in cancer treatments where drug efflux is critical.

4. **Metformin and SLC22A1:**

   a. Genetic testing for SLC22A1 variants can optimize metformin dosing in diabetic patients, enhancing glucose control and reducing the risk of side effects.

Challenges and Future Directions

1. **Complex Interactions:**

a. Drug response is influenced by multiple genes and environmental factors. Comprehensive models considering these interactions are needed to accurately predict outcomes.

2. **Ethical Considerations:**

   a. Issues related to genetic privacy, consent, and potential discrimination must be addressed to ensure ethical implementation of pharmacogenomic testing.

3. **Clinical Integration:**

   a. Incorporating pharmacogenomic testing into routine clinical practice requires education for healthcare providers, development of guidelines, and availability of testing infrastructure.

4. **Research and Validation:**

   a. Ongoing research is needed to discover new genetic variants, validate their clinical relevance, and expand the knowledge base across diverse populations to ensure equitable healthcare benefits.

GENETIC VARIATION IN G PROTEIN COUPLED RECEPTORS

Introduction

G protein-coupled receptors (GPCRs) are a large family of cell surface receptors that play crucial roles in cellular signaling and are targets for a significant proportion of modern pharmaceuticals. Genetic variations in GPCRs can influence individual responses to drugs that target these receptors, affecting both therapeutic efficacy and the risk of adverse effects. Understanding these variations is essential in pharmacogenomics to tailor treatments to individual genetic profiles.

Overview of GPCRs

1. **Structure and Function:**

   a. GPCRs consist of seven transmembrane helices and are involved in transmitting signals from various extracellular stimuli, including hormones, neurotransmitters, and environmental signals, to intracellular signaling pathways.

2. **Role in Pharmacology:**

    a. GPCRs mediate the effects of numerous drugs across various therapeutic areas, including cardiovascular, neurological, metabolic, and psychiatric disorders. Examples include beta-adrenergic receptors (beta-blockers), serotonin receptors (antidepressants), and angiotensin receptors (antihypertensives).

Types of Genetic Variations in GPCRs

1. **Single Nucleotide Polymorphisms (SNPs):**

    a. **Definition:** SNPs are variations at a single nucleotide position in the DNA sequence.

    b. **Impact**: SNPs can alter receptor function, expression levels, or ligand binding affinity.

2. **Insertions and Deletions (Indels):**

    a. **Definition**: Indels involve the addition or deletion of small DNA segments.

    b. **Impact**: Indels can affect receptor structure and function, potentially leading to altered drug responses.

3. **Copy Number Variations (CNVs):**

    a. **Definition:** CNVs are larger segments of DNA that are duplicated or deleted.

    b. **Impact:** CNVs can influence the dosage and expression of GPCRs, affecting drug sensitivity.

Examples of GPCR Variants and Their Clinical Relevance

Beta-Adrenergic Receptors (ADRB1 and ADRB2)

1. **ADRB1:**

    a. **Function**: Mediates the effects of catecholamines like adrenaline and noradrenaline on the heart and kidneys.

b. **Genetic Variations**:

    i. **Ser49Gly (S49G):** This SNP affects receptor desensitization and is associated with varying responses to beta-blockers.

    ii. **Arg389Gly (R389G):** This SNP influences the receptor's coupling efficiency with G proteins, affecting heart rate and blood pressure response to beta-blockers.

2. **ADRB2:**

a. **Function**: Regulates smooth muscle relaxation, metabolic processes, and lipolysis.

b. **Genetic Variations:**

    i. **Arg16Gly (R16G) and Gln27Glu (Q27E):** These SNPs affect receptor downregulation and are associated with differences in bronchodilator response in asthma and COPD treatment.

Serotonin Receptors (5-HT2A and 5-HT2C)

1. **5-HT2A:**

a. **Function**: Involved in the regulation of mood, cognition, and perception.

b. **Genetic Variations:**

    i. **T102C and A1438G**: These SNPs are associated with varying responses to antipsychotic drugs and antidepressants.

2. **5-HT2C:**

a. **Function**: Plays a role in appetite regulation and mood.

b. **Genetic Variations:**

    i. **Cys23Ser (C23S)**: This SNP affects receptor function and has been linked to differences in response to antipsychotic-induced weight gain and efficacy of certain antidepressants.

Angiotensin II Receptor Type 1 (AGTR1)

a. **Function:** Mediates the effects of angiotensin II on blood pressure and electrolyte balance.

b. **Genetic Variations**:

    i. **A1166C:** This SNP is associated with varying responses to angiotensin receptor blockers (ARBs) used in hypertension and heart failure management.

Clinical Implications of GPCR Variations

1. **Drug Efficacy:**

   a. Genetic variations can lead to differences in receptor function and signaling, influencing the therapeutic response to drugs targeting GPCRs.

2. **Example:** Patients with the ADRB1 Arg389Gly variant may require different dosages of beta-blockers for optimal management of hypertension and heart failure.

3. **Drug Safety:**

   a. Variations can predispose individuals to adverse drug reactions by altering receptor sensitivity or expression.

4. **Example:** The 5-HT2C Cys23Ser variant can influence susceptibility to weight gain from antipsychotic medications, necessitating careful drug selection and monitoring.

5. **Personalized Treatment**:

   a. Pharmacogenomic testing for GPCR variants can guide personalized treatment plans, improving efficacy and reducing the risk of adverse effects.

6. **Example**: Screening for ADRB2 polymorphisms can help tailor asthma treatment by identifying patients likely to benefit from specific bronchodilators.

Examples of Pharmacogenomic Applications

1. **Beta-Blockers and ADRB1/ADRB2:**

a. Genetic testing for ADRB1 and ADRB2 variants can help optimize beta-blocker therapy in cardiovascular diseases by predicting individual responses and tailoring dosages.

2. **Antidepressants and Serotonin Receptors:**

a. Testing for 5-HT2A and 5-HT2C variants can assist in selecting the most effective antidepressant with the fewest side effects, particularly in patients with treatment-resistant depression.

3. **ARBs and AGTR1:**

a. Genetic screening for AGTR1 variants can guide the use of ARBs in hypertension and heart failure, improving therapeutic outcomes.

Challenges and Future Directions

1. **Complex Interactions:**

a. Drug response is influenced by multiple genetic and environmental factors. Comprehensive models considering these interactions are needed for accurate predictions.

2. **Ethical Considerations:**

a. Issues related to genetic privacy, consent, and potential discrimination must be addressed to ensure ethical implementation of pharmacogenomic testing.

3. **Integration into Clinical Practice:**

a. Incorporating pharmacogenomic testing into routine clinical practice requires education for healthcare providers, development of guidelines, and availability of testing infrastructure.

4. **Research and Validation:**

a. Ongoing research is needed to discover new genetic variants, validate their clinical relevance, and expand knowledge across diverse populations to ensure equitable healthcare benefits.

APPLICATIONS OF PROTEOMICS SCIENCE: GENOMICS, PROTEOMICS, METABOLOMICS, FUNCTIONOMICS, NUTRIGENOMICS

Pharmacogenomics is the study of how genes affect a person's response to drugs. It combines pharmacology and genomics to develop effective, safe medications and doses tailored to a person's genetic makeup. Integrating other omics sciences, such as proteomics, metabolomics, functionomics, and nutrigenomics, enhances the understanding of drug responses and helps in developing personalized medicine.

Genomics in Pharmacogenomics

Genomics involves the comprehensive analysis of an organism's complete set of DNA, including all of its genes. In pharmacogenomics:

1. **Identification of Genetic Variants:**
   a. Understanding single nucleotide polymorphisms (SNPs), copy number variations (CNVs), and other genetic mutations that influence drug metabolism, efficacy, and toxicity.
   b. **Example**: Variants in CYP2C19 affecting response to the antiplatelet drug clopidogrel.

2. **Drug Response Prediction:**
   a. Predicting how different individuals will respond to specific medications based on their genetic profiles.
   b. **Example:** Variants in the VKORC1 gene influencing warfarin dosing.

3. **Target Identification:**
   a. Identifying new drug targets by studying genes and their functions.
   b. **Example**: Oncogenes and tumor suppressor genes as targets for cancer therapy.

Proteomics in Pharmacogenomics

Proteomics is the large-scale study of proteins, particularly their structures and functions. In pharmacogenomics:

1. **Biomarker Discovery:**
   a. Identifying protein biomarkers for disease states and drug response.
   b. **Example**: HER2 protein levels guiding the use of trastuzumab in breast cancer.

2. **Understanding Drug Mechanisms:**
   a. Studying how drugs affect protein expression and function to understand their mechanisms of action.
   b. **Example**: Analyzing the proteome changes induced by chemotherapy drugs to understand resistance mechanisms.

3. **Personalized Therapy:**
   a. Tailoring drug therapy based on the proteomic profile of a patient.
   b. **Example:** Using proteomic profiles to guide the use of targeted therapies in cancer.

Metabolomics in Pharmacogenomics

Metabolomics is the study of metabolites, the small molecule substrates, intermediates, and products of metabolism. In pharmacogenomics:

1. **Metabolic Profiling:**
   a. Profiling the metabolic responses to drugs to understand individual differences in drug metabolism.
   b. **Example:** Metabolic profiling to optimize doses of antidepressants.

2. **Biomarker Identification:**
   a. Identifying metabolic biomarkers that predict drug response and toxicity.
   b. **Example**: Identifying metabolites associated with adverse reactions to statins.

3. **Pathway Analysis:**

a. Understanding the metabolic pathways affected by drugs to improve drug design and therapy.

b. **Example:** Investigating metabolic changes in response to cancer therapies to identify new treatment strategies.

Functionomics in Pharmacogenomics

Functionomics refers to the study of the functional aspects of the genome, including the interactions and activities of genes and proteins. In pharmacogenomics:

1. **Functional Assays:**

    a. Using functional assays to study the impact of genetic variations on protein function and drug response.

    b. **Example:** Assays to measure the functional activity of CYP450 enzymes with different genetic variants.

2. **Gene-Protein Interaction Networks:**

    a. Mapping gene-protein interaction networks to understand the complex interactions affecting drug response.

    b. **Example**: Studying the interaction network of cancer-related genes and proteins to identify key drivers of drug resistance.

3. **Functional Genomics:**

    a. Using techniques such as CRISPR/Cas9 to manipulate genes and study their role in drug response.

    b. **Example**: Using CRISPR to knock out specific genes in cell lines to study their impact on chemotherapy resistance.

Nutrigenomics in Pharmacogenomics

Nutrigenomics is the study of the effects of foods and food constituents on gene expression. In pharmacogenomics:

1. **Diet-Drug Interactions:**

    a. Understanding how diet affects drug metabolism and response.

b. **Example**: The impact of grapefruit juice on the metabolism of drugs metabolized by CYP3A4.

2. **Personalized Nutrition:**

   a. Developing personalized dietary recommendations based on genetic profiles to optimize drug therapy.

   b. **Example**: Tailoring dietary advice for patients taking anticoagulants like warfarin to manage vitamin K intake.

3. **Nutrient-Gene Interactions:**

   a. Studying how nutrients influence gene expression and how this affects drug response.

   b. **Example**: Investigating how folate intake affects the efficacy of methotrexate in cancer therapy.

Integration of Omics Sciences in Pharmacogenomics

1. **Holistic Understanding:**

   a. Integrating data from genomics, proteomics, metabolomics, and other omics to gain a comprehensive understanding of drug response mechanisms.

2. **Personalized Medicine:**

   a. Using multi-omics approaches to develop personalized treatment plans that consider genetic, proteomic, and metabolic profiles.

3. **Systems Biology:**

   a. Applying systems biology approaches to integrate omics data and model complex biological systems to predict drug responses.

4. **Biomarker Discovery:**

   a. Identifying multi-omics biomarkers that provide more accurate predictions of drug response and toxicity.

IMMUNOTHERAPEUTIC

Introduction

Immunotherapeutics, also known as immunotherapies, are treatments that harness the body's immune system to fight diseases, particularly cancers. Pharmacogenomics plays a crucial role in understanding individual responses to these therapies, optimizing treatment regimens, and minimizing adverse effects. This integration enables personalized immunotherapy, improving efficacy and patient outcomes.

Types of Immunotherapeutics

1. **Checkpoint Inhibitors:**
   a. **Mechanism**: These drugs block proteins that inhibit immune responses, such as PD-1/PD-L1 and CTLA-4, thereby enhancing the immune system's ability to attack cancer cells.
   b. **Examples**: Pembrolizumab (Keytruda), Nivolumab (Opdivo), Ipilimumab (Yervoy).

2. **CAR-T Cell Therapy:**
   a. **Mechanism**: Patient's T cells are genetically engineered to express chimeric antigen receptors (CARs) that target specific cancer antigens.
   b. **Examples**: Tisagenlecleucel (Kymriah), Axicabtagene ciloleucel (Yescarta).

3. **Cancer Vaccines:**
   a. **Mechanism**: These vaccines stimulate the immune system to recognize and attack cancer-specific antigens.
   b. **Examples:** Sipuleucel-T (Provenge) for prostate cancer.

4. **Monoclonal Antibodies:**
   a. **Mechanism**: These antibodies bind to specific antigens on cancer cells, marking them for destruction by the immune system.
   b. **Examples**: Trastuzumab (Herceptin), Rituximab (Rituxan).

Role of Pharmacogenomics in Immunotherapeutics

1. **Predicting Response to Therapy:**

a. **Genomic Biomarkers:**

   i. Identifying genetic markers that predict patient response to immunotherapies.

   ii. **Example**: Tumor mutational burden (TMB) and microsatellite instability (MSI) are associated with better responses to checkpoint inhibitors.

2. **Minimizing Adverse Effects:**

   a. **Genetic Risk Factors:**

      i. Identifying genetic variants that predispose patients to immune-related adverse events (irAEs).

      ii. **Example:** HLA genotypes associated with higher risk of autoimmune reactions in patients receiving checkpoint inhibitors.

3. **Optimizing Dosage and Treatment Schedules:**

   a. **Pharmacokinetic and Pharmacodynamic Genes:**

      i. Studying genes that affect drug metabolism and action to personalize dosing regimens.

      ii. **Example:** Variants in FcγR genes can influence the efficacy and safety of monoclonal antibody therapies.

4. **Enhancing Drug Development:**

   a. **Target Identification:**

      i. Using genomic data to identify new targets for immunotherapy.

      ii. **Example**: Identifying novel tumor antigens or immune checkpoints through cancer genomics.

Examples of Pharmacogenomic Applications in Immunotherapy

1. **PD-1/PD-L1 Inhibitors:**

   a. **Genomic Markers:**

i. High PD-L1 expression, high TMB, and MSI-high status are associated with better responses to PD-1/PD-L1 inhibitors.

ii. **Example**: Pembrolizumab is approved for tumors with high TMB regardless of cancer type.

2. **CAR-T Cell Therapy:**

a. **Genetic Profiling:**

i. Genetic profiling of tumors to identify antigens that can be targeted by CAR-T cells.

ii. **Example**: CD19 is a common target for CAR-T therapies in B-cell malignancies.

3. **Monoclonal Antibodies:**

a. **Pharmacogenetic Variants:**

i. FcγR polymorphisms can affect the binding affinity of monoclonal antibodies, influencing their therapeutic efficacy.

ii. **Example**: FcγRIIIa V158F polymorphism affects response to rituximab in non-Hodgkin lymphoma.

Challenges and Future Directions

1. **Complexity of Immune Response:**

a. The immune response to cancer is highly complex and influenced by multiple genetic and environmental factors, making it challenging to predict outcomes accurately.

2. **Inter-individual Variability:**

a. Significant variability in immune system function between individuals necessitates comprehensive genetic profiling to personalize immunotherapy effectively.

3. **Integration into Clinical Practice:**

a. Integrating pharmacogenomic testing into routine clinical practice requires significant investment in infrastructure, education for healthcare providers, and development of clinical guidelines.

4. Ethical and Privacy Concerns:

a. Genetic testing raises concerns about patient privacy and the potential for genetic discrimination, necessitating robust ethical frameworks and regulations.

Future Directions

1. Comprehensive Multi-Omics Approaches:

a. Combining genomics with proteomics, metabolomics, and other omics data to gain a holistic understanding of the immune response and optimize immunotherapy.

2. Advanced Genomic Technologies:

a. Leveraging technologies such as next-generation sequencing (NGS) and CRISPR to identify new genetic markers and therapeutic targets.

3. Personalized Vaccine Development:

a. Developing personalized cancer vaccines based on the patient's unique tumor genomics and immune profile.

4. AI and Machine Learning:

a. Utilizing artificial intelligence and machine learning to analyze large-scale genomic data and predict patient responses to immunotherapies more accurately.

TYPES OF IMMUNOTHERAPEUTIC

Immunotherapeutics are a class of treatments that utilize the body's immune system to fight diseases, particularly cancers. Pharmacogenomics, the study of how genes influence drug response, plays a critical role in understanding and optimizing these therapies for individual patients. Below are the key types of immunotherapeutics and their roles in pharmacogenomics.

1. Checkpoint Inhibitors

Mechanism of Action

Checkpoint inhibitors block proteins that act as brakes on the immune system, such as PD-1/PD-L1 and CTLA-4. By inhibiting these checkpoints, the immune system can more effectively attack cancer cells.

Examples

1. **Pembrolizumab (Keytruda):** Targets PD-1.
2. **Nivolumab (Opdivo):** Targets PD-1.
3. **Ipilimumab (Yervoy):** Targets CTLA-4.

Pharmacogenomics Applications

1. **Biomarker Identification**: Genetic markers like high PD-L1 expression, high tumor mutational burden (TMB), and microsatellite instability (MSI) are associated with better responses to checkpoint inhibitors.
   a. **Example**: Pembrolizumab is effective in tumors with high TMB, which can be determined through genomic testing.
2. **Adverse Effect Prediction**: Variants in genes such as HLA can indicate a higher risk of immune-related adverse events (irAEs).

2. CAR-T Cell Therapy

Mechanism of Action

CAR-T cell therapy involves modifying a patient's T cells to express chimeric antigen receptors (CARs) that specifically target cancer cells.

Examples

1. **Tisagenlecleucel (Kymriah):** Targets CD19 in B-cell malignancies.
2. **Axicabtagene ciloleucel (Yescarta):** Targets CD19 in B-cell lymphomas.

Pharmacogenomics Applications

1. **Target Identification**: Genetic profiling of tumors to identify specific antigens that can be targeted by CAR-T cells.
   a. **Example:** CD19 is a common target for B-cell malignancies.

2. **Efficacy Prediction**: Genomic analysis can help predict which patients are more likely to respond to CAR-T cell therapy.

3. Cancer Vaccines

Mechanism of Action

Cancer vaccines aim to stimulate the immune system to recognize and attack cancer cells by presenting tumor-specific antigens.

Examples

1. **Sipuleucel-T (Provenge):** Approved for prostate cancer, it targets prostatic acid phosphatase (PAP).

Pharmacogenomics Applications

1. **Personalized Vaccines**: Developing vaccines based on the unique mutational profile of an individual's tumor.

    a. **Example:** Neoantigen vaccines are tailored to the specific mutations found in a patient's tumor.

4. Monoclonal Antibodies

Mechanism of Action

Monoclonal antibodies are designed to bind to specific antigens on cancer cells, marking them for destruction by the immune system or blocking signaling pathways essential for tumor growth.

Examples

1. **Trastuzumab (Herceptin)**: Targets HER2 in breast cancer.
2. **Rituximab (Rituxan)**: Targets CD20 in B-cell non-Hodgkin lymphoma.

Pharmacogenomics Applications

1. **Efficacy Optimization**: Genetic variants in Fcγ receptors (FcγR) can affect the binding affinity and therapeutic efficacy of monoclonal antibodies.

    a. **Example**: FcγRIIIa V158F polymorphism influences response to rituximab.

2. **Resistance Mechanisms**: Genomic analysis can identify mutations that confer resistance to monoclonal antibodies, guiding alternative treatment strategies.

5. Cytokines

Mechanism of Action

Cytokines are signaling proteins that modulate the immune response. Therapeutic cytokines enhance the immune system's ability to fight cancer.

Examples

1. **Interferon-alpha (IFN-α):** Used in certain types of cancer and viral infections.

2. **Interleukin-2 (IL-2):** Promotes the proliferation of T cells and is used in metastatic melanoma and renal cell carcinoma.

Pharmacogenomics Applications

1. **Predicting Response**: Genetic variations in cytokine receptors and downstream signaling pathways can influence patient responses to cytokine therapy.

    a. **Example:** Polymorphisms in IL2RA may affect response to IL-2 therapy.

6. Adoptive Cell Transfer (ACT)

Mechanism of Action

ACT involves transferring immune cells (e.g., T cells) into a patient after enhancing their cancer-fighting abilities in the laboratory.

Examples

1. **Tumor-Infiltrating Lymphocytes (TILs):** T cells extracted from a tumor, expanded, and reintroduced into the patient.

2. **Engineered T Cell Receptors (TCRs):** T cells modified to express specific TCRs that target cancer antigens.

Pharmacogenomics Applications

1. **Patient Selection**: Genomic profiling helps identify patients who are likely to benefit from ACT.

    a. **Example:** Patients with tumors expressing specific neoantigens may be ideal candidates for TCR-based therapies.

2. **Monitoring and Adaptation**: Genetic monitoring of infused cells to assess persistence, proliferation, and potential for immune escape.

Challenges and Future Directions

1. **Complexity of Immune Response:**

    a. The immune system's complexity and its interaction with cancer and other diseases present challenges in predicting and optimizing responses to immunotherapies.

2. **Inter-individual Variability:**

    a. Genetic diversity among individuals requires personalized approaches to accurately predict and enhance treatment outcomes.

3. **Integration into Clinical Practice:**

    a. Implementing pharmacogenomic testing in routine clinical practice requires infrastructure, education, and guidelines.

4. **Ethical and Privacy Concerns:**

    a. Genetic testing involves ethical considerations regarding privacy and potential discrimination, necessitating robust ethical frameworks and policies.

HUMANISATION ANTIBODY THERAPY

Introduction

Humanization of antibody therapy is a technique used to modify monoclonal antibodies derived from non-human species, such as mice, to make them more similar to human antibodies. This reduces the immune response against the therapeutic antibody when administered to humans, enhancing its efficacy and safety. Pharmacogenomics, the study of how genetic differences influence individual responses to drugs, plays a crucial role in optimizing humanized antibody therapies for personalized medicine.

Monoclonal Antibodies and Their Humanization

Monoclonal Antibodies (mAbs)

Monoclonal antibodies are antibodies produced by identical immune cells that are clones of a unique parent cell. They have high specificity for a particular antigen and are used in the treatment of various diseases, including cancers, autoimmune disorders, and infectious diseases.

Humanization Techniques

Humanization involves modifying non-human antibodies to reduce their immunogenicity while retaining their antigen-binding specificity. Techniques include:

1. **Chimeric Antibodies:**
   a. Combining murine variable regions with human constant regions.
   b. **Example:** Rituximab (Rituxan) is a chimeric antibody targeting CD20.

2. **Humanized Antibodies:**
   a. Grafting murine complementarity-determining regions (CDRs) into human antibody frameworks.
   b. **Example**: Trastuzumab (Herceptin) targets HER2 and is used in breast cancer treatment.

3. **Fully Human Antibodies:**
   a. Generated using transgenic mice with human immunoglobulin genes or phage display libraries.
   b. **Example:** Adalimumab (Humira) targets TNF-alpha and is used in autoimmune diseases.

Role of Pharmacogenomics in Humanized Antibody Therapy

Pharmacogenomics enhances the development and application of humanized antibody therapies by identifying genetic factors that influence drug response and optimizing treatment strategies for individual patients.

Predicting Therapeutic Efficacy

1. **Fcγ Receptor Polymorphisms:**
    a. Genetic variations in Fcγ receptors (FcγRs) affect the binding of antibodies and influence their therapeutic efficacy.
    b. **Example:** FcγRIIIa V158F polymorphism affects the clinical response to rituximab in non-Hodgkin lymphoma.

2. **Tumor Antigen Expression:**
    a. Genetic profiling of tumors to assess the expression of target antigens can predict response to antibody therapy.
    b. **Example:** HER2 amplification in breast cancer predicts a positive response to trastuzumab.

Minimizing Adverse Effects

1. **Immunogenicity:**
    a. Identifying genetic markers associated with immune responses to humanized antibodies helps in predicting and managing adverse effects.
    b. **Example**: Anti-drug antibodies (ADAs) can reduce the efficacy of biologics like infliximab and adalimumab.

2. **Pharmacokinetic Variants:**
    a. Genetic variants in drug metabolism and clearance pathways can affect antibody levels and toxicity.
    b. **Example**: Polymorphisms in the FCGR2A gene can influence the clearance of therapeutic antibodies.

Optimizing Dosage and Treatment Regimens

1. **Pharmacodynamic Markers:**

a. Genetic factors influencing the pharmacodynamics of antibodies can guide dosing strategies to maximize efficacy and minimize toxicity.

b. **Example**: Genetic variants affecting immune checkpoint pathways can inform the use of PD-1/PD-L1 inhibitors.

2. Personalized Dosing:

a. Pharmacogenomic profiling enables personalized dosing regimens based on an individual's genetic makeup, improving therapeutic outcomes.

b. **Example:** Adjusting doses of anti-TNF therapies based on genetic markers associated with drug metabolism.

Clinical Applications of Humanized Antibody Therapy

Cancer Treatment

1. Trastuzumab (Herceptin):

a. Targets HER2-positive breast cancer.

b. **Pharmacogenomics**: HER2 gene amplification and overexpression are predictors of response.

2. Rituximab (Rituxan):

a. Targets CD20 in B-cell non-Hodgkin lymphoma.

b. **Pharmacogenomics:** FcγR polymorphisms influence response and outcomes.

3. Pembrolizumab (Keytruda):

a. Targets PD-1 in various cancers.

b. **Pharmacogenomics**: High TMB and MSI status are associated with better responses.

Autoimmune Diseases

1. Adalimumab (Humira):

a. Targets TNF-alpha in rheumatoid arthritis, Crohn's disease, and psoriasis.

b. **Pharmacogenomics**: HLA variants can predict response and risk of adverse effects.

2. Infliximab (Remicade):

a. Targets TNF-alpha in autoimmune diseases.

b. **Pharmacogenomics**: Genetic markers can influence the development of ADAs and therapeutic efficacy.

Future Directions and Challenges

Advanced Genomic Technologies

1. Next-Generation Sequencing (NGS):

a. Comprehensive genomic profiling to identify new biomarkers for predicting responses to antibody therapies.

b. **Example:** Using NGS to discover novel genetic variants associated with treatment outcomes.

2. CRISPR/Cas9:

a. Gene editing to validate the functional impact of genetic variants on antibody therapy response.

b. **Example:** Using CRISPR to study the effects of specific polymorphisms on FcγR function.

Integrating Multi-Omics Data

1. Proteomics and Metabolomics:

a. Combining genomic data with proteomic and metabolomic profiles to gain a holistic understanding of drug response.

b. **Example**: Integrating data to identify biomarkers for personalized immunotherapy.

2. Systems Biology:

a. Applying systems biology approaches to model complex interactions between genetic, proteomic, and metabolic factors influencing antibody therapy.

b. **Example**: Using computational models to predict patient-specific responses.

Ethical and Privacy Considerations

1. **Genetic Privacy:**

    a. Ensuring the confidentiality and security of genetic data used for pharmacogenomic testing.

    b. **Example:** Implementing robust data protection measures in clinical practice.

2. **Equitable Access:**

    a. Addressing disparities in access to pharmacogenomic testing and personalized therapies.

    b. **Example:** Developing policies to ensure equitable access across different populations.

IMMUNOTHERAPEUTIC IN CLINICAL PRACTICE

Immunotherapy has emerged as a groundbreaking approach in the treatment of various diseases, including cancer, autoimmune disorders, and infectious diseases. It harnesses the body's immune system to target and destroy diseased cells while sparing healthy tissues. Pharmacogenomics, the study of how genetic variations affect drug responses, plays a crucial role in optimizing the efficacy and safety of immunotherapies in clinical practice. Here's an in-depth look at how immunotherapy is integrated with pharmacogenomics:

1. Checkpoint Inhibitors

Introduction

Checkpoint inhibitors have revolutionized cancer treatment by unleashing the body's immune system to target and destroy cancer cells. Pharmacogenomics, the study of how genetic variations affect drug responses, plays a crucial role in guiding the use of checkpoint inhibitors in clinical practice. Here's a detailed exploration of how pharmacogenomics informs the use of checkpoint inhibitors:

Mechanism of Action

PD-1/PD-L1 Pathway

1. Programmed cell death protein 1 (PD-1) is a checkpoint receptor expressed on T cells.

2. Programmed death-ligand 1 (PD-L1) is expressed on tumor cells, suppressing T cell activity.

3. Checkpoint inhibitors block PD-1 or PD-L1, restoring T cell function and enhancing anti-tumor immunity.

Pharmacogenomic Considerations

Biomarker Identification

1. **Tumor Mutational Burden (TMB):** High TMB is associated with increased neoantigen formation and improved response to checkpoint inhibitors.

2. **Microsatellite Instability (MSI):** MSI-high tumors exhibit defective DNA repair mechanisms and are more responsive to checkpoint blockade.

HLA Genotypes

1. **Human Leukocyte Antigen (HLA) Polymorphisms**: Variations in HLA genes influence immune recognition of tumor antigens and response to checkpoint inhibitors.

2. **Example: HLA-B*57**:01 allele is associated with a higher risk of cutaneous adverse reactions to pembrolizumab.

PD-L1 Expression

1. **Tumor PD-L1 Expression**: High levels of PD-L1 expression on tumor cells correlate with improved response to PD-1/PD-L1 inhibitors.

2. Pharmacogenomic testing helps stratify patients based on PD-L1 status to guide treatment decisions.

Clinical Applications

Patient Selection

1. Pharmacogenomic testing helps identify patients most likely to benefit from checkpoint inhibitors.
2. **Example**: Patients with high TMB or MSI-high tumors are prioritized for PD-1/PD-L1 inhibitor therapy.

Predicting Treatment Response

1. Genetic markers such as TMB and PD-L1 expression levels predict response to checkpoint inhibitors.
2. Pharmacogenomic testing guides personalized treatment strategies to maximize efficacy.

Minimizing Adverse Events

1. Pharmacogenomics identifies genetic factors associated with immune-related adverse events (irAEs) and helps manage treatment toxicity.
2. **Example:** Genetic variants in HLA genes inform the risk of developing irAEs.

Challenges and Future Directions

Data Integration

1. Integrating pharmacogenomic data with other omics information (e.g., proteomics, metabolomics) to enhance predictive models and treatment outcomes.

Novel Biomarkers

1. Discovering new genetic biomarkers to improve patient stratification and response prediction beyond TMB and PD-L1 expression.

Real-time Monitoring

1. Developing methods for real-time monitoring of pharmacogenomic markers during treatment to guide therapy adjustments and minimize toxicity.

2. CAR-T Cell Therapy

Introduction

CAR-T cell therapy represents a revolutionary approach to cancer treatment, offering personalized and targeted therapy by harnessing the patient's own immune cells to fight cancer. Pharmacogenomics, the study of how genetic variations influence drug responses, plays a crucial role in optimizing the efficacy and safety of CAR-T cell therapy in clinical practice. Here's an in-depth exploration of how pharmacogenomics informs the use of CAR-T cell therapy:

Mechanism of Action

CAR-T Cell Engineering

1. Chimeric Antigen Receptor (CAR) T cells are engineered to express synthetic receptors that recognize specific tumor antigens.
2. Upon recognition of the target antigen, CAR-T cells become activated, leading to the destruction of tumor cells.

Pharmacogenomic Considerations

Antigen Selection

1. **Tumor Antigen Expression**: Genetic profiling helps identify tumor-specific antigens for CAR-T cell targeting.
2. Pharmacogenomic testing guides the selection of antigens that are highly expressed in the patient's tumor.

Host Immune Response

1. **Genetic Variations in Immune Genes**: Polymorphisms in genes involved in immune activation or regulation may influence CAR-T cell persistence and efficacy.
2. **Example**: Variants in cytokine receptor genes may impact cytokine release syndrome (CRS) severity.

Immunogenicity and Toxicity

1. **HLA Genotypes**: Variations in human leukocyte antigen (HLA) genes affect the presentation of antigens and the risk of adverse events.

2. Pharmacogenomic testing helps predict the likelihood of immune-related adverse events (irAEs) and inform risk mitigation strategies.

Clinical Applications

Patient Selection

1. Pharmacogenomic profiling guides patient selection by identifying individuals most likely to respond to CAR-T cell therapy.
2. Example: Patients with tumors expressing high levels of the target antigen are more likely to benefit.

Treatment Response Prediction

1. Genetic markers such as HLA genotypes and immune gene polymorphisms predict response to CAR-T cell therapy.
2. Pharmacogenomic testing helps tailor treatment strategies to maximize efficacy and minimize toxicity.

Adverse Event Management

1. Pharmacogenomics informs the management of immune-related adverse events (irAEs) by identifying genetic factors associated with treatment toxicity.
2. Example: HLA typing helps predict the risk of CRS and neurotoxicity.

Challenges and Future Directions

Off-Target Effects

1. Developing strategies to minimize off-target effects and improve the specificity of CAR-T cell therapy.
2. Pharmacogenomic approaches may identify genetic variants associated with off-target toxicity.

Resistance Mechanisms

1. Understanding the mechanisms of resistance to CAR-T cell therapy and developing strategies to overcome resistance.
2. Pharmacogenomic studies may reveal genetic factors contributing to resistance and guide the development of combination therapies.

Long-Term Monitoring

1. Establishing protocols for long-term monitoring of pharmacogenomic markers to assess treatment durability and inform retreatment decisions.

2. Pharmacogenomic testing may help identify markers of relapse or resistance during follow-up.

3. Monoclonal Antibodies

Introduction

Monoclonal antibodies (mAbs) have revolutionized the treatment of various diseases, including cancer, autoimmune disorders, and infectious diseases. Pharmacogenomics, the study of how genetic variations influence drug responses, plays a crucial role in optimizing the efficacy and safety of monoclonal antibody therapy in clinical practice. Here's a comprehensive exploration of how pharmacogenomics informs the use of monoclonal antibodies in immunotherapy:

Mechanism of Action

Monoclonal Antibodies

1. Monoclonal antibodies are engineered to target specific antigens on cancer cells, immune cells, or pathogens.

2. They can induce direct cytotoxic effects, block signaling pathways, or trigger immune-mediated destruction of target cells.

Pharmacogenomic Considerations

Fcγ Receptor Polymorphisms

1. **Fcγ Receptors (FcγRs):** Variations in FcγR genes influence the binding affinity of monoclonal antibodies to immune cells.

2. Pharmacogenomic testing helps predict the efficacy and safety of antibody-dependent cellular cytotoxicity (ADCC) and other immune-mediated mechanisms.

3. **Example**: FcγRIIIa V158F polymorphism affects the clinical response to rituximab in non-Hodgkin lymphoma.

HLA Genotypes

1. **Human Leukocyte Antigen (HLA) Genes**: Variations in HLA genes impact immune recognition of therapeutic antibodies and the risk of immune-related adverse events (irAEs).

2. Pharmacogenomic testing guides patient selection and risk stratification for monoclonal antibody therapy.

3. **Example**: HLA-B*57:01 allele is associated with a higher risk of cutaneous adverse reactions to pembrolizumab.

ADAs and Immunogenicity

1. **Anti-Drug Antibodies (ADAs):** Genetic factors influence the development of ADAs, which can reduce the efficacy and increase the risk of adverse events.

2. Pharmacogenomic testing helps identify patients at risk of developing ADAs and informs treatment strategies to mitigate immunogenicity.

3. **Example:** Genetic variants associated with immune response pathways may predispose individuals to ADA formation.

Clinical Applications

Patient Selection

1. Pharmacogenomic profiling guides patient selection by identifying individuals most likely to respond to monoclonal antibody therapy.

2. **Example:** HLA typing helps predict the risk of immune-related adverse events and informs treatment decisions.

Predicting Treatment Response

1. Genetic markers such as FcγR polymorphisms and HLA genotypes predict response to monoclonal antibody therapy.

2. **Pharmacogenomic** testing helps tailor treatment strategies to maximize efficacy and minimize toxicity.

Adverse Event Management

1. Pharmacogenomics informs the management of immune-related adverse events (irAEs) by identifying genetic factors associated with treatment toxicity.

2. **Example**: HLA typing helps predict the risk of infusion reactions, cytokine release syndrome (CRS), and other irAEs.

Challenges and Future Directions

Biomarker Discovery

1. Identifying novel genetic biomarkers associated with response to monoclonal antibody therapy and treatment-related adverse events.

2. Pharmacogenomic studies may reveal new targets for personalized immunotherapy.

Real-Time Monitoring

1. Developing methods for real-time monitoring of pharmacogenomic markers during treatment to guide therapy adjustments and minimize toxicity.

2. Pharmacogenomic testing may help identify markers of treatment response or resistance early in the course of therapy.

Combination Therapies

1. Investigating the synergistic effects of combining monoclonal antibody therapy with other targeted agents or immunotherapies.

2. Pharmacogenomics may guide the selection of optimal combination therapies based on individual genetic profiles.

4. Cancer Vaccines

Introduction

Cancer vaccines represent an innovative approach to cancer treatment by stimulating the immune system to recognize and attack tumor cells. Pharmacogenomics, the study of how genetic variations influence drug responses, plays a critical role in optimizing the efficacy and safety of cancer vaccines in clinical practice. Here's an in-depth exploration of how pharmacogenomics informs the use of cancer vaccines in immunotherapy:

Mechanism of Action

Cancer Vaccines

1. Cancer vaccines aim to induce specific immune responses against tumor-associated antigens (TAAs) or neoantigens present on cancer cells.
2. They activate antigen-presenting cells (APCs) to prime cytotoxic T cells and memory T cells, resulting in tumor cell destruction.

Pharmacogenomic Considerations

Neoantigen Prediction

1. **Genomic Profiling**: Identifying tumor-specific neoantigens through genomic sequencing helps personalize cancer vaccine development.
2. Pharmacogenomic testing guides the selection of neoantigens that are highly immunogenic and specific to the patient's tumor.
3. **Example**: Next-generation sequencing (NGS) identifies somatic mutations and neoantigens for personalized vaccine design.

HLA Typing

1. **Human Leukocyte Antigen (HLA) Genes**: Variations in HLA genes influence immune recognition of vaccine antigens and the efficacy of antigen presentation.
2. Pharmacogenomic testing helps identify HLA alleles associated with enhanced immune responses to vaccine antigens.
3. **Example**: HLA typing informs the selection of vaccine peptides that match the patient's HLA genotype for optimal T cell recognition.

Immune Response Modulation

1. **Immune Gene Polymorphisms**: Genetic variants in immune-related genes may affect the magnitude and quality of immune responses to cancer vaccines.

2. Pharmacogenomic testing helps predict individual responses to vaccination and tailor adjuvant therapies to enhance vaccine efficacy.

3. **Example:** Variants in cytokine genes influence cytokine production and immune cell activation in response to vaccination.

Clinical Applications

Patient Selection

1. Pharmacogenomic profiling guides patient selection by identifying individuals most likely to benefit from cancer vaccines.

2. **Example**: HLA typing helps match vaccine antigens to the patient's HLA genotype for optimal immune recognition.

Predicting Treatment Response

1. Genetic markers such as HLA genotypes and immune gene polymorphisms predict immune responses to cancer vaccines.

2. Pharmacogenomic testing helps personalize vaccine regimens and monitor treatment efficacy over time.

Adverse Event Management

1. Pharmacogenomics informs the management of vaccine-related adverse events by identifying genetic factors associated with treatment toxicity.

2. **Example:** Genetic variants in immune-related genes may predispose individuals to vaccine-induced inflammation or autoimmune reactions.

Challenges and Future Directions

Biomarker Discovery

1. Identifying novel genetic biomarkers associated with vaccine responsiveness and treatment outcomes.

2. Pharmacogenomic studies may reveal new targets for personalized vaccine development and combination therapies.

Vaccine Delivery and Formulation

1. Optimizing vaccine delivery methods and formulations to enhance immune responses and overcome immune tolerance mechanisms.

2. Pharmacogenomics may guide the selection of adjuvants and vaccine platforms based on individual genetic profiles.

Immune Monitoring

1. Developing assays for monitoring immune responses to cancer vaccines and predicting treatment responses.

2. Pharmacogenomic testing may help identify genetic markers of vaccine-induced immunity and correlate them with clinical outcomes.

Clinical Applications

Clinical applications of pharmacogenomics in immunotherapy encompass a broad range of areas, from patient selection and treatment response prediction to adverse event management and personalized dosing strategies. Let's delve into each of these aspects in detail:

1. Patient Selection

Pharmacogenomic testing assists clinicians in identifying patients who are most likely to benefit from immunotherapy based on their genetic makeup. This includes:

a. **Biomarker Identification**: Genetic markers associated with treatment response or resistance help stratify patients into responder and non-responder groups.

b. **HLA Typing**: Determining the patient's HLA genotype aids in predicting immune responses to therapeutic agents, such as checkpoint inhibitors and cancer vaccines.

c. **Tumor Profiling**: Genomic analysis of tumor tissue helps identify specific mutations or biomarkers that may predict responsiveness to immunotherapy.

2. Treatment Response Prediction

Pharmacogenomics enables the prediction of individual responses to immunotherapy, allowing for tailored treatment strategies:

a. **Predictive Biomarkers**: Genetic variants associated with treatment response, such as PD-L1 expression levels or TMB, help forecast the likelihood of a positive response.

b. **Host Immune Response**: Variations in immune-related genes influence the efficacy of immunotherapeutic agents by modulating immune cell function and cytokine production.

c. **Monitoring Markers**: Genetic markers can be used to monitor treatment efficacy over time and detect early signs of treatment resistance or relapse.

3. Adverse Event Management

Pharmacogenomic testing assists in identifying patients at increased risk of developing treatment-related adverse events, enabling proactive management strategies:

a. **HLA Genotyping**: HLA alleles associated with hypersensitivity reactions or immune-related adverse events help guide treatment decisions and risk mitigation strategies.

b. **Immune Gene Polymorphisms**: Variants in immune-related genes may predispose individuals to immune-mediated toxicities, such as cytokine release syndrome or infusion reactions.

c. **ADAs and Immunogenicity**: Genetic factors influencing the formation of anti-drug antibodies help predict the risk of immunogenicity and guide therapeutic interventions.

4. Personalized Dosing Strategies

Pharmacogenomic information informs personalized dosing regimens tailored to individual patient characteristics:

a. **Metabolic Variants**: Genetic variations in drug metabolism enzymes influence drug clearance and may require dose adjustments to optimize treatment outcomes.

b. **Drug Transporters**: Polymorphisms in drug transporter genes affect drug distribution and elimination, influencing drug exposure and response.

c. **Pharmacokinetic Markers**: Genetic markers associated with drug pharmacokinetics guide dose optimization and minimize the risk of under- or overexposure.

Challenges and Future Directions

a. **Data Integration**: Integrating pharmacogenomic data with clinical and molecular information to develop comprehensive treatment strategies.

b. **Real-time Monitoring**: Implementing methods for real-time monitoring of pharmacogenomic markers during treatment to guide therapy adjustments.

c. **Ethical and Regulatory Considerations**: Addressing ethical, legal, and social implications of pharmacogenomic testing, including patient consent, data privacy, and equitable access.

Challenges and Future Directions

The integration of pharmacogenomics into immunotherapeutic clinical practice presents several challenges and opportunities for future development. Let's delve into these aspects in detail:

Challenges:

1. **Data Integration and Interpretation:**

   a. *Complexity of Data:* Integrating genomic, transcriptomic, proteomic, and clinical data poses challenges due to the complexity and volume of information.

   b. *Interpretation:* Interpreting multi-omics data and identifying clinically actionable insights require advanced analytical tools and expertise.

2. **Biomarker Validation:**

a. *Clinical Utility:* Validating pharmacogenomic biomarkers for immunotherapy response prediction and adverse event management in large, diverse patient populations is essential for clinical implementation.

b. **Replication:** Ensuring reproducibility and consistency of pharmacogenomic findings across different studies and cohorts is crucial for reliable biomarker validation.

3. Real-Time Monitoring:

a. ***Dynamic Nature of Responses:*** Monitoring pharmacogenomic markers in real-time during treatment to guide therapy adjustments and predict treatment responses presents logistical and technical challenges.

b. *Clinical Implementation:* Developing point-of-care assays and technologies for rapid and cost-effective pharmacogenomic testing in clinical settings is essential for real-time monitoring.

4. Data Privacy and Security:

a. **Genetic Privacy:** Protecting patient genetic data and ensuring confidentiality and security against unauthorized access or misuse.

b. *Ethical Considerations:* Addressing ethical concerns related to genetic testing, including informed consent, data ownership, and potential discrimination.

5. Equitable Access and Implementation:

a. *Healthcare Disparities:* Ensuring equitable access to pharmacogenomic testing and personalized immunotherapy for all patients, irrespective of geographic location or socioeconomic status.

b. *Resource Allocation:* Addressing resource constraints and infrastructure limitations in healthcare systems to facilitate the widespread adoption of pharmacogenomics in clinical practice.

Future Directions:

1. **Advanced Genomic Technologies:**

    a. *Next-Generation Sequencing (NGS):* Advancing NGS technologies for comprehensive genomic profiling and identification of novel pharmacogenomic markers.

    b. *Single-Cell Genomics:* Harnessing single-cell sequencing techniques to characterize immune cell heterogeneity and identify rare cell populations involved in immunotherapy response.

2. **Machine Learning and AI:**

    a. *Predictive Modeling:* Developing machine learning algorithms and artificial intelligence (AI) approaches to predict treatment responses, identify treatment-resistant subtypes, and optimize personalized treatment strategies.

    b. *Data Integration:* Integrating multi-omics data using AI-driven approaches to identify complex interactions between genetic, molecular, and clinical factors influencing immunotherapy outcomes.

3. **Biobanking and Data Sharing:**

    a. *Large-Scale Biobanks:* Establishing large-scale biobanks with comprehensive clinical and genomic data to facilitate biomarker discovery, validation, and replication studies.

    b. *Data Sharing Initiatives:* Promoting data sharing and collaboration among researchers, institutions, and pharmaceutical companies to accelerate translational research and improve patient care.

4. **Clinical Trials Design:**

    a. *Biomarker-Driven Trials:* Designing biomarker-driven clinical trials to prospectively evaluate the clinical utility of pharmacogenomic markers in guiding immunotherapy treatment decisions.

b. ***Adaptive Trial Designs****:* Implementing adaptive trial designs that incorporate real-time pharmacogenomic data to optimize treatment regimens and patient outcomes.

5. Patient Education and Engagement:

a. ***Genomic Literacy****:* Educating patients and healthcare providers about the role of pharmacogenomics in immunotherapy, including its benefits, limitations, and ethical considerations.

b. ***Shared Decision-Making****:* Engaging patients in shared decision-making processes regarding pharmacogenomic testing, treatment options, and personalized care plans.

Multiple Choice Questions (MCQs)

1. What is the primary focus of pharmacogenomics?

   A) Analyzing environmental impacts on health

   B) Developing non-genetic therapies

   C) Understanding how genetic makeup affects drug response

   D) Studying non-human genetic systems

2. Which enzyme family is commonly studied in pharmacogenomics for its role in drug metabolism?

   A) Amylase

   B) Cytochrome P450

   C) Lactase

   D) Helicase

3. What type of genetic variations directly affect drug transport mechanisms?

   A) Drug metabolism enzymes

   B) Transporter proteins

   C) Cell membrane structures

   D) Hormone levels

4. Which technique is not used in pharmacogenomic research?

    A) Genotyping

    B) Sequencing

    C) Light microscopy

    D) Bioinformatics

5. What is a common application of pharmacogenomics?

    A) Enhancing cosmetic products

    B) Tailoring drug therapy to genetic profiles

    C) Developing agricultural pesticides

    D) Mapping geological data

6. Which of the following is not a challenge in pharmacogenomics?

    A) Complexity of genetic interactions

    B) High cost of computational resources

    C) Ethical and legal issues

    D) Clinical implementation

7. What future direction is pharmacogenomics likely to take?

    A) Decrease focus on technology

    B) Reduce genetic database sizes

    C) Integrate with other omics sciences

    D) Limit personalized medicine applications

8. What role do drug transporters like ABC and SLC families play in pharmacogenomics?

    A) Modifying drug synthesis pathways

    B) Affecting the absorption and elimination of drugs

    C) Influencing genetic transcription processes

    D) Directly altering protein binding sites

9. Which pharmacogenomics technology involves determining the entire DNA sequence?

    A) Genotyping

B) PCR amplification

C) Sequencing

D) Microarray analysis

10. Which application does not belong to the field of pharmacogenomics?

    A) Predicting disease susceptibility

    B) Personalizing drug dosages

    C) Designing fitness programs

    D) Identifying genetic factors in drug development

11. What is the primary benefit of personalized medicine in pharmacogenomics?

    A) Lowering the cost of healthcare significantly

    B) Maximizing drug efficacy and minimizing adverse effects

    C) Completely eliminating genetic diseases

    D) Enhancing pharmaceutical marketing strategies

12. What significant milestone helped advance the field of pharmacogenomics in 2003? A) Invention of the microscope

    B) Completion of the Human Genome Project

    C) Discovery of penicillin

    D) Introduction of the first antibiotic

13. Which factor complicates the clinical implementation of pharmacogenomics?

    A) Rapid results of genetic tests

    B) Simplified patient consent forms

    C) Education and infrastructure needs

    D) Decreased data analysis requirements

14. What does gene mapping help in pharmacogenomics?

    A) Determining the physical locations of genes on chromosomes

    B) Measuring the activity level of genes

    C) Identifying non-genetic factors in drug response

D) Directly creating new drug compounds

15. Which method is particularly effective for complex diseases in gene mapping?

A) Linkage analysis

B) Association studies

C) Electrophoresis

D) Cloning

16. How do gene cloning techniques benefit pharmacogenomics?

A) By eliminating all genetic diseases

B) By studying gene function and drug response

C) By increasing genetic diversity

D) By replacing all traditional treatment methods

17. What is not a focus area in pharmacogenomics?

A) Drug development

B) Environmental conservation

C) Personalized medicine

D) Disease susceptibility

18. Which is not a typical gene mapping technique?

A) Fine mapping

B) Association studies

C) Light spectroscopy

D) Linkage analysis

19. What does the future of pharmacogenomics likely involve?

A) Moving away from genetic studies

B) Decreasing reliance on technology

C) Increasing diversity and size of genetic databases

D) Reducing the use of bioinformatics tools

20. How does pharmacogenomics contribute to drug safety?

A) By predicting drug responses and avoiding adverse reactions

B) By lowering the cost of drug production

C) By speeding up drug approval processes

D) By reducing the need for clinical trials

Short Answer Type Questions

1. What is the basic definition of pharmacogenomics?

2. How did the completion of the Human Genome Project influence pharmacogenomics?

3. Name two enzymes that are significant in pharmacogenomic studies of drug metabolism.

4. What is the role of the VKORC1 gene in pharmacogenomics?

5. Describe one application of pharmacogenomics in clinical practice.

6. List two technologies used in pharmacogenomic research.

7. What are some challenges facing the implementation of pharmacogenomics in clinical settings?

8. How does pharmacogenomics contribute to personalized medicine?

9. Define gene mapping and its purpose in pharmacogenomics.

10. What is the difference between linkage analysis and association studies in gene mapping?

11. Describe the function of microsatellites in gene mapping.

12. Explain the principle behind PCR-based cloning.

13. How do cytochrome P450 enzymes affect drug metabolism?

14. What impact do genetic variations in drug transporters have on drug efficacy?

15. Give an example of a drug that requires dose adjustment based on genetic testing.

16. What are copy number variations and how do they impact health?

17. What role do epigenetic modifications play in pharmacogenomics?

18. How can genetic variations influence disease susceptibility?

19. Describe the process and purpose of pharmacogenomic testing panels in clinical practice.

20. What future directions is pharmacogenomics likely to take in integrating with other sciences?

Long Answer Type Questions

1. Discuss the historical context of pharmacogenomics and how genetic understanding has evolved to influence drug therapy.

2. Explain the significance of the cytochrome P450 enzyme family in the field of pharmacogenomics, particularly focusing on their role in drug metabolism.

3. Describe the impact of drug transporter proteins in pharmacogenomics, including examples of how genetic variations in these transporters can alter drug absorption and efficacy.

4. Outline the technologies and methods used in pharmacogenomic research, emphasizing genotyping and sequencing.

5. Discuss the challenges and limitations of pharmacogenomics, including ethical, legal, and clinical implementation issues.

6. Explain how pharmacogenomics can be used to tailor drug therapy to individual genetic profiles, including examples of drugs that are commonly adjusted based on genetic testing.

7. Discuss the role of gene mapping in identifying genes associated with disease susceptibility and drug response, including the methodologies involved.

8. Describe how gene cloning techniques are employed in pharmacogenomics to study gene function and drug response.

9. Explain the role of genetic variation in health and pharmacology, focusing on different types of genetic variations and their impacts on drug metabolism and disease progression.

10.Discuss the future directions of pharmacogenomics, including how it might integrate with other omics sciences and what this means for the advancement of personalized medicine.

Answer Key

1. (C) Understanding how genetic makeup affects drug response
2. (B) Cytochrome P450
3. (B) Transporter proteins
4. (C) Light microscopy
5. (B) Tailoring drug therapy to genetic profiles
6. (B) High cost of computational resources
7. (C) Integrate with other omics sciences
8. (B) Affecting the absorption and elimination of drugs
9. (C) Sequencing
10.(C) Designing fitness programs
11.(B) Maximizing drug efficacy and minimizing adverse effects
12.(B) Completion of the Human Genome Project
13.(C) Education and infrastructure needs
14.(A) Determining the physical locations of genes on chromosomes
15.(B) Association studies
16.(B) By studying gene function and drug response
17.(B) Environmental conservation
18.(C) Light spectroscopy
19.(C) Increasing diversity and size of genetic databases
20.(A) By predicting drug responses and avoiding adverse reactions

CHAPTER – 5

CELL CULTURE

INTRODUCTION:

Cell culture is a fundamental laboratory technique in biological research and biotechnology, involving the growth and maintenance of cells in a controlled, artificial environment. This method is pivotal for studying cellular mechanisms, drug development, cancer research, and the production of biological products such as vaccines and therapeutic proteins. Below is a detailed introduction to cell culture, covering its key aspects:

1. Basics of Cell Culture

Definition: Cell culture refers to the process of growing cells derived from multicellular organisms in vitro (outside their natural environment) in a controlled setting, typically within culture dishes or flasks containing a nutrient-rich medium.

Types of Cell Cultures:

a. **Primary Cell Culture**: Cells directly isolated from tissues and cultured. They closely mimic the in vivo state but have limited lifespan.

b. **Secondary Cell Culture (Subculturing):** Cells derived from primary cultures after multiple passages. They adapt to the culture conditions but may lose some in vivo characteristics.

c. **Cell Lines**: Cells that have undergone genetic modifications to proliferate indefinitely (immortalized), such as HeLa or CHO cells.

2. Equipment and Materials

Culture Vessels:

a. Petri dishes, T-flasks, multi-well plates, roller bottles.

Culture Medium:

a. **Basal Medium**: Provides essential nutrients, amino acids, vitamins, salts, glucose, and buffering agents (e.g., DMEM, RPMI-1640).

b. **Serum**: Often fetal bovine serum (FBS), providing growth factors, hormones, and additional nutrients.

c. **Serum-Free Media**: Used to minimize variability and specific applications.

Sterilization and Aseptic Techniques:

a. Use of laminar flow hoods, autoclaves, and proper handling to prevent contamination.

3. Cell Culture Techniques

Isolation of Cells:

a. Enzymatic digestion (e.g., trypsin) or mechanical methods to dissociate cells from tissues.

Seeding Cells:

a. Dispensing a specified number of cells into culture vessels with the appropriate medium.

Subculturing (Passaging):

a. Transferring cells to new vessels to prevent over-confluence and maintain growth.

Cryopreservation:

a. Freezing cells in a cryoprotectant (e.g., DMSO) for long-term storage and future use.

4. Cell Growth and Monitoring

Growth Phases:

a. **Lag Phase**: Adaptation period with little growth.

b. **Log (Exponential) Phase**: Rapid cell division and growth.

c. **Stationary Phase**: Growth rate slows due to nutrient depletion or waste accumulation.

d. **Death Phase**: Cell death exceeds cell division.

Monitoring:

  a. **Microscopy**: Regular observation to assess cell morphology and confluence.

  b. **Viability Assays**: Trypan blue exclusion, MTT assay to evaluate cell health.

  c. **Automated Cell Counters**: Devices for accurate cell counting.

5. Applications

Research:

  a. Understanding cellular mechanisms, gene expression, and protein function.

Drug Development:

  a. Screening potential pharmaceuticals for efficacy and toxicity.

Cancer Studies:

  a. Investigating tumor biology and testing anti-cancer agents.

Production of Biologics:

  a. Manufacturing vaccines, antibodies, and recombinant proteins.

Regenerative Medicine:

  a. Culturing stem cells for tissue engineering and regenerative therapies.

6. Challenges and Considerations

Contamination:

  a. Microbial (bacteria, fungi, mycoplasma) and cross-contamination between cell lines.

Genetic and Phenotypic Drift:

  a. Changes over prolonged culture can affect experimental outcomes.

Ethical Considerations:

  a. Use of animal-derived products and human tissues requires ethical approvals and considerations.

Conclusion

Cell culture is a versatile and powerful tool that has revolutionized biological sciences and biotechnology. Mastery of cell culture techniques enables researchers to explore complex biological processes, develop new therapies, and produce valuable biological products, all while providing a controlled environment that mimics the physiological conditions of living organisms.

CELL CULTURE TECHNIQUES

Cell culture techniques encompass a range of practices essential for the successful growth, maintenance, and manipulation of cells in vitro. These techniques ensure that cells are provided with the necessary environment to thrive and be used for various research and industrial applications. Here is a detailed overview of key cell culture techniques:

1. Cell Isolation and Preparation

Tissue Dissociation:

a. **Enzymatic Digestion**: Using enzymes like trypsin, collagenase, or dispase to break down the extracellular matrix and release cells from tissues.

b. **Mechanical Methods**: Cutting, mincing, or using a homogenizer to physically separate cells.

Cell Suspension Preparation:

a. **Filtration**: Passing the cell suspension through a filter to remove large debris and clumps.

b. **Centrifugation**: Spinning the cell suspension to pellet cells and remove supernatant containing unwanted materials.

2. Cell Seeding

Determining Cell Density:

a. **Cell Counting**: Using a hemocytometer or an automated cell counter to determine the concentration of cells.

b. **Dilution:** Adjusting the cell concentration to the desired seeding density.

Seeding Process:

   a. **Dispensing Cells**: Evenly distributing the cell suspension into culture vessels (e.g., petri dishes, T-flasks, multi-well plates).

   b. **Incubation**: Placing the culture vessels in an incubator with controlled temperature (usually 37°C), CO_2 (typically 5%), and humidity.

3. Media Preparation and Maintenance

Media Composition:

   a. **Basal Medium**: Provides essential nutrients and buffering agents.

   b. **Supplementation:** Adding fetal bovine serum (FBS), growth factors, hormones, antibiotics, and other supplements as required.

Media Change:

   a. **Frequency**: Regularly changing the medium to remove waste products and replenish nutrients.

   b. **Technique**: Carefully aspirating old media and adding fresh media without disturbing the cell monolayer or cell suspension.

4. Subculturing (Passaging) Cells

Passaging Protocol:

   a. **Trypsinization:** Adding trypsin or other dissociating agents to detach adherent cells from the culture surface.

   b. **Neutralization**: Using a medium containing serum or trypsin inhibitor to neutralize the trypsin.

   c. **Centrifugation**: Collecting cells by centrifugation, discarding the supernatant, and resuspending cells in fresh medium.

   d. **Reseeding:** Dispensing the cell suspension into new culture vessels at an appropriate density.

5. Cryopreservation and Thawing

Cryopreservation:

   a. **Freezing Medium**: Preparing a medium containing cryoprotectants like dimethyl sulfoxide (DMSO) to protect cells during freezing.

b. **Freezing Protocol:** Gradually cooling cells to -80°C using a controlled rate freezer or a step-wise freezing protocol before transferring to liquid nitrogen for long-term storage.

Thawing:

a. **Rapid Thawing**: Quickly thawing frozen cells in a 37°C water bath to minimize ice crystal formation.

b. **Recovery**: Gently transferring the thawed cells to a culture vessel with fresh medium and allowing them to recover in an incubator.

6. Contamination Control

Aseptic Techniques:

a. **Laminar Flow Hood**: Working within a sterile laminar flow hood to minimize exposure to contaminants.

b. **Sterile Equipment**: Using autoclaved or sterile disposable pipettes, culture vessels, and media.

c. **Good Laboratory Practices**: Regularly cleaning the work area with disinfectants, wearing gloves, and practicing good personal hygiene.

Contamination Monitoring:

a. **Regular Observation**: Frequently checking cultures under a microscope for signs of contamination (e.g., changes in pH, turbidity, or unexpected cell death).

b. **Testing:** Periodically testing for mycoplasma and other contaminants using specific assays.

7. Cell Viability and Growth Monitoring

Viability Assays:

a. **Trypan Blue Exclusion**: Staining cells with trypan blue and counting viable (unstained) and non-viable (stained) cells using a hemocytometer.

b. **MTT/XTT Assays**: Measuring metabolic activity as an indicator of cell viability.

Growth Monitoring:

a. **Microscopy**: Observing cell morphology, confluence, and health.

b. **Automated Systems**: Using automated cell culture monitoring systems to track cell growth and conditions.

8. Specialized Cell Culture Techniques

Co-culture:

a. **Multiple Cell Types**: Culturing different cell types together to study interactions (e.g., epithelial cells with fibroblasts).

3D Cell Culture:

a. **Spheroids and Organoids**: Culturing cells in three dimensions using scaffolds or specialized matrices to mimic in vivo conditions more closely.

Stem Cell Culture:

a. **Maintenance and Differentiation**: Special protocols for maintaining pluripotency or inducing differentiation in stem cells.

High-Throughput Screening:

a. **Automation**: Using robotic systems to handle large numbers of cultures for drug screening or genetic studies.

BASIC EQUIPMENT'S USED IN CELL CULTURE LAB

A cell culture lab is equipped with a variety of specialized equipment to create a controlled environment for growing and maintaining cells. Each piece of equipment plays a crucial role in ensuring the success and reproducibility of cell culture experiments. Here's a detailed overview of the basic equipment used in a cell culture lab:

1. Biological Safety Cabinet (Laminar Flow Hood)

a. **Purpose**: Provides a sterile working environment by filtering air through HEPA filters to protect both the cells and the user from contamination.

b. **Types**: Class I, II, and III, with Class II being the most commonly used in cell culture labs for providing both product and personnel protection.

2. Incubator

a. **Purpose**: Maintains the optimal temperature, humidity, and CO_2 levels required for cell growth.

b. **Types**:

    i. **CO_2 Incubators**: Regulate CO_2 levels (usually 5%) to maintain the pH of the culture medium.

    ii. Humidity-Controlled Incubators: Prevents evaporation of the culture medium.

3. Microscope

a. **Purpose:** Allows observation of cell morphology, confluence, and contamination.

b. **Types:**

    i. **Inverted Microscope**: Ideal for observing cells in culture dishes or flasks.

    ii. **Phase-Contrast Microscope**: Enhances contrast in unstained cells, useful for live cell observation.

4. Autoclave

a. **Purpose:** Sterilizes equipment, media, and solutions by using high-pressure saturated steam.

b. **Types:** Bench-top and vertical autoclaves, depending on the lab size and requirements.

5. Water Bath

a. **Purpose**: Provides a controlled temperature environment for thawing cells, heating media, or reagents.

b. **Types:** Standard and shaking water baths for varying applications.

6. Centrifuge

a. **Purpose:** Separates cells from the culture medium or other components by spinning at high speeds.

b. **Types:**

i. **Refrigerated Centrifuge**: Maintains samples at low temperatures during centrifugation.

ii. **Microcentrifuge**: For small volume samples.

7. Pipettes and Pipette Aids

a. **Purpose:** Accurate measurement and transfer of liquids.

b. **Types:**

    i. **Manual Pipettes**: Single and multi-channel for varying volumes.

    ii. **Electronic Pipettes**: Provide higher precision and ease of use.

    iii. **Pipette Aids**: Used with serological pipettes for larger volumes.

8. Cell Counters

a. **Purpose**: Determines cell concentration and viability.

b. **Types:**

    i. **Hemocytometer:** Manual counting using a specialized glass slide.

    ii. **Automated Cell Counters**: Provide rapid and accurate cell counts, often with viability assessment using dyes like trypan blue.

9. Refrigerators and Freezers

a. **Purpose**: Storage of reagents, media, and cells.

b. **Types:**

    i. **4°C Refrigerators**: For short-term storage of reagents and media.

    ii. **-20°C Freezers**: For longer-term storage of reagents and media.

    iii. **-80°C Ultra-Low Freezers**: For long-term storage of cell lines and sensitive reagents.

10. Cryostorage Systems

a. **Purpose**: Long-term storage of cells in liquid nitrogen.

b. **Types:**

    i. **Cryovials**: Small vials designed for freezing cells.

    ii. **Liquid Nitrogen Freezers**: Tanks or containers that store cryovials at very low temperatures.

11. pH Meter and Osmometer

a. **Purpose:**

    i.   **pH Meter**: Measures the acidity/alkalinity of the culture medium.

    ii.   **Osmometer**: Measures the osmolality of the culture medium to ensure it is within the optimal range for cell growth.

12. Water Purification System

a. **Purpose:** Provides ultra-pure water required for preparing media and reagents.

b. **Types**: Systems that use reverse osmosis, deionization, and filtration to purify water.

13. Sterile Disposable Supplies

a. **Purpose**: Ensure sterility and convenience.

b. **Types**: Culture dishes, flasks, multi-well plates, serological pipettes, pipette tips, and filter units.

14. Culture Vessels

a. **Purpose**: Contain and support the growth of cells.

b. **Types:**

    i.   **Petri Dishes**: For surface culture of adherent cells.

    ii.   **T-Flasks**: For larger scale adherent cell cultures.

    iii.   **Multi-Well Plates**: For high-throughput experiments.

    iv.   **Spinner Flasks and Bioreactors**: For suspension cell cultures and large-scale production.

15. Laboratory Consumables

a. **Purpose**: Various tasks and experiments.

b. **Types:** Sterile gloves, lab coats, sterile filters, and reagents like trypsin, EDTA, and media components.

CELL CULTURE MEDIA

Cell culture media provide the necessary nutrients, growth factors, and environmental conditions for cells to grow and proliferate in vitro. The choice of media depends on the specific requirements of the cell type being cultured.

Here is a detailed overview of the components, types, preparation, and usage of cell culture media:

1. Components of Cell Culture Media

Basic Components:

a. **Inorganic Salts**: Maintain osmotic balance and provide essential ions (e.g., Na^+, K^+, Mg^{2+}, Ca^{2+}, Cl^-).

b. **Buffering Agents**: Maintain pH stability (e.g., bicarbonate, HEPES).

c. **Amino Acids**: Essential for protein synthesis (e.g., L-glutamine, which is often added separately due to its instability).

d. **Vitamins**: Essential for various metabolic processes (e.g., B-vitamins, ascorbic acid).

e. **Glucose or Other Energy Sources**: Provide energy for cellular metabolism.

f. **Trace Elements**: Required in minute quantities for enzyme function (e.g., zinc, selenium).

Supplementary Components:

a. **Serum**: Provides growth factors, hormones, attachment factors, and additional nutrients. Fetal bovine serum (FBS) is the most commonly used, but alternatives like human serum or serum-free supplements are also used.

b. **Antibiotics and Antimycotics**: Prevent bacterial and fungal contamination (e.g., penicillin, streptomycin, amphotericin B). Use cautiously to avoid masking low-level contamination.

c. **Growth Factors and Hormones**: Added to serum-free media to support specific cell types (e.g., EGF, FGF, insulin).

2. Types of Cell Culture Media

Basal Media:

a. **DMEM (Dulbecco's Modified Eagle Medium):** High or low glucose formulations for various cell types.

b. **RPMI-1640 (Roswell Park Memorial Institute)**: Suitable for lymphocyte culture.

c. **MEM (Minimum Essential Medium):** Commonly used for adherent cells.

d. **Ham's F12 and DMEM/F12**: Often used for co-culture or mixed cell populations.

Serum-Free Media:

a. Designed to minimize variability and support specific cell lines without the use of animal serum. These media contain defined supplements to replace serum functions.

Specialized Media:

a. **Stem Cell Media**: Formulated to maintain pluripotency or induce differentiation (e.g., mTeSR for human embryonic stem cells).

b. **Primary Cell Media**: Tailored for cells directly isolated from tissues (e.g., keratinocyte serum-free medium for skin cells).

c. **Hybridoma Media**: Supports the growth and monoclonal antibody production of hybridoma cells.

3. Preparation and Storage of Media

Preparation:

a. **Reconstitution**: Powdered media need to be reconstituted with sterile water, followed by filtration to ensure sterility.

b. **Sterile Filtration**: Liquid media are often filter-sterilized using a 0.22-micron filter to remove contaminants.

c. **Additives:** Supplements like serum, antibiotics, and L-glutamine are added after filtration to avoid degradation during sterilization.

Storage:

a. **Liquid Media**: Typically stored at 2-8°C and protected from light to prevent degradation of light-sensitive components.

b. **Powdered Media**: Stored at room temperature or as specified by the manufacturer, in a dry, dark place.

4. pH and Osmolality

pH Maintenance:

a. The pH of culture media is usually maintained around 7.2-7.4.

b. **CO₂ Levels**: In CO_2 incubators, the bicarbonate buffer system requires 5% CO_2 to maintain pH.

c. **HEPES Buffer**: Often added for additional buffering capacity, especially in open systems.

Osmolality:

a. Ensures proper cellular hydration and function, typically around 280-320 mOsm/kg.

5. Media Change and Monitoring

Frequency of Media Change:

a. Regular media changes are crucial to replenish nutrients and remove waste products. Frequency depends on cell type and growth rate, usually every 2-3 days.

Monitoring:

a. **Color Indicators**: Phenol red is commonly used as a pH indicator; a yellow color indicates acidic conditions, while purple indicates alkaline conditions.

b. **Microscopy**: Regular microscopic examination to check for cell health and contamination.

6. Troubleshooting Common Media Issues

Contamination:

a. **Bacterial and Fungal Contamination**: Cloudiness, pH shifts, and altered cell morphology indicate contamination.

b. **Mycoplasma Contamination**: Often not visible, requires specific detection assays (e.g., PCR, DNA staining).

Nutrient Depletion:

a. Signs include slowed cell growth, changes in morphology, and reduced viability. Ensure regular media changes and proper storage of media components.

VARIOUS TYPES OF CELL CULTURE

Cell culture techniques can be categorized based on the type of cells being cultured, the conditions in which they are grown, and their applications. Understanding the various types of cell culture helps researchers choose the appropriate methods and conditions for their specific needs. Here's a detailed overview:

1. Primary Cell Culture

Definition:

a. Cells are directly isolated from tissues of an organism and cultured. These cells maintain many of the physiological characteristics of the tissue of origin.

Characteristics:

a. Limited lifespan (finite number of cell divisions).

b. Closely mimic the in vivo environment.

c. High variability between batches.

Applications:

a. Studying normal cell physiology and pathology.

b. Drug testing and toxicology studies.

c. Vaccine production.

2. Secondary Cell Culture (Subculture or Passage)

Definition:

a. Cells derived from primary cultures after they have been enzymatically or mechanically disaggregated and transferred to a new culture vessel to continue growth.

Characteristics:

    a. Can undergo multiple passages but eventually senesce.

    b. Often used to increase the cell population for experiments.

Applications:

    a. Expansion of cell numbers for further experimentation.

    b. Intermediate stage before establishing a cell line.

3. Cell Lines

Definition:

    a. Cells that have been adapted to in vitro conditions and can proliferate indefinitely due to genetic modifications or spontaneous mutations (immortalized).

Characteristics:

    a. Continuous growth and division.

    b. Easier to handle and more reproducible than primary cells.

    c. Can be maintained for extended periods.

Applications:

    a. Molecular biology studies.

    b. Drug screening and high-throughput assays.

    c. Genetic manipulation and functional studies.

Examples:

    a. HeLa (cervical cancer cells), CHO (Chinese Hamster Ovary cells), HEK 293 (Human Embryonic Kidney cells).

4. Adherent vs. Suspension Cultures

Adherent Cultures:

    a. Cells that require attachment to a solid surface to grow.

    b. Common for epithelial and fibroblast cells.

    c. Grown in culture flasks, petri dishes, or multi-well plates coated with attachment factors.

Suspension Cultures:

a. Cells that grow freely floating in the culture medium.

b. Common for hematopoietic and some cancer cell lines.

c. Grown in spinner flasks or bioreactors for large-scale production.

5. 3D Cell Culture

Definition:

a. Cells are grown in a three-dimensional environment, which more closely mimics the in vivo conditions compared to traditional 2D cultures.

Types:

a. **Spheroids**: Aggregates of cells that form a 3D structure naturally.

b. **Organoids**: Miniature, simplified versions of an organ produced from stem cells.

c. **Scaffold-based**: Cells grown on biocompatible scaffolds.

d. **Matrix-embedded**: Cells embedded within a hydrogel matrix (e.g., Matrigel).

Applications:

a. Cancer research and drug testing.

b. Tissue engineering and regenerative medicine.

c. Studying cell-cell and cell-matrix interactions.

6. Co-culture Systems

Definition:

a. Culturing two or more different cell types together to study their interactions.

Types:

a. **Direct Co-culture**: Different cell types are in direct contact.

b. **Indirect Co-culture**: Cells are separated by a permeable membrane, allowing exchange of soluble factors but preventing direct contact.

Applications:

a. Studying cell signaling and interaction.

b. Tissue engineering.

c. Disease modeling.

7. Stem Cell Culture

Types:

a. **Embryonic Stem Cells (ESCs):** Pluripotent cells derived from the inner cell mass of the blastocyst.

b. **Induced Pluripotent Stem Cells (iPSCs):** Somatic cells reprogrammed to a pluripotent state.

c. **Adult Stem Cells**: Multipotent cells found in specific tissues (e.g., hematopoietic stem cells).

Applications:

a. Regenerative medicine and tissue engineering.

b. Disease modeling and drug testing.

c. Studying differentiation and development.

8. Organotypic Culture

Definition:

a. Culturing whole tissues or organ explants to maintain the architecture and function of the original tissue.

Applications:

a. Studying tissue development and pathology.

b. Drug testing in a more physiologically relevant context.

c. Neuroscience research using brain slices.

9. Perfusion Culture

Definition:

a. Continuous or intermittent flow of fresh medium through the culture to provide nutrients and remove waste products.

Applications:

a. Large-scale production of cells or secreted products.

b. Maintaining long-term cultures with high viability.

10. High-Throughput Culture

Definition:

a. Automation and miniaturization of cell culture techniques to allow for the simultaneous processing of multiple samples.

Applications:

a. Drug discovery and screening.

b. Genetic and functional assays.

c. Large-scale studies on cell behavior and response.

GENERAL PROCEDURE FOR CELL CULTURES

The general procedure for cell culture involves a series of steps to ensure the successful growth and maintenance of cells in vitro. Here's a detailed guide covering the key stages of cell culture:

1. Preparation

1.1 Sterilization:

a. **Autoclave Equipment**: Sterilize all reusable equipment (e.g., glassware, instruments) using an autoclave.

b. **Disinfect Work Area**: Clean the biological safety cabinet with 70% ethanol or another appropriate disinfectant.

c. **Sterile Techniques**: Use sterile disposable pipettes, pipette tips, and culture vessels to avoid contamination.

1.2 Media Preparation:

a. **Prepare Culture Medium**: Reconstitute powdered media with sterile water if necessary, and add supplements (e.g., serum, antibiotics, L-glutamine).

b. **Sterile Filtration**: Filter the medium using a 0.22-micron filter to ensure sterility.

c. **Storage**: Store prepared media at 2-8°C and protect from light if necessary.

2. Cell Thawing and Initial Seeding

2.1 Thawing Cells:

a. **Warm Water Bath**: Quickly thaw frozen cells in a 37°C water bath until only a small ice crystal remains.

b. **Transfer to Culture Vessel**: Transfer the cell suspension to a culture vessel containing pre-warmed complete medium.

c. **Centrifugation (Optional):** Centrifuge cells at 200-300 x g for 5 minutes, discard the supernatant, and resuspend the cell pellet in fresh medium to remove DMSO (cryoprotectant).

2.2 Seeding Cells:

a. **Cell Density:** Count cells using a hemocytometer or automated cell counter to determine the cell density.

b. **Seeding:** Dispense the appropriate volume of cell suspension into culture vessels to achieve the desired cell density.

2.3 Incubation:

a. **Incubator Conditions**: Place culture vessels in an incubator set to 37°C, 5% CO_2, and appropriate humidity.

3. Routine Maintenance

3.1 Feeding Cells:

a. **Medium Change Frequency**: Change the culture medium every 2-3 days or as required based on cell growth and confluence.

b. **Technique**: Carefully aspirate the old medium and replace it with fresh, pre-warmed medium without disturbing the cells.

3.2 Monitoring:

a. **Microscopic Observation**: Regularly examine cells under a microscope to check for morphology, confluence, and contamination.

b. **pH and Contamination Indicators**: Check for color changes in the medium (e.g., phenol red turning yellow or purple) and any signs of contamination (e.g., cloudiness, unexpected cell behavior).

4. Subculturing (Passaging) Cells

4.1 Preparing for Subculture:

a. **Confluence:** Subculture cells when they reach approximately 70-90% confluence to prevent overgrowth and nutrient depletion.

b. **Preparation:** Pre-warm trypsin-EDTA solution and fresh culture medium.

4.2 Detaching Cells:

a. **Aspirate Medium**: Remove the old medium from the culture vessel.

b. **Add Trypsin-EDTA**: Add enough trypsin-EDTA to cover the cell layer and incubate at 37°C for 2-5 minutes or until cells detach.

c. **Observe Detachment:** Gently tap the vessel to help dislodge cells, and observe under a microscope to ensure cells are detached.

4.3 Neutralizing Trypsin:

a. **Add Medium**: Add an equal volume of medium containing serum to neutralize trypsin.

b. **Collect Cells**: Transfer the cell suspension to a centrifuge tube.

4.4 Centrifugation:

a. **Spin:** Centrifuge cells at 200-300 x g for 5 minutes.

b. **Resuspend:** Discard the supernatant and resuspend the cell pellet in fresh medium.

4.5 Reseeding:

a. **Count Cells**: Determine the cell density using a hemocytometer or automated cell counter.

b. **Dilute and Seed**: Dilute the cell suspension to the desired concentration and dispense into new culture vessels.

5. Cryopreservation

5.1 Preparing Cells:

a. **High Viability**: Ensure cells are in the log phase of growth and are healthy before freezing.

b. **Harvest Cells**: Detach and collect cells as described in the subculturing section.

5.2 Freezing Medium:

a. **Prepare Medium**: Use a freezing medium containing 10% DMSO and 90% FBS or complete medium.

5.3 Freezing Process:

a. **Aliquot Cells**: Resuspend cells in freezing medium and aliquot into cryovials.

b. **Controlled Rate Freezing**: Place cryovials in a controlled-rate freezing container (e.g., Mr. Frosty) and store at -80°C overnight before transferring to liquid nitrogen for long-term storage.

6. Quality Control and Troubleshooting

6.1 Contamination Checks:

a. **Regular Testing**: Test cultures periodically for mycoplasma and other contaminants using specific assays (e.g., PCR, ELISA).

6.2 Viability and Proliferation:

a. **Viability Assays**: Use trypan blue exclusion, MTT, or similar assays to assess cell health.

b. **Growth Curves**: Monitor cell growth rates to ensure consistency and optimal conditions.

ISOLATION OF CELLS

Isolation of cells for cell culture involves obtaining cells from tissues or organs and preparing them for growth under controlled in vitro conditions. The process can be quite complex and varies depending on the type of cells being isolated. Here is a detailed overview of the general procedures for isolating cells from tissues:

1. Preparation

1.1 Materials and Reagents:

a. **Enzymes:** Such as trypsin, collagenase, dispase, or hyaluronidase for tissue dissociation.

b. **Buffers:** Phosphate-buffered saline (PBS) or Hank's balanced salt solution (HBSS) for washing tissues.

c. **Culture Media:** Appropriate complete media for the specific cell type.

d. **Sterile Equipment**: Scalpels, forceps, scissors, Petri dishes, and cell strainers.

e. **Instruments**: Centrifuge, incubator, biological safety cabinet, and pipettes.

1.2 Sterilization and Setup:

a. **Sterilize Instruments**: Autoclave or sterilize all instruments and prepare a sterile work area.

b. **Prepare Reagents**: Pre-warm media and enzymatic solutions to 37°C.

2. Tissue Collection

2.1 Animal or Human Tissue:

a. **Source:** Obtain tissue samples from euthanized animals or human biopsy/surgical samples, ensuring ethical and legal compliance.

b. **Transport:** Keep tissue samples on ice in sterile containers filled with transport medium or PBS to maintain viability until processing.

3. Tissue Processing

3.1 Washing:

a. **Rinse Tissue**: Thoroughly rinse tissue samples with sterile PBS or HBSS to remove blood and debris.

3.2 Mince Tissue:

a. **Mechanical Disaggregation**: Use sterile scalpels or scissors to finely mince the tissue into small pieces ($1\text{-}2$ mm^3) in a sterile Petri dish.

4. Enzymatic Digestion

4.1 Selection of Enzyme:

a. **Collagenase**: Commonly used for many tissues (e.g., liver, pancreas).

b. **Trypsin**: Often used for epithelial tissues.

c. **Dispase or Hyaluronidase**: Used for specific tissues like skin or connective tissue.

4.2 Digestion Process:

a. **Incubation**: Transfer minced tissue to a sterile flask containing the enzyme solution and incubate at 37°C with gentle agitation (e.g., shaking water bath or orbital shaker).

b. **Duration**: Incubation time varies from 30 minutes to several hours, depending on the tissue type and enzyme used.

4.3 Termination:

a. **Stop Enzymatic Reaction**: Dilute or neutralize the enzyme by adding an excess of complete culture medium containing serum (which inhibits enzyme activity).

5. Cell Separation

5.1 Filtration:

a. **Strain Through Filter**: Pass the digested tissue suspension through a cell strainer (e.g., 70 μm or 100 μm) to remove undigested tissue fragments and obtain a single-cell suspension.

5.2 Centrifugation:

a. **Pellet Cells**: Centrifuge the cell suspension at 200-300 x g for 5-10 minutes to pellet the cells.

b. **Resuspend Pellet**: Discard the supernatant and gently resuspend the cell pellet in fresh complete medium.

6. Cell Counting and Viability

6.1 Cell Count:

a. **Hemocytometer:** Count cells using a hemocytometer and trypan blue exclusion to assess viability.

b. **Automated Cell Counter:** Use an automated cell counter for accurate and quick cell counting.

6.2 Viability Assessment:

a. **Trypan Blue**: Stain cells with trypan blue to distinguish live (unstained) from dead (blue-stained) cells.

7. Seeding and Culture Initiation

7.1 Seeding Density:

a. **Calculate Density**: Determine the appropriate seeding density based on the cell type and surface area of the culture vessel.

7.2 Plating Cells:

a. **Distribute Cells:** Evenly distribute the cell suspension into culture flasks, dishes, or multi-well plates containing pre-warmed complete medium.

7.3 Incubation:

a. **Culture Conditions**: Place the culture vessels in an incubator set to $37°C$ with 5% CO_2 and appropriate humidity.

8. Initial Culture Maintenance

8.1 Media Changes:

a. **First Change**: Perform the first medium change after 24 hours to remove non-adherent cells and debris.

b. **Regular Feeding**: Subsequently change the medium every 2-3 days or as required.

8.2 Monitoring:

a. **Microscopy**: Regularly observe cells under a microscope to monitor attachment, growth, morphology, and contamination.

9. Purification and Subculture

9.1 Purification:

a. **Selective Adherence**: Use selective adherence properties of different cell types to enrich the desired cell population.

b. **Density Gradient Centrifugation**: Use density gradients (e.g., Ficoll, Percoll) to separate cells based on their density.

9.2 Subculturing:

a. **Passaging**: When cells reach 70-90% confluence, subculture them by enzymatic detachment (e.g., trypsinization) and reseed into new culture vessels.

10. Cryopreservation (Optional)

10.1 Preparation for Freezing:

a. **Healthy Cells**: Ensure cells are healthy and in the log phase of growth.

b. **Freezing Medium**: Use a medium containing 10% DMSO and 90% FBS or complete medium.

10.2 Freezing Process:

a. **Aliquot Cells**: Resuspend cells in freezing medium and aliquot into cryovials.

b. **Controlled Rate Freezing**: Freeze cells slowly using a controlled-rate freezing container before transferring to liquid nitrogen for long-term storage.

SUBCULTURE

Subculturing, also known as passaging, is the process of transferring cells from a crowded culture environment to a new vessel to provide fresh nutrients and more space for continued growth. This is a routine procedure necessary for maintaining healthy, proliferating cell cultures. Here's a detailed guide on subculturing cells:

1. Preparation

1.1 Materials and Reagents:

a. **Culture Medium**: Pre-warmed complete medium appropriate for the cell type.

b. **Trypsin-EDTA**: Pre-warmed enzymatic solution for detaching adherent cells.

c. **Phosphate-Buffered Saline (PBS):** For washing cells.

d. **Sterile Equipment**: Pipettes, pipette tips, culture vessels (flasks, dishes, or multi-well plates).

1.2 Sterilization and Setup:

a. **Biological Safety Cabinet**: Ensure the work area is sterile by cleaning with 70% ethanol.

b. **Sterile Techniques**: Use sterile, disposable pipettes and pipette tips to avoid contamination.

2. Monitoring and Assessment

2.1 Check Confluence:

a. **Microscopic Observation**: Ensure cells are at 70-90% confluence. Over-confluent cultures may experience nutrient depletion and waste accumulation, affecting cell health.

2.2 Morphology Check:

a. **Health Assessment**: Look for healthy cell morphology and absence of contamination or cell debris.

3. Subculturing Procedure for Adherent Cells

3.1 Aspiration:

a. **Remove Medium**: Carefully aspirate the spent culture medium without disturbing the cell monolayer.

3.2 Washing:

a. **PBS Wash**: Gently add PBS to wash away residual medium and serum, which can inhibit trypsin activity. Aspirate the PBS completely.

3.3 Detachment:

a. **Add Trypsin-EDTA**: Add enough trypsin-EDTA to cover the cell monolayer.

b. **Incubate**: Place the culture vessel in the incubator (37°C) for 2-5 minutes, monitoring the cells under a microscope. Gently tap the vessel to help dislodge cells.

3.4 Neutralization:

a. **Add Medium**: Once cells are detached, add an equal volume of complete medium containing serum to neutralize the trypsin.

b. **Collect Cells**: Transfer the cell suspension to a sterile centrifuge tube.

3.5 Centrifugation:

a. **Spin**: Centrifuge at 200-300 x g for 5 minutes.

b. **Resuspend:** Discard the supernatant and gently resuspend the cell pellet in fresh, pre-warmed complete medium.

4. Subculturing Procedure for Suspension Cells

4.1 Collection:

a. **Resuspend Cells**: Gently pipette the culture medium to resuspend cells evenly.

4.2 Centrifugation:

a. **Spin:** Centrifuge the cell suspension at 200-300 x g for 5 minutes.

b. **Resuspend**: Discard the supernatant and resuspend the cell pellet in fresh complete medium.

5. Seeding New Culture Vessels

5.1 Cell Counting:

a. **Count Cells**: Use a hemocytometer or automated cell counter to determine the cell density. Assess viability with trypan blue exclusion if necessary.

5.2 Dilution:

a. **Calculate Dilution**: Dilute the cell suspension to the desired concentration for seeding. The seeding density depends on the cell type and experiment requirements.

5.3 Seeding:

a. **Distribute Cells**: Dispense the appropriate volume of cell suspension into new culture vessels containing pre-warmed complete medium.

6. Post-Subculture Maintenance

6.1 Incubation:

a. **Incubator Conditions**: Place culture vessels in an incubator set to 37°C with 5% CO_2 and appropriate humidity.

6.2 Monitoring:

a. **Microscopic Observation**: Regularly check cell attachment, morphology, and growth.

6.3 Media Changes:

a. **Regular Feeding**: Change the culture medium every 2-3 days or as needed to provide fresh nutrients and remove waste products.

7. Troubleshooting

7.1 Low Viability or Poor Attachment:

a. **Check Conditions**: Ensure proper enzyme concentration and incubation time. Verify the quality and temperature of media and reagents.

7.2 Contamination:

a. **Sterile Techniques**: Maintain strict aseptic conditions. Regularly check for contamination and discard any contaminated cultures.

7.3 Slow Growth:

a. **Nutrient Depletion**: Ensure regular media changes. Check for proper CO_2 levels and incubator conditions.

CRYOPRESERVATION

Cryopreservation is a method used to preserve cells, tissues, or other biological constructs by cooling them to sub-zero temperatures, typically -196°C using liquid nitrogen. This process is essential for maintaining the viability and functionality of cells for long-term storage, and it allows for the conservation of genetic material and the ability to restart cell cultures when needed. Here's a detailed guide on cryopreservation in cell culture:

1. Preparation

1.1 Materials and Reagents:

a. **Cryoprotective Agent (CPA):** Commonly used CPAs include dimethyl sulfoxide (DMSO) and glycerol.

b. **Freezing Medium**: Typically composed of 90% complete culture medium and 10% DMSO.

c. **Cryovials:** Sterile, labeled cryogenic vials suitable for low-temperature storage.

d. **Isopropanol Freezing Container**: For controlled rate cooling (e.g., Mr. Frosty).

e. **Liquid Nitrogen Storage**: Liquid nitrogen tank or cryogenic freezer.

1.2 Sterilization and Setup:

a. **Biological Safety Cabinet**: Ensure the work area is sterile by cleaning with 70% ethanol.

b. **Pre-warm Medium**: Pre-warm complete culture medium to 37°C.

2. Cell Preparation

2.1 Cell Health Check:

a. **Culture Condition**: Ensure cells are healthy and in the log phase of growth. Avoid cryopreserving over-confluent or stressed cells.

2.2 Harvesting Cells:

a. **Adherent Cells:**

  i. **Remove Medium**: Aspirate the spent medium.

  ii. **Wash with PBS**: Rinse cells with PBS to remove residual serum.

  iii. **Add Trypsin-EDTA**: Incubate with trypsin-EDTA until cells detach.

  iv. **Neutralize Trypsin**: Add complete medium with serum to stop the enzymatic reaction.

  v. **Collect Cells**: Transfer the cell suspension to a centrifuge tube.

b. **Suspension Cells:**

  i. **Resuspend Cells**: Gently pipette the culture to ensure even cell suspension.

2.3 Centrifugation:

a. **Spin:** Centrifuge at 200-300 x g for 5 minutes.

b. **Resuspend:** Discard the supernatant and resuspend the cell pellet in fresh, pre-warmed complete medium.

3. Cryoprotectant Addition

3.1 Prepare Freezing Medium:

a. **Formulation:** Prepare freezing medium containing 90% complete medium and 10% DMSO.

b. **Pre-cool Freezing Medium**: Chill the freezing medium to 4°C to reduce the shock to the cells.

3.2 Mixing with Cells:

a. **Cell Density**: Resuspend cells at a concentration of $1\text{-}5 \times 10^6$ cells/mL in the freezing medium.

b. **Slow Addition:** Slowly add the freezing medium to the cell suspension to avoid osmotic shock.

4. Aliquoting

4.1 Distribute Cells:

a. **Cryovials**: Aliquot 1-1.5 mL of the cell suspension into sterile, labeled cryovials.

5. Freezing Process

5.1 Controlled Rate Freezing:

a. **Isopropanol Freezing Container**: Place cryovials in an isopropanol freezing container (e.g., Mr. Frosty) to ensure a gradual cooling rate of approximately -1°C/minute.

b. **Freezer:** Place the container in a -80°C freezer overnight.

6. Storage

6.1 Transfer to Liquid Nitrogen:

a. **Long-term Storage**: Transfer cryovials from the -80°C freezer to a liquid nitrogen storage tank or a cryogenic freezer for long-term storage at -196°C.

7. Thawing Cells

7.1 Rapid Thawing:

a. **Water Bath**: Quickly thaw cryovials in a 37°C water bath until only a small ice crystal remains. Rapid thawing minimizes the formation of ice crystals, which can damage cell membranes.

7.2 Transfer to Culture Vessel:

a. **Resuspend**: Transfer the cell suspension to a culture vessel containing pre-warmed complete medium.

7.3 Centrifugation (Optional):

a. **Spin**: Centrifuge cells at 200-300 x g for 5 minutes to remove DMSO, then resuspend the cell pellet in fresh medium.

8. Post-Thaw Care

8.1 Medium Change:

a. **First Change**: After 24 hours, change the medium to remove any remaining DMSO and non-viable cells.

8.2 Monitoring:

a. **Microscopic Observation**: Regularly check cell attachment, morphology, and growth.

9. Quality Control

9.1 Viability Assessment:

a. **Trypan Blue Exclusion**: Use trypan blue staining to assess cell viability post-thaw.

9.2 Functional Assays:

a. **Proliferation and Function**: Conduct assays to ensure cells retain their proliferative capacity and functionality after thawing.

CHARACTERIZATION OF CELLS AND THEIR APPLICATION

Characterization of cells in cell culture is essential to confirm their identity, purity, and functionality. Proper characterization ensures that the cells being used for research or therapeutic applications are the correct type and are free from contamination. The following sections provide a detailed overview of the methods used to characterize cells and their applications in cell culture.

1. Morphological Characterization

1.1 Microscopic Examination:

a. **Phase-Contrast Microscopy**: Used to observe living cells and their morphology without staining.

b. **Fluorescence Microscopy**: Allows visualization of specific cellular components using fluorescent dyes or proteins.

1.2 Morphological Criteria:

a. **Shape**: Cells may be round, spindle-shaped, polygonal, etc.

b. **Size**: Measured using calibrated microscopes or image analysis software.

c. **Growth Patterns**: Adherent cells typically form monolayers, while suspension cells grow in clusters or singly.

2. Phenotypic Characterization

2.1 Immunocytochemistry (ICC):

a. **Antibody Staining**: Uses antibodies specific to cell surface or intracellular markers to identify cell types.

b. **Fluorescent Labels**: Conjugated with fluorophores for visualization under a fluorescence microscope.

2.2 Flow Cytometry:

a. **Cell Surface Markers**: Quantifies and sorts cells based on the expression of specific markers using fluorescently labeled antibodies.

b. **Multicolor Analysis**: Allows simultaneous detection of multiple markers.

2.3 Western Blotting:

a. **Protein Expression**: Detects specific proteins in cell lysates, providing information on the presence and relative abundance of cell type-specific markers.

3. Genotypic Characterization

3.1 Polymerase Chain Reaction (PCR):

a. **DNA Analysis**: Detects specific DNA sequences to confirm cell identity and check for contamination (e.g., mycoplasma).

b. **RT-PCR**: Measures mRNA levels of specific genes, providing information on gene expression.

3.2 Karyotyping:

a. **Chromosome Analysis**: Examines chromosomal structure and number to identify genetic stability and integrity.

3.3 Short Tandem Repeat (STR) Profiling:

a. **Cell Line Authentication**: Uses STR markers to verify the identity of cell lines and detect cross-contamination.

4. Functional Characterization

4.1 Proliferation Assays:

a. **MTT/XTT Assays**: Measure cell viability and proliferation based on metabolic activity.

b. **Cell Counting**: Manual or automated counting of cells over time to assess growth rates.

4.2 Differentiation Assays:

a. **Induction of Differentiation**: For stem cells or progenitor cells, induce differentiation and assess the formation of specialized cell types using specific markers and functional assays.

4.3 Migration and Invasion Assays:

a. **Wound Healing Assay**: Measures the migration ability of cells.

b. **Transwell Assay**: Assesses both migration and invasion through a membrane or matrix-coated insert.

5. Metabolic Characterization

5.1 Metabolite Analysis:

a. **Glucose Consumption and Lactate Production**: Indicators of metabolic activity.

b. **Oxygen Consumption Rate (OCR):** Assesses mitochondrial respiration using tools like Seahorse XF Analyzer.

5.2 Enzyme Activity Assays:

a. **Specific Enzymes**: Measure the activity of enzymes relevant to the cell type or metabolic pathway of interest.

6. Applications of Characterized Cells in Cell Culture

6.1 Basic Research:

a. **Cell Biology**: Studying cellular processes such as division, signaling, and apoptosis.

b. **Disease Models**: Using cell lines derived from patients to study disease mechanisms and potential treatments.

6.2 Drug Development:

a. **High-Throughput Screening**: Testing thousands of compounds for biological activity using characterized cell lines.

b. **Toxicity Testing**: Assessing the safety of new drugs by evaluating their effects on cultured cells.

6.3 Regenerative Medicine:

a. **Stem Cell Therapy**: Using characterized stem cells for transplantation and tissue regeneration.

b. **Tissue Engineering**: Creating tissue constructs from characterized cells for repair or replacement of damaged tissues.

6.4 Personalized Medicine:

a. **Patient-Derived Cells**: Culturing cells from individual patients to tailor treatments based on the patient's cellular responses.

6.5 Biotechnology:

a. **Production of Biologics**: Using characterized cell lines to produce therapeutic proteins, antibodies, or vaccines.

6.6 Diagnostic Applications:

a. **Biomarker Discovery**: Identifying markers for disease diagnosis or prognosis using characterized cells.

b. **Diagnostic Assays**: Developing assays that use cultured cells to detect pathogens or other diagnostic targets.

PRINCIPLES AND APPLICATIONS OF CELL VIABILITY ASSAYS

Cell viability assays are essential techniques used in cell culture to assess the health and viability of cells. These assays provide valuable information about the effects of experimental treatments, environmental conditions, or therapeutic interventions on cell survival and function. Here, we'll delve into the principles behind cell viability assays and explore their applications in detail.

1. Principles of Cell Viability Assays

1.1 Measurement of Cellular Metabolic Activity:

a. **Metabolic Assays:** Many viability assays measure cellular metabolic activity as an indicator of cell health.

b. **Tetrazolium Salts**: Tetrazolium salts such as MTT, XTT, or WST-1 are reduced by metabolically active cells to form formazan dyes, which can be quantified spectrophotometrically.

1.2 Membrane Integrity:

a. **Membrane Permeability**: Viability assays may assess cell membrane integrity by detecting the release of intracellular contents (e.g., lactate dehydrogenase, LDH) into the culture medium upon cell death.

b. **Fluorescent Dyes**: Fluorescent dyes like propidium iodide (PI) or SYTOX Green can selectively enter cells with compromised membranes and emit fluorescence upon binding to nucleic acids.

1.3 Enzyme Activity:

a. **Intracellular Enzymes**: Some viability assays measure the activity of intracellular enzymes that are indicative of cell viability.

b. **AlamarBlue Assay**: AlamarBlue is reduced by metabolically active cells, leading to a color change that can be quantified.

2. Common Cell Viability Assays

2.1 MTT Assay (3-(4,5-Dimethylthiazol-2-yl)-2,5-diphenyltetrazolium bromide):

a. **Principle:** MTT is reduced by mitochondrial dehydrogenases in metabolically active cells to form purple formazan crystals.

b. **Measurement:** After solubilization, formazan absorbance is quantified spectrophotometrically at a wavelength around 570 nm.

2.2 Trypan Blue Exclusion:

a. **Principle:** Trypan blue selectively stains dead cells with compromised membranes while viable cells exclude the dye.

b. **Measurement**: Live and dead cells are counted using a hemocytometer or automated cell counter.

2.3 LDH Cytotoxicity Assay:

a. **Principle**: LDH released from damaged cells converts lactate to pyruvate, which reacts with a substrate to produce a colored product.

b. **Measurement:** LDH activity is measured spectrophotometrically at a wavelength around 490 nm.

2.4 Calcein-AM/PI Viability Assay:

a. **Principle:** Calcein-AM is cleaved by intracellular esterases in live cells to produce green fluorescence, while PI stains dead cells with red fluorescence.

b. **Measurement:** Live and dead cells are visualized and quantified using fluorescence microscopy or flow cytometry.

2.5 Annexin V/PI Apoptosis Assay:

a. **Principle**: Annexin V binds to phosphatidylserine exposed on the outer membrane of apoptotic cells, while PI stains necrotic cells.

b. **Measurement**: Live, apoptotic, and necrotic cells are quantified using flow cytometry.

3. Applications of Cell Viability Assays

3.1 Drug Screening and Toxicity Testing:

a. **High-Throughput Screening**: Assess the effects of compounds on cell viability to identify potential drug candidates or toxic substances.

b. **Dose-Response Studies**: Determine the concentration-dependent effects of drugs or chemicals on cell viability.

3.2 Cell Culture Optimization:

a. **Media Formulation**: Evaluate the cytotoxicity of culture media components and optimize culture conditions.

b. **Substrate Compatibility**: Assess the biocompatibility of substrates for cell culture applications.

3.3 Cell-based Assays:

a. **Cell Signaling Studies**: Investigate the effects of signaling molecules, growth factors, or cytokines on cell viability and proliferation.

b. **Apoptosis and Cell Death**: Study the mechanisms of apoptosis induction or inhibition in response to various stimuli.

3.4 Regenerative Medicine and Tissue Engineering:

- **Stem Cell Viability**: Assess the survival and differentiation of stem cells in culture for regenerative therapies.

- **Tissue Constructs:** Evaluate the viability of tissue constructs or engineered organs for transplantation.

3.5 Disease Modeling and Research:

a. **Cancer Research**: Assess the response of cancer cells to chemotherapeutic agents or targeted therapies.

b. **Neuroscience**: Study neurodegenerative diseases by evaluating neuronal cell viability and apoptosis.

3.6 Microbial Viability:

a. **Microbiology**: Assess the efficacy of antimicrobial agents or disinfectants against bacterial or fungal pathogens.

PRINCIPLES AND APPLICATIONS OF GLUCOSE UPTAKE ASSAY

Glucose uptake assays are valuable tools used in cell culture to measure the cellular uptake of glucose, which is a fundamental process in cellular metabolism. These assays provide insights into glucose utilization by cells under different experimental conditions and can be applied in various research areas. Here, we'll explore the principles behind glucose uptake assays and their applications in detail:

1. Principles of Glucose Uptake Assays

1.1 Glucose Transporters:

a. Glucose uptake into cells is primarily mediated by glucose transporters (GLUTs).

b. GLUTs facilitate the transport of glucose across the plasma membrane, maintaining intracellular glucose homeostasis.

1.2 Radioactive and Non-radioactive Assays:

a. Glucose uptake assays can be radioactive or non-radioactive.

b. Radioactive assays utilize radiolabeled glucose (e.g., [^{3}H]- or [^{14}C]-labeled glucose), while non-radioactive assays use fluorescent or colorimetric detection methods.

1.3 Measurement of Glucose Uptake:

a. Radiolabeled glucose is taken up by cells and trapped intracellularly, allowing quantification by scintillation counting.

b. Non-radioactive assays measure the accumulation of a fluorescent or colorimetric product generated upon glucose uptake.

2. Common Glucose Uptake Assays

2.1 Radioactive Glucose Uptake Assay:

a. **Principle:** Cells are incubated with radiolabeled glucose ([^{3}H]- or [^{14}C]-glucose) and the uptake is measured by quantifying the radioactivity trapped within the cells.

b. **Measurement:** After incubation, cells are washed to remove extracellular radioactivity, lysed, and the radioactivity is quantified using liquid scintillation counting.

2.2 2-Deoxyglucose (2-DG) Uptake Assay:

a. **Principle:** 2-DG, a non-metabolizable glucose analog, is taken up by cells through glucose transporters but cannot be further metabolized.

b. **Measurement:** Intracellular 2-DG is phosphorylated by hexokinase, trapping it intracellularly. The accumulation of phosphorylated 2-DG is quantified using colorimetric or fluorescent detection methods.

2.3 Fluorescent Glucose Uptake Assay:

a. **Principle**: Fluorescently labeled glucose analogs (e.g., 2-NBDG) are taken up by cells and accumulate intracellularly.

b. **Measurement:** Intracellular fluorescence is quantified using fluorescence microscopy or flow cytometry.

2.4 Colorimetric Glucose Uptake Assay:

a. **Principle**: Glucose uptake assays based on enzymatic reactions produce a colorimetric product proportional to glucose uptake.

b. **Measurement**: The colorimetric product is quantified using a microplate reader, and glucose uptake is calculated based on the absorbance.

3. Applications of Glucose Uptake Assays

3.1 Metabolic Studies:

a. Assess the effects of hormones, growth factors, or signaling pathways on cellular glucose uptake.

b. Investigate alterations in glucose metabolism associated with diseases such as diabetes, cancer, or metabolic disorders.

3.2 Drug Screening and Target Identification:

a. Screen for compounds that modulate glucose uptake as potential therapeutics for metabolic diseases or cancer.

b. Identify novel targets involved in glucose transport for drug development.

3.3 Nutrient Sensing and Signaling:

a. Study nutrient sensing pathways (e.g., AMP-activated protein kinase, mTOR) and their regulation of glucose uptake.

b. Investigate the cross-talk between glucose metabolism and other cellular processes.

3.4 Exercise Physiology and Sports Science:

a. Assess glucose uptake in skeletal muscle cells to understand the metabolic adaptations to exercise.

b. Study the effects of sports supplements or nutritional interventions on cellular glucose uptake.

3.5 Stem Cell Biology and Tissue Engineering:

a. Monitor glucose uptake during stem cell differentiation or tissue development processes.

b. Optimize culture conditions for stem cell expansion or tissue engineering applications.

3.6 Infectious Diseases and Host-Pathogen Interactions:

a. Investigate the role of glucose uptake in pathogen replication and host immune responses.

b. Identify therapeutic targets to modulate glucose metabolism in infectious diseases.

PRINCIPLES AND APPLICATIONS OF CALCIUM INFLUX ASSAYS

Calcium influx assays are vital techniques used in cell culture to monitor changes in intracellular calcium levels. Calcium ions (Ca^{2+}) are ubiquitous second messengers involved in regulating numerous cellular processes, including signaling, neurotransmission, muscle contraction, and gene expression. These assays enable the investigation of calcium signaling dynamics in response to various stimuli and are widely used in cell biology research. Here's a detailed exploration of the principles behind calcium influx assays and their applications:

1. Principles of Calcium Influx Assays

1.1 Calcium Signaling Pathways:

a. Calcium influx into the cytoplasm occurs through various channels, including voltage-gated calcium channels (VGCCs), ligand-gated ion channels (e.g., NMDA receptors), store-operated calcium channels (SOCCs), and transient receptor potential (TRP) channels.

b. Intracellular calcium stores, such as the endoplasmic reticulum (ER) and mitochondria, also contribute to calcium signaling.

1.2 Calcium-sensitive Dyes:

a. Calcium influx assays typically employ calcium-sensitive fluorescent dyes that undergo a conformational change or fluorescence emission upon binding to calcium ions.

b. Common calcium indicators include Fluo-3, Fluo-4, Fura-2, and Rhod-2, which exhibit increased fluorescence intensity upon calcium binding.

1.3 Fluorescence Imaging and Detection:

a. Changes in intracellular calcium levels are detected using fluorescence microscopy or microplate readers equipped with fluorescence detection capabilities.

b. Real-time imaging allows the visualization of dynamic calcium signals in individual cells or cell populations.

1.4 Calcium Calibration:

a. Calibration of calcium indicators is essential to convert fluorescence signals into absolute calcium concentrations. This is achieved by measuring the fluorescence intensity at defined calcium concentrations using calibration buffers.

2. Common Calcium Influx Assays

2.1 Single-cell Fluorescence Imaging:

a. **Principle**: Cells loaded with calcium-sensitive fluorescent dyes are imaged using fluorescence microscopy or live-cell imaging systems.

b. **Measurement:** Changes in fluorescence intensity over time indicate alterations in intracellular calcium levels in response to stimuli.

2.2 Plate-based Assays:

a. **Principle:** Cells plated in multi-well plates are loaded with calcium indicators and treated with test compounds or stimuli.

b. **Measurement**: Fluorescence intensity is measured using a microplate reader before and after stimulation to quantify changes in calcium levels.

2.3 Flow Cytometry:

a. **Principle:** Cells labeled with calcium indicators are analyzed using flow cytometry to assess calcium influx in large cell populations.

b. **Measurement:** Changes in fluorescence intensity are quantified for individual cells, allowing high-throughput analysis.

3. Applications of Calcium Influx Assays

3.1 Cellular Signaling Studies:

a. Investigate the role of calcium signaling in cell proliferation, differentiation, apoptosis, and gene expression.

b. Characterize calcium dynamics in response to neurotransmitters, hormones, growth factors, or pharmacological agents.

3.2 Neurobiology and Neuroscience:

a. Study synaptic transmission and neuronal excitability by monitoring calcium influx in neurons in response to neurotransmitters or electrical stimulation.

b. Investigate the pathophysiology of neurological disorders such as Alzheimer's disease, Parkinson's disease, and epilepsy.

3.3 Cardiovascular Research:

a. Assess the regulation of cardiac contractility by monitoring calcium influx in cardiomyocytes.

b. Investigate calcium handling abnormalities associated with cardiac arrhythmias and heart failure.

3.4 Immunology and Inflammation:

a. Examine calcium signaling in immune cells (e.g., T cells, B cells, macrophages) during activation, proliferation, and cytokine production.

b. Investigate the role of calcium signaling in inflammatory responses and immune cell migration.

3.5 Drug Discovery and Pharmacology:

a. Screen compounds for their effects on calcium signaling pathways as potential therapeutics for various diseases.

b. Identify modulators of calcium channels or calcium-dependent enzymes for drug development.

3.6 Cancer Biology:

a. Investigate aberrant calcium signaling in cancer cells and its role in tumor growth, invasion, and metastasis.

b. Screen anti-cancer drugs targeting calcium signaling pathways for therapeutic efficacy.

PRINCIPLES OF FLOW CYTOMETRY

Flow cytometry is a powerful technique used in cell culture and various other fields of biology and medicine for analyzing and sorting cells based on their physical and chemical properties. It provides quantitative and qualitative information about individual cells within heterogeneous populations. Here's a detailed overview of the principles behind flow cytometry:

1. Basics of Flow Cytometry

1.1 Fluidics System:

a. Flow cytometry involves the hydrodynamic focusing of cells into a single-file stream.

b. Cells pass through an interrogation point where they are analyzed by lasers.

1.2 Light Scattering:

a. **Forward Scatter (FSC):** Measures the relative size of cells. Larger cells scatter more light in the forward direction.

b. **Side Scatter (SSC)**: Reflects the granularity or complexity of cells. Cells with more internal complexity scatter more light sideways.

1.3 Fluorescence Detection:

a. Fluorescent dyes or proteins are used to label specific cellular components.

b. Cells are excited by lasers, causing fluorophores to emit fluorescent light at specific wavelengths.

c. Detectors capture emitted fluorescence at different wavelengths, providing information about the labeled components.

2. Components of a Flow Cytometer

2.1 Light Sources:

a. Lasers of various wavelengths (e.g., violet, blue, green, red) are used to excite fluorophores.

b. Each laser excites specific fluorophores based on their excitation spectra.

2.2 Optics:

a. Lenses and mirrors direct and focus light onto the cells and detectors.

b. Optical filters separate emitted fluorescence into different channels based on wavelength.

2.3 Fluidics System:

a. Cells are hydrodynamically focused into a single-file stream to ensure accurate analysis.

b. Sheath fluid surrounds the sample stream, maintaining a stable flow rate and preventing cell clumping.

2.4 Detectors:

a. Photomultiplier tubes (PMTs) or avalanche photodiodes (APDs) detect emitted fluorescence.

b. Each detector is specific for a particular fluorescent channel.

2.5 Electronics and Data Analysis:

a. Signals from detectors are converted into electronic signals and processed by a computer.

b. Data analysis software interprets the signals, allowing the quantification of cellular parameters.

3. Applications of Flow Cytometry in Cell Culture

3.1 Cell Counting and Viability:

a. Flow cytometry can accurately count cells and assess viability using fluorescent dyes like propidium iodide (PI) or 7-AAD.

3.2 Immunophenotyping:

a. Identify and quantify specific cell populations based on surface markers using fluorescently labeled antibodies.

b. Useful for characterizing immune cell subsets and stem cell populations.

3.3 Cell Cycle Analysis:

a. Determine the distribution of cells in different phases of the cell cycle based on DNA content using fluorescent DNA dyes (e.g., propidium iodide) or BrdU/EdU incorporation.

3.4 Apoptosis and Cell Death:

a. Assess apoptosis by detecting externalization of phosphatidylserine using Annexin V and membrane integrity using PI or 7-AAD.

3.5 Functional Assays:

a. Measure intracellular calcium levels, reactive oxygen species (ROS), mitochondrial membrane potential, and other functional parameters using fluorescent indicators.

3.6 Sorting:

a. Sort cells based on specific characteristics or fluorescence intensity using a flow cytometer equipped with a cell sorter.

b. Allows isolation of pure cell populations for downstream applications.

APPLICATIONS OF FLOW CYTOMETRY

Flow cytometry is a versatile technique with numerous applications in cell culture. It allows for the rapid and quantitative analysis of individual cells within heterogeneous populations. Here's a detailed exploration of the various applications of flow cytometry in cell culture:

1. Cell Counting and Viability Assessment

1.1 Absolute Cell Counting:

a. Flow cytometry provides accurate and rapid quantification of cell numbers, allowing researchers to monitor cell growth, proliferation, and viability over time.

1.2 Viability Assessment:

a. Fluorescent dyes such as propidium iodide (PI) or 7-aminoactinomycin D (7-AAD) can be used to distinguish between live and dead cells based on membrane integrity.

2. Immunophenotyping and Cell Surface Marker Analysis

2.1 Identification of Cell Types:

a. Flow cytometry enables the characterization and quantification of different cell populations based on the expression of specific cell surface markers.

2.2 Stem Cell Analysis:

a. Characterization of stem cell populations based on surface marker expression, facilitating the study of differentiation, self-renewal, and pluripotency.

3. Cell Cycle Analysis

3.1 DNA Content Analysis:

a. Flow cytometry allows for the determination of cell cycle distribution by measuring DNA content using DNA-binding dyes like propidium iodide (PI) or DAPI.

3.2 Cell Proliferation Studies:

a. Assess cell proliferation rates, identify cell cycle phase distributions, and investigate the effects of drugs or experimental treatments on cell cycle progression.

4. Apoptosis and Cell Death Analysis

4.1 Apoptosis Detection:

a. Flow cytometry can distinguish apoptotic cells by detecting changes in cell membrane integrity (Annexin V staining) and DNA fragmentation (TUNEL assay).

4.2 Necrosis Assessment:

a. Differentiate between apoptotic and necrotic cell death using various fluorescent dyes, such as Annexin V/PI staining.

5. Functional Assays

5.1 Intracellular Signaling Pathways:

a. Measure intracellular calcium levels, reactive oxygen species (ROS), mitochondrial membrane potential, and pH using fluorescent indicators.

5.2 Cell Metabolism:

a. Assess cellular metabolic activity, glucose uptake, and mitochondrial function using specific fluorescent probes.

6. Cell Sorting

6.1 Purification of Cell Subpopulations:

a. Sort specific cell populations based on surface marker expression, size, granularity, or functional properties for downstream analyses or culture.

6.2 Clonal Expansion:

a. Isolate single cells or clonal populations for clonal expansion or monoclonal antibody production.

7. Drug Discovery and Toxicology

7.1 High-Throughput Screening:

a. Screen compound libraries to identify potential drug candidates based on their effects on cell viability, proliferation, apoptosis, or specific signaling pathways.

7.2 Toxicity Assessment:

a. Evaluate the cytotoxicity and genotoxicity of drugs, chemicals, or environmental pollutants on cultured cells.

8. Stem Cell Research and Tissue Engineering

8.1 Characterization of Stem Cells:

a. Analyze the expression of pluripotency markers and differentiation potential in stem cell populations.

8.2 Tissue Engineering:

a. Assess cell viability, proliferation, and differentiation within tissue-engineered constructs to optimize culture conditions and scaffold design.

9. Microbial Analysis

9.1 Microbial Enumeration:

a. Quantify microbial populations in environmental samples, food, or water by labeling with fluorescent dyes or antibodies.

9.2 Functional Microbial Assays:

a. Measure microbial metabolic activity, antibiotic susceptibility, and virulence factor expression using flow cytometry.

Conclusion

Flow cytometry is a powerful tool with diverse applications in cell culture, spanning from basic research to clinical diagnostics. Its ability to analyze multiple parameters simultaneously at the single-cell level provides valuable insights into cellular functions, dynamics, and interactions. By leveraging flow cytometry, researchers can advance our understanding of cell biology, disease mechanisms, drug discovery, and therapeutic interventions.

BIOSIMILARS

Biosimilars are biological products that are highly similar to and have no clinically meaningful differences from an existing approved reference product. In cell culture, the development of biosimilars involves complex processes to ensure similarity in structure, function, and efficacy compared to the reference product. Here's a detailed exploration of biosimilars in cell culture:

1. Introduction to Biosimilars

1.1 Definition:

a. Biosimilars are biological products that are highly similar to an already approved reference biologic (also known as the originator or reference product).

b. They must demonstrate similarity in terms of quality, safety, and efficacy to the reference product through comprehensive analytical and preclinical studies.

1.2 Regulatory Pathway:

a. Regulatory agencies, such as the FDA in the United States and the EMA in Europe, have established guidelines for the approval of biosimilars, outlining the requirements for demonstrating similarity to the reference product.

b. Biosimilars undergo a stepwise regulatory approval process, including analytical characterization, preclinical studies, and clinical trials to establish safety and efficacy.

2. Development of Biosimilars in Cell Culture

2.1 Cell Line Selection:

a. The choice of cell line for biosimilar production is critical and should ideally match the cell line used for the reference product.

b. Common cell lines used in biosimilar production include Chinese hamster ovary (CHO) cells, NS0 cells, and Sp2/0 cells.

2.2 Process Development:

a. The manufacturing process for biosimilars aims to replicate the process used for the reference product as closely as possible.

b. Process parameters such as cell culture conditions, media composition, and purification methods are optimized to ensure consistent product quality.

2.3 Analytical Characterization:

a. Extensive analytical testing is performed to compare the biosimilar with the reference product in terms of physicochemical properties, structural characteristics, and biological activity.

b. Analytical techniques such as mass spectrometry, chromatography, spectroscopy, and bioassays are employed to assess similarity.

2.4 Preclinical Studies:

a. Preclinical studies are conducted to evaluate the pharmacokinetics, pharmacodynamics, and toxicity of the biosimilar in relevant animal models.

b. These studies aim to establish similarity in terms of pharmacological activity, immunogenicity, and safety compared to the reference product.

3. Clinical Development and Approval

3.1 Clinical Trials:

a. Clinical trials are conducted to demonstrate the safety, efficacy, and immunogenicity of the biosimilar in human subjects.

b. Trials typically include pharmacokinetic and pharmacodynamic studies, as well as comparative efficacy and safety studies against the reference product in relevant patient populations.

3.2 Immunogenicity Assessment:

a. Immunogenicity studies assess the potential of the biosimilar to induce immune responses and the development of anti-drug antibodies (ADAs).

b. These studies evaluate the incidence and impact of immunogenicity on safety, efficacy, and patient outcomes.

3.3 Regulatory Approval:

a. Upon successful completion of analytical, preclinical, and clinical studies, regulatory authorities review the data to determine whether the biosimilar meets the criteria for approval.

b. Approval is granted based on a demonstration of similarity to the reference product in terms of quality, safety, and efficacy.

4. Market Access and Commercialization

4.1 Market Entry:

a. Biosimilars are introduced to the market following regulatory approval, offering cost-effective alternatives to the reference product.

b. Market access strategies may include pricing and reimbursement negotiations with payers, education and awareness campaigns, and targeted marketing efforts.

4.2 Post-Marketing Surveillance:

a. Ongoing pharmacovigilance and post-marketing surveillance are essential to monitor the safety and effectiveness of biosimilars in real-world clinical practice.

b. Surveillance programs track adverse events, immunogenicity, and patient outcomes to ensure continued safety and quality.

5. Challenges and Considerations

5.1 Analytical Similarity:

a. Achieving analytical similarity to the reference product can be challenging due to the complexity of biological molecules and variability in manufacturing processes.

b. Advanced analytical techniques and robust comparability studies are required to demonstrate similarity.

5.2 Immunogenicity Risk:

a. Immunogenicity is a critical consideration for biosimilars, as differences in manufacturing processes or impurities may impact immunogenicity profiles compared to the reference product.

b. Comprehensive immunogenicity assessments are necessary to evaluate the risk of immune responses and their potential impact on safety and efficacy.

Multiple-Choice Questions (MCQs)

1. What is the primary purpose of a biological safety cabinet in a cell culture lab?

   A) To provide light for microscopic observation

   B) To supply CO_2 for cell growth

   C) To offer a sterile working environment

   D) To store cells at low temperatures

2. Which type of microscope is ideal for observing cells in culture dishes or flasks?

   A) Electron microscope

   B) Inverted microscope

   C) Telescope

   D) Compound microscope

3. What is the main role of fetal bovine serum (FBS) in cell culture media?

   A) To provide essential nutrients and growth factors

   B) To maintain the pH of the medium

   C) To provide a color indicator for pH

   D) To sterilize the medium

4. During the subculturing process, what is the purpose of adding trypsin to adherent cells?

   A) To nourish the cells

   B) To freeze the cells

C) To detach the cells from the culture surface

D) To count the cells

5. What type of cells require attachment to a solid surface to grow, which is common for epithelial and fibroblast cells?

   A) Suspension cultures

   B) Adherent cultures

   C) Spheroid cultures

   D) Stem cell cultures

6. What is the purpose of using cryoprotectants like DMSO during the cryopreservation process?

   A) To enhance cell growth

   B) To color the cells for identification

   C) To protect cells during freezing

   D) To stimulate cell division

7. Which assay would you use to measure cell viability based on metabolic activity?

   A) PCR assay

   B) MTT assay

   C) Gram staining

   D) Western blotting

8. What is the purpose of using antibiotics in cell culture?

   A) To provide nutrients

   B) To prevent bacterial contamination

   C) To color the media

   D) To increase cell growth rate

9. What is the primary function of the incubator in cell culture?

   A) To sterilize instruments

   B) To maintain optimal growth conditions like temperature and CO_2 levels

C) To view cells under a microscope

D) To store reagents

10. What type of cell culture involves cells that are grown freely floating in the culture medium?

A) Adherent culture

B) Suspension culture

C) Spheroid culture

D) 3D culture

11. What is the purpose of a hemocytometer in cell culture?

A) To measure pH

B) To count cells

C) To warm media

D) To freeze cells

12. Which medium is used commonly for lymphocyte culture?

A) DMEM

B) RPMI-1640

C) MEM

D) F12

13. What is a key feature of primary cell culture?

A) Cells can proliferate indefinitely

B) Cells are derived from an existing cell line

C) Cells are directly isolated from tissues

D) Cells require no nutrient media

14. What phase do cells enter where growth rate slows due to nutrient depletion or waste accumulation?

A) Log phase

B) Death phase

C) Lag phase

D) Stationary phase

15. What is the purpose of the trypsin neutralization step during the subculturing of cells? A) To enhance the detachment of cells

    B) To maintain the pH of the medium

    C) To stop the action of trypsin

    D) To provide nutrients to cells

16. What characteristic is primarily analyzed using a flow cytometer?

    A) Weight of the cells

    B) Size and granularity of the cells

    C) Color of the cells

    D) Texture of the cells

17. What does a color change in phenol red in the culture medium indicate?

    A) A change in glucose levels

    B) A change in cell confluence

    C) A change in pH

    D) A change in temperature

18. In what type of cell culture do cells form a 3D structure naturally?

    A) Monolayer culture

    B) Suspension culture

    C) Spheroid culture

    D) Adherent culture

19. Which instrument is used to separate cells from the culture medium by spinning at high speeds?

    A) Centrifuge

    B) Microscope

    C) Autoclave

    D) Incubator

20. What is an essential step before adding trypsin to detach adherent cells during subculturing?

    A) Aspirating the old medium

B) Increasing the CO_2 levels

C) Adding more cells to the culture

D) Changing the pH of the medium

Short Answer Type Questions

1. What is cell culture and why is it important in biological research?

2. Describe the difference between primary and secondary cell cultures.

3. What is the role of a biological safety cabinet in cell culture?

4. Explain the function of fetal bovine serum in cell culture media.

5. How does an inverted microscope aid in cell culture?

6. What is trypsin and why is it used in cell culture?

7. Define what a cell line is and give an example.

8. What are the four main phases of cell growth in culture?

9. Describe the importance of cryopreservation in cell culture.

10. What are the ethical considerations in cell culture involving human tissues?

11. Explain the purpose of using antibiotics in cell culture.

12. What is a hemocytometer and how is it used in cell culture?

13. Why is RPMI-1640 media often used for lymphocyte culture?

14. Describe how a centrifuge is used in cell culture.

15. What is the significance of the color change in phenol red in culture media?

16. Explain the process of subculturing or passaging in cell culture.

17. How do adherent cultures differ from suspension cultures?

18. What is the purpose of a viability assay in cell culture?

19. Describe the process of preparing cell culture media.

20. What are the potential sources of contamination in a cell culture lab?

Long Answer Type Questions

1. Discuss the importance and methods of maintaining sterility in a cell culture environment.

2. Explain the process and significance of enzymatic digestion in the isolation of cells from tissues.

3. Describe the steps involved in the cryopreservation and thawing of cells and why each step is critical.

4. Detail the process of cell seeding and the factors that influence how cells are seeded in culture vessels.

5. Outline the various types of cell culture media and their specific applications in cell culture.

6. Explain the role and mechanism of action of trypsin in detaching adherent cells during the subculturing process.

7. Discuss the applications and limitations of using fetal bovine serum in cell culture media.

8. Describe the various phases of cell growth in a culture and their biological significance.

9. Explain how automated cell counters work and their advantages over manual counting methods.

10. Detail the process and purpose of subculturing cells, including the steps to ensure cell health and viability.

Answer Key

1. (C) To offer a sterile working environment

2. (B) Inverted microscope

3. (A) To provide essential nutrients and growth factors

4. (C) To detach the cells from the culture surface

5. (B) Adherent cultures

6. (C) To protect cells during freezing

7. (B) MTT assay

8. (B) To prevent bacterial contamination

9. (B) To maintain optimal growth conditions like temperature and CO_2 levels

10.(B) Suspension culture

11.(B) To count cells

12.(B) RPMI-1640

13.(C) Cells are directly isolated from tissues

14.(D) Stationary phase

15.(C) To stop the action of trypsin

16.(B) Size and granularity of the cells

17.(C) A change in pH

18.(C) Spheroid culture

19.(A) Centrifuge

20.(A) Aspirating the old medium